Development and Faith

Where Mind, Heart, and Soul Work Together

Development and Faith

Where Mind, Heart, and Soul Work Together

Katherine Marshall
Marisa Van Saanen

THE WORLD BANK
Washington, D.C.

© 2007 The International Bank for Reconstruction and Development / The World Bank
1818 H Street, NW
Washington, DC 20433
Telephone: 202-473-1000
Internet: www.worldbank.org
E-mail: feedback@worldbank.org

Cover design by Naylor Design, Inc.

ISBN-10: 0-8213-7173-8
ISBN-13: 978-0-8213-7173-2
e-ISBN: 0-8213-7174-6
e-ISBN-13: 978-0-8213-7174-9
DOI: 10.1596/978-0-8213-7173-2

Cataloging-in-Publication Data has been applied for.

Contents

Foreword   *xi*

Acknowledgments   *xv*

Abbreviations and Acronyms   *xvii*

1. **Bridging the Worlds of Development and Faith**   1
   Religious Groups Face Development   2
   The World Bank's Journey to Partnership with Faith Institutions   5
   Practical Challenges   9
   The Rationale for this Book   10
   The Book's Organization and Goals   15

PART I – PARTNERS ON MILLENNIUM CHALLENGES   **17**

   Introduction   **19**

2. **Faith Communities Engage the Millennium Development Goals**   23
   Global Faith Advocacy and Mobilization   24
   Monitoring Progress   28
   Country and Regional Engagement   29
   Scaling Up   30
   Faith Participation in Policy Making and Programs   31

3. **Strategic Challenges for Faith-Based Health Care**   33
   Ancient Roots   35
   Information Challenges   36
   Challenges for Faith-Run Health Care   40
   The Morality Conundrum   43
   The Promise of Partnerships   44
   Looking Ahead   45

4. Partnerships in Battling AIDS   49
   Mapping the Terrain   51
   Integrating Faith-Run Programs into National HIV/AIDS Strategies   53
   Emphasizing Advocacy and Messages   54
   Engaging Faith Leaders in National, Regional, and Global Forums   56
   Forming Innovative Secular-Faith Partnerships   58
   Tackling the Core Challenges of HIV/AIDS Work   60
   Boosting the Faith-Based Capacity to Respond   62

5. Together Against Malaria: Faith-Led Community Mobilization
   in Mozambique   67
   The Challenge   68
   The Washington National Cathedral and Interfaith Activists in
      Mozambique   69
   The Inter-Religious Campaign against Malaria in Mozambique   70
   Creating a Sustainable Interfaith Infrastructure   74

6. Education, Values, and Global Citizenship: Centro Magis and
   the Council of 100   77
   Education for Change in Latin America   78
   Education and Relations between Western and Islamic Nations   83

7. Ghana's Interfaith Initiative to Manage Waste and Care for
   the Environment   87
   Roots of the Response   88
   The Program   90
   Lessons beyond Ghana   91

8. New Alliances to Tackle the Housing Dimensions of Poverty   93
   The Challenge   94
   Applying Principles in Practice   96
   Interfaith Community Action in the Philippines   96
   Interfaith Dreams in Lebanon   100

PART II – FAITH COMMUNITIES IN ACTION   103

   Introduction   105

9. Shifting Community Attitudes: The Tostan Story in West Africa   109
   Tostan   110
   Addressing Female Genital Cutting   111
   Public Declarations and Community Engagement   113

10. Grassroots Matters: Sarvodaya, the Tsunami, and
    Development in Sri Lanka   117
    Introducing Sarvodaya   119
    Linking Peace and Community Building   121
    Post-Tsunami Sri Lanka   122
    Learning from the Disaster   125
    The Road Ahead   126

11. Madrasa Challenges and Reforms in Pakistan   129
      Origins of ICRD   130
      How the Program Works   131
      Medium-Term Goals   133
      The Impact of the Program   136
      A Respectful and Inclusive Approach   137

12. Integrating HIV/AIDS Care, Treatment, and Support:
      The Coptic Orthodox Church in Africa   139
      The Challenges   140
      The Coptic Orthodox Mission   141

13. Alliances for Development: Case Studies from
      the United States   145
      The Interfaith Summit on Africa   151
      The 2006 Global Summit on AIDS and the Church:
        A Race Against Time   153

14. Learning from the Extreme Poor: Participatory Approaches
      to Fostering Child Health in Madagascar   159
      ATD Fourth World's Approach to Learning from People Mired in
        Extreme Poverty   160
      Health and Living Conditions in Antananarivo, Madagascar 161
      Lessons for Other Programs   168

PART III – EXTENDING THE REACH: GLOBAL DIALOGUE,
PARTNERSHIPS, AND MOVEMENTS   171

      Introduction   173

15. Responding to the Orphan Crisis in Africa   177
      The Impact of HIV/AIDS on African Children and Communities 179
      What Draws Religious Organizations to Offer Programs
        for Children?   180
      How Have Faith Organizations Responded?   182
      What Do Faith-Based Children's Programs Do?   186
      Challenges in Scaling Up   192
      Building Local Capacity   193

16. A Pathfinding Dialogue among the World Council of
      Churches, the IMF, and the World Bank   195
      Origins of the Process   196
      The Dialogue Process   198
      The Finale: A High-Level Encounter in Geneva   201
      Next Steps?   207

17. Faith and Finance: Unlikely Partners   209
      Leading Up to the Present   213
      The International Interfaith Investment Group   215

18. Paths to Hope through Music and Culture: Dialogue at Fès 221
The Idea 222
Rumi's Elephant 223
Paths to Hope? 225
The 2006 Forum 226
Sustaining the Forum 229

19. New Alliances for Integrity, Against Corruption 231
Common Religious Ethical Teachings and Public Integrity 233
Exploring Differences 234
Mobilizing the Organizations of the World's Faiths 236
Education and Religious Teaching 236
Integrity within Faith Communities and Programs 237
Faith Engagement in Monitoring Poverty and Public Sector
Expenditures 238
Integrity, Ethics, and Accountability: HIV/AIDS and
Gender-Linked Violence 239

20. From Community Initiatives to Movements:
Faith-Inspired Work for Social Transformation 241
Two Sets of Case Studies 242
Tyndale's *Visions of Development* 244
Dharma and Development 251
A Holistic View of Development 255

PART IV – CONFLICT, REBUILDING, AND RECONCILIATION 263

Introduction 265

21. Hope for Peace and Faith-Based Reconciliation in
Northern Uganda 269
The Conflict 269
The Faith Contribution 271
Religious Leaders in Peace Processes 273
Turning to Rebuilding 274
Reconciliation and Truth Commissions 275
The Future Role of Religious Groups in Northern Uganda 276

22. Religion, Reconciliation, and Rebuilding 279
Forgiveness at Fès 280
Religion and Reconciliation: Different Approaches 284

23. Bridging Civilizations and Cultures 291
Alliance of Civilizations 292
The Council of 100 294

24. Concluding Thoughts 305

Selected Bibliography 315
Index 319

BOXES

1.1 What on Earth is the Friday Morning Group? 6
1.2 Principles for Partnerships 12
3.1 Mapping Religious Health Assets in Zambia and Lesotho:
The Importance of Local Wisdom 37
3.2 Uganda's Faith-Based Health Partners: A Workable System
Confronts a Crisis 41
5.1 Global Partnerships against Malaria 71
13.1 Bread for the World: A Christian Citizens' Movement to End Hunger 146
13.2 Heartland Tour with Bono and Gateway Ambassadors 149
16.1 Joint Statement by the General Secretary of the World Council of
Churches, President of the World Bank, and Deputy Managing Director
of the International Monetary Fund, Geneva, October 22, 2004 202
17.1 Faith-Based Microcredit: Five Talents 210
17.2 Faith-Consistent Investing in Development: Responsible Forestry 216
20.1. Mayan Spirituality Meets Catholic Teaching in
San Marcos, Guatemala 245
20.2 A Partnership to Address Senegal's Number-One Social Issue:
Getting Children off the Streets 256
20.3 Turkey's Street Children 258
23.1 The Imam and the Pastor 297
23.2 A Wall of Peace: Reflections of Mahatma Gandhi's Grandson 299
23.3 Caravan Safe Community: Youth, Faith Groups, and Armed Violence 301
24.1 What Can One Person Do? 308
24.2 Challenges for Minds, Hearts, Soul and Hands 310

FIGURES

15.1 Faith Adherents in Six African Countries (Kenya, Malawi,
Mozambique, Namibia, Swaziland, and Uganda) 183
15.2 Number of Vulnerable Children Supported by
Different Types of FBOs 185
15.3 Main Activities of FBOs to Address the Needs of Orphans
and Vulnerable Children 186

TABLES

15.1 Sample of Large-Scale Faith-Based Initiatives Serving Orphaned
and Vulnerable Children 189
15.2 Best Practices for Child-Friendly Institutions Caring for
HIV/AIDS Orphans 191
15.3 Priority Needs of FBOs Serving Orphans and Vulnerable
Children (Percent) 193

Foreword

Global poverty is a moral outrage. The suffering of people who lack basic necessities cries out to our conscience. The lost opportunities in human development—represented by children underserved and underschooled; men, women, and children who suffer from diseases that are easily prevented; and jobless and underemployed individuals around the globe—are daunting and difficult to reconcile with a world that in other ways is so technologically advanced, connected, fast-paced, and rich. We understand well, from the different perspectives of our contrasting backgrounds and present missions, that poverty and inequity are matters of conscience.

Beyond our real human empathy for a world where too many suffer, we also recognize that global poverty is a practical threat to peace, as the welfare of each citizen is affected by the condition of people the world over, including those who live far away. The despair and anger of those who contrast the suffering within their own families and communities with images of plenty beyond their reach translate into instability.

Poverty and social injustice thus demand a vigorous response. Of course, if these problems were simple, we could long since have relegated them to history. But the challenges are vast, the actors many, and the landscape includes complex bureaucracies, limited infrastructure, and constraints on human and organizational capacity. Where development efforts have succeeded, they have relied on careful planning and analysis, and a concerted effort to focus on results and institutional collaboration.

The World Bank has not traditionally engaged in dialogue with leaders of the major faiths—the worlds of faith and international financial institutions seemed far apart—but today there is broadening recognition that these different voices belong at the same policy table. The world's great faiths have billions of followers, and inherit centuries of tradition and understanding. At a very practical level, they have long been doing the work of development by caring for the sick, setting up schools near and far, and living in and supporting poor communities. And the focus of faith institutions and leaders on spiritual concerns is as important as their grasp of practical life issues and their pivotal role in providing basic services.

Just as the World Bank held religious leaders at a distance, many faith leaders have long looked askance at multilateral development institutions, convinced that their work was perhaps irrelevant and even detrimental to their communities. The development institutions were too often seen as enigmatic, overly confident, and imposing solutions that did not safeguard the well-being of the most vulnerable. Today, however, more and more faith leaders recognize the common bonds that link them to development work. These leaders also recognize that development institutions have made conscious efforts to include the voices of the poor in policy making, and to ensure that countries drive their own development. We sense a readiness for dialogue and partnership that did not exist in the past.

Thus, for nearly a decade, the World Bank and concerned leaders of world faiths have worked together to seek common understanding of the causes of poverty and how to fight it. Our aim has been to learn from each other. We also aim at practical solutions: we want to see progress toward the Millennium Development Goals, which set such clear targets for the global community, and we want to exceed those benchmarks.

This book aims to advance the shared understanding that is emerging from our dialogue on global development issues. It takes stock of a decade of exchanges and partnerships that have marked the effort to bridge what were too often diverging worlds. It recognizes the complexity and challenge inherent in dialogue on difficult issues, where conflicting views and areas of uncertainty abound. But it also highlights the wealth of experience that we have gained.

This is a book about partnerships between development and faith institutions. It is grounded in our common, abiding resolve to deepen our efforts to combat poverty, and it highlights several areas of shared focus and endeavor. Three stand out. First, we share a special commitment to development of Africa, and a conviction that progress on that continent must take into account the role of religious institutions and organizations, especially in the key arenas of education and health. Second, we both firmly hold the conviction that new forms of partnership are critical to addressing the development challenges of the twenty-first century. No institution, government, or country can succeed alone, and the challenges of our time demand innovative ways of working together. Finally, we know that quality matters. We must work well and carefully to achieve the results we desire. Programs must be run well and honestly if they are to succeed.

Reason and conscience, knowledge and belief, ideas and practice all converge in meeting development challenges. This simple statement lies at the core of the convictions on which our work, and this book, are based. Mind, heart, soul, and hands need to work together to achieve results.

Joy Phumaphi
Vice-President
Human Development Network
World Bank

Lord Carey of Clifton
Chair
World Faiths Development Dialogue

Acknowledgments

The purpose of this book is to explore and celebrate the remarkable new partnerships that are emerging in the world of development. Each case study presented reflects the work of committed people whose work is often too little known. The selection of cases reflects above all the direct engagement of the authors; but in some cases fascinating stories we encountered about faith development partnerships seemed so noteworthy that we included at least a sketch of what we learned second hand about the experience.

The key partners who led the work involved are noted in each chapter, especially those who were engaged at the writing stage. However, many others contributed ideas and goaded thinking. We gratefully acknowledge both their remarkable work and their support to the production of this book.

Special thanks go to Nicholas Krafft in the World Bank, who supported the project as it progressed, and Tom Banchoff, who directs Georgetown University's Berkley Center for Religion, Peace and World Affairs and offered inspiration at every stage. Sandra Hackman and Michael Alwan lent their keen editorial eyes, Paola Scalabrin and Michael Alwan shepherded the book through the production process, and Jan-Marie Hopkins helped solve the inevitable administrative hurdles along the way.

Abbreviations and Acronyms

ADRA	Adventist Development and Relief Agency
AEE	Africa Evangelistic Enterprise
AIDS	Acquired immunodeficiency syndrome
ARC	Alliance of Religions and Conservation
ARHAP	African Religious Health Assets Programme
AUSJAL	Latin American Jesuit university network
ARLPI	Acholi Religious Leaders Peace Initiative
AVINA	Foundation working in Latin America
BAPS	Bochasanwasi Shri Akshar Purushottam Swaminarayan Sanstha
CAA	Catholic AIDS Action
CBO	Community-based organization
CGJR	Center for Global Justice and Reconciliation
DREAM	Drug Resource Enhancement against AIDS and Malnutrition
FBO	Faith-based organization
HIV	Human immunodeficiency virus
IACC	International Anti-Corruption Conference
ICCR	Interfaith Center on Corporate Responsibility
IDA	International Development Association
IDB	Inter-American Development Bank
3iG	International Interfaith Investment Group
IMF	International Monetary Fund
IRCMM	Inter-Religious Campaign against Malaria in Mozambique
LIRNEasia	Learning Initiatives on Reforms for Network Economies
LRA	Lord's Resistance Army
MAP	Multi-country AIDS Project

NACO	India's national HIV/AIDS organization
NCCK	National Council of Churches of Kenya
NGO	Nongovernmental organization
NU	Nahdlatul Ulama
OVC	Orphans and vulnerable children
PACANet	Pan African Christian AIDS Network
PRSP	Poverty Reduction Strategy Paper
RCBs	Religious coordinating bodies
TAFREN	Task Force for Rebuilding the Nation
TAM	Together against Malaria
TAP	Treatment Acceleration Program
TKMOAMS	Tate Kalungu Mweneka Omukithi wo "AIDS" Moshilongo Shetu (Our Mighty Father Protect Our Nation from the Deadly Disease "AIDS")
UNAIDS	Joint United Nations Programme on HIV/AIDS
UNDP	United Nations Development Programme
UNICEF	United Nations Children's Fund
URI	United Religions Initiative
WCRP	World Conference of Religions for Peace
WEF	World Economic Forum
WHO	World Health Organization

World Bank Group, includes International Bank for Reconstruction and Development (IBRD), International Development Association (IDA), International Finance Corporation (IFC)

CHAPTER 1

Bridging the Worlds of Development and Faith

Religious voices, topics, and institutions were largely absent from the agenda and work of secular development and financial institutions over much of their history. Of course, faith-based groups often overlapped with secular nongovernmental, national, and international organizations in their respective work to advance social and economic development. However, contacts among these very different institutions were relatively isolated and ephemeral, and efforts to document and analyze the interactions that did occur have been sparse.

However, significant shifts are occurring—especially in the United States, but also globally—in how the broad foreign policy community views religion and its relationship to international events. There is mounting interest in far-ranging topics, including the role of church and state in modernizing societies, the role of religion and values in educational curricula, religion in conflict and peacemaking, faith roles in situations of disaster, and potential faith roles in global warming.[1] There is also a heightened interest in how religion affects development, how development institutions should approach faith-based ideas and institutions, and (to a lesser extent) the impact of development on religious groups themselves. Examples of such reflection include policy reviews in the UK's Department for International Development, the Netherlands Ministry of Foreign Affairs, and the Swiss Development Agency, as well as active debates within many agencies of the U.S. government.

Both United Nations headquarters and its agencies have also considered how to engage with religious organizations and introduced changes as a result. For example, the UN launched the Tripartite Forum on Interfaith Cooperation for Peace in June 2005, which brings together member states, UN agencies, and faith-based nongovernmental organizations (NGOs).[2] Academic institutions, think tanks, and foundations are also showing keen interest in religion and development, and international and national youth organizations are similarly focusing on ethical and spiritual issues. Media attention is sharply on the rise.

Examination of religion as a critical factor in development has not been systematic or universal, and it faces significant challenges. Some secular development institutions specifically mention faith and faith-based groups in their formal structures, policies, and programs, while others treat them as subsets of NGOs and civil society; in some quarters they are explicitly excluded. The future stance of the development world toward religion remains uncertain. Still, the new wave of interest has stimulated real shifts in operational work, with the HIV/AIDS pandemic perhaps the most significant example as faith organizations and issues are increasingly seen as critical to the global response.

RELIGIOUS GROUPS FACE DEVELOPMENT

A similarly complex picture emerges from the vantage point of religious organizations. Faith groups across the world have long engaged in what we would today term development, working at all levels ranging from families, neighborhoods, and communities through global movements. These faith institutions have been deeply involved in humanitarian assistance and social services, especially in the arenas of education and health, with their engagement reflecting both ancient religious teachings and contemporary lived religion and practice. However, while a fairly clear evolution of thinking about development and global poverty can be charted for the World Bank and other secular organizations since 1945, which stands as an important turning point for modern concepts of development and foreign aid, tracing a parallel path in the vast and variegated worlds of faith institutions is far more difficult. There are many very different philosophies and approaches and the whole presents a dynamic and intertwined picture.

The increasing interest among faith communities in issues of global poverty can be traced in many ways; but two notable examples are the focus of Catholic social teaching on development, and the ecumenical work by the World Council of Churches in the decades following World War II.[3] That both examples fall within the Christian tradition is no accident, because other faith traditions—while deeply involved in social justice work—have not tended to frame their activities as development in such explicit terms. Overall, the variety and differences of approach to development work among the panoply of faith institutions stand out more than any common approach.

Nonetheless, beginning perhaps in the 1980s, two patterns did begin to emerge. The first took the form of critiques of significant parts of the mainstream development agenda, particularly what was termed the "Washington consensus"[4]—that is, economic reforms recommended or required by major development institutions, especially the World Bank and the International Monetary Fund, as part of their financing programs. Of particular concern to faith organizations have been "structural adjustment policies," which many in faith communities view as above all emphasizing privatization of state-owned assets and services (like water), budget cutting that forces reductions in government services, and an emphasis on economic growth as a cure-all. Conflicts around dam building and the displacement of indigenous people, in particular, resonated deeply within many faith institutions, as did the mounting indebtedness of many poor countries, and perceived links between economic growth and environmental damage. These critiques spurred, among other responses, the global Jubilee 2000 movement, which called on secular development institutions to rethink their overall approach to poor countries, including their debt burdens.[5]

The second pattern emerged largely after the Jubilee 2000 movement, which had heightened interest in the global dimensions of poverty and spurred widely differing faith organizations to take a more systematic interest in the work of secular development institutions. This has occurred in tandem with greater willingness among such institutions to engage religious leaders in policy discussions, away from the picket lines. Faith communities are also continuing their prominent roles in pressing for more attention to global poverty and social justice—specifically the Millennium Development Goals (MDGs), established with the United Nations Summit in September 2000.

Faith institutions today are increasingly likely to collaborate among themselves and with development institutions to address poverty and humanitarian needs more forcefully. The specific engagement of three global interfaith organizations in such work is an important marker of this interest. The United Religions Initiative at its Rio assembly in 2002, the World Parliament of the Religions at its Barcelona assembly in 2004, and the World Conference of Religions for Peace (WCRP) at its Kyoto assembly in 2006 all tackled development issues, including debt, the environment, HIV/AIDS, water, and gender roles. This work builds on the historic engagement of these organizations in addressing interfaith conflicts and peacemaking, which leads them to reflection and action on the underlying causes of social tensions at both local and international levels.

A wide range of interfaith groups, including the Micah Challenge (a Christian organization), the WCRP, and the World Parliament of the Religions are also focusing on the aspirations and global commitment that underlie the MDGs, as are many individual denominations and congregations. This interest is spurring faith institutions to seek a seat at the policy table, while they are also, in many instances, asking development institutions to work and support faith groups in scaling up their community advocacy and social justice operations.

The picture that emerges is of converging agendas on economic and social development among the vast array of secular agencies and faith institutions. Common ground lies in deep concern for the suffering of poor people, and frustration with slow progress on the MDGs.

However, relationships among development and faith institutions are far from harmonious. Different languages (of disciplines, not tongues) and complex institutional bureaucracies help keep the two worlds separate. Contentious issues such as HIV/AIDS prevention strategies, approaches to ethical norms, environmental protection, and gender roles divide faith organizations themselves, as well as development and faith institutions. Indeed, no issue has served as a stronger lightening rod for such tensions than women's rights to reproductive health. Still, the overriding concern among all parties with poverty and inequity offers a rich avenue for dialogue and engagement.

THE WORLD BANK'S JOURNEY TO PARTNERSHIP WITH FAITH INSTITUTIONS

The history of the World Bank illustrates the traditional separation between faith and formal development work, as well as the bumpy path toward greater understanding and cooperation. For much of the Bank's history, religion was simply absent from its public statements, formal policies, operating documents, and research agendas. That omission reflected two major concerns. The first was the Bank's technical approach to virtually all aspects of development and its grounding in economics as a leading discipline. The second was the view among many Bank officers that a focus on faith could breach the Articles of Agreement, which prohibit the Bank from becoming involved in the internal political affairs of its member countries.

Still, formal policy notwithstanding, the World Bank has long engaged with faith institutions and issues, although it documented these efforts poorly, so they are not readily apparent to outside and even inside observers. These encounters included conferences that explored spirituality, contacts and policy discussions with faith leaders and institutions in many countries, community-grounded work on culture and environment, and some joint projects. A small but not insignificant number of Bank staff members have some training in theology, and many more are committed members of faith communities or are inspired and motivated by the values that have drawn them to development work. This is reflected in the Values in Development Group, also known as the Friday Morning Group (FMG)—a remarkable and durable if entirely informal group of people who meet every Friday at 8:00 am at Bank headquarters to explore issues that often involve religion and spirituality (see box 1.1).

Personal leadership beginning a decade ago by James D. Wolfensohn, then president of the World Bank, launched a more systematic attempt to engage the world of religion. This work has helped forge better relationships

BOX 1.1:
WHAT ON EARTH IS THE FRIDAY MORNING GROUP?

Virtually everyone who works in the development field confronts tensions and uncertainties in the course of their work, because so many complex issues are embedded in even the most technical matters. The struggle to reconcile competing objectives, and to tie them to one's core values, is often a lonely one.

The World Bank's long-standing, informal network known as the Friday Morning Group, or FMG, emerged from widespread concern about how individuals' values come into play during global development work.[a] Gainsaying traditional images of the World Bank, the FMG has endured for more than 25 years as a practical, ethereal, pugnacious, supportive, and questioning forum for exploring tough development challenges.

The FMG got started in 1981, when six very different people agreed to meet to explore how their differing religious traditions and values (or their reactions against such traditions) helped them grapple with practical daily dilemmas. Six short sessions over coffee, on six Fridays before work, they thought, would suffice to help them to answer their questions. They found, instead, that their joint musings struck a chord, and others joined the group. The FMG's founders produced a book about their early days of dialogue, which still stands as an unusual and enduring publication emanating from the World Bank.[b]

The Values for Development Group, as the FMG is more formally known, convenes in a World Bank dining room, always on Friday mornings, always at 8:00 am sharp, always for exactly one hour, and always beginning with a minute of silence. The group is wonderfully diverse, its members counting staff working at the World Bank and retirees, people from other organizations, women and men, religious and distinctly not religious, spiritual and questioning. It is a group of members and friends.

What brings the group together is a constant questing interest in exploring the purposes and directions of development work. What

(Box continues on the following page.)

(box continued)

are our values? Where are the areas of difficulty, the areas of difference? How do they play out in how we and our development partners do our work?

Meetings fall into roughly three categories. First, the group invites a wide range of speakers. Recent visitors included a Salvation Army officer, the former Archbishop of Canterbury, the local representative of the World Trade Organization, and the Bank staff member responsible for working with people with disabilities.

Second, members make personal presentations about their lives and the intersection of their work and values. Third, meetings can take the form of open discussion, when members raise whatever is on their minds. Every topic under the sun can surface, from war to nutrition, microcredit to domestic violence. FMG participants thrashed out many issues that have challenged the World Bank—participatory approaches to development, environmental consequences, military expenditures, corruption, harassment and bullying, leadership, responses to conflict, and many other topics. Friday morning is a pivotal part of the lives and work of many members. It is a rare safe space—a place of respectful support for ideas and gentle and not so gentle challenges and questions.

a. See http://vle.worldbank.org/gdln/vd.htm.

b. David Beckmann, Ramgopal Agarwala, Sven Burmester, and Ismail Serageldin, 1991, *Friday Morning Reflections at the World Bank: Essays on Values and Development* (Washington, DC: Seven Locks Press).

with faith groups, and encouraged a wide range of partnerships on development projects. While no one has formally evaluated the impact of these efforts on development results (and probably could not, given their breadth and diversity), a number of quite varied indicators do suggest that they have enhanced the quality and reach of development programs.

The first step in this invigorated interest was a meeting with leaders of the world's major faiths at Lambeth Palace in London in February 1998, co-chaired by James D. Wolfensohn and George Carey, then Archbishop of Canterbury. That meeting—exploratory and private—gave rise to two convictions. First, common interest in fighting poverty was a powerful impetus for collaboration; and second, major efforts to bridge gaps between secular and faith organizations in communication styles as well as practical perspectives were essential if the common interest was to go beyond words.

A second meeting in Washington, DC, in November 1999 brought together a somewhat larger group, which agreed on the need for a more formal institutional venue. That led to creation of the World Faiths Development Dialogue (WFDD), which initially operated as an informal hub but later organized as a British charity based in Oxford and then Birmingham. Then, in early 2007, the WFDD was relaunched as a U.S. NGO, based at Georgetown University's Berkley Center for Religion, Peace and World Affairs.[6]

Debates within the World Bank on the role of WFDD in late 2000 and early 2001 focused on whether formal partnerships with faith institutions at a global level were wise or necessary.[7] The upshot was refined objectives for WFDD and a more hands-off relationship between the World Bank and WFDD. The World Bank would focus on translating insights from high-level meetings into practice through the Development Dialogue on Values and Ethics, a small unit within the Bank with a mandate to examine ethics and values for development, rather than faith per se.

Two further international meetings of faith and development leaders, at Canterbury in October 2002 and Dublin in January 2005, were instrumental in linking the challenges inherent in the MDGs to the ideas and work of religious leaders and institutions.[8] These meetings led to pilot faith-development partnerships in specific arenas. The most significant example was a series of workshops on HIV/AIDS in Africa that engaged faith institutions who were working with on-the-ground programs, often but by no means exclusively with the World Bank. Consultations on the annual World Bank flagship World Development Reports and on how well faith institutions and leaders were able to engage in the Poverty Reduction Strategy Paper (PRSP) process made tangible contributions and advanced the overall action agenda. Country-based pilot efforts also enlisted interfaith coalitions to address food security and health.

The internal debates, however, have left a legacy of some uncertainty about how the World Bank would approach faith institutions in the future.

After Paul Wolfowitz became World Bank president in June 2005, he affirmed his commitment to the ongoing dialogue with representatives of the world's major faiths, and urged that partnerships deepen, particularly in Africa and in the Islamic world. The limbo surrounding the faith engagement, nonetheless, has yet to be fully resolved.

PRACTICAL CHALLENGES

The term "dialogue" in the titles of both the WFDD and the World Bank Development Dialogue reflects the goal of deepening engagement to help bridge the gulfs that have separated development and faith institutions, always with poverty the central focus. Dialogue has been used in a sense commonly understood in faith circles as an active exchange that aims to transform both understanding and action. The term dialogue, however, can sit uneasily if interpreted as talk alone. A part of the objective, clearly, is to translate abundant rhetoric and conclusions from dialogue into action. The WFDD and the World Bank unit have been catalysts in this effort. Their mission has been quite different from that of some other faith focused activities, notably the White House Office of Faith Based Initiatives, which was designed in large measure to help faith-based entities to secure public funding; the WFDD and World Bank effort has largely not involved funding of specific development programs but focuses instead on learning and ideas.

The World Bank and the WFDD's inaugural work focused on articulating why poverty persists and what should be done about it, with a priority to addressing disagreements among faiths and between faiths and development institutions on the topic. For the 2000 World Development Report on Poverty, the WFDD conducted regional consultations that elicited a range of perspectives. The resulting WFDD publication, *Poverty and Development*, offers a fresh and thoughtful view (and appears, among other places, in university syllabuses around the world).[9] The approach has strong synergy with the World Bank's Comprehensive Development Framework, which stresses the relationships between economic and social development, and the need to anchor all poverty work in a robust multisectoral approach.

WFDD also undertook work on culture, spirituality, and development, and has explored practice and issues on the MDGs, the Bank's PRSP process, and HIV/AIDS. The first explicit initiative of the relaunched, Washington, DC–based WFDD (early 2007) focuses on mapping faith-based children's programs in selected countries, to highlight knowledge and policy issues and opportunities for new partnerships. The WFDD also hopes to facilitate more active participation by faith communities in the PRSP process, based on their community-level and country-level work with the very poor. At the heart of both the World Bank and the WFDD's vision is the desire to bring the voices and experience of poor communities on a broad range of life issues, including spirituality, more forcefully and formally into development work.

Cooperative work between faith and development institutions under the joint leadership of the WFDD and the World Bank in Guatemala, Ethiopia, and Tanzania (between 2000 and 2003) proved complex to manage but yielded many lessons and insights. These efforts affirmed the large gulf between faith and development worlds in many developing countries: in particular, secular and religious organizations simply do not understand their respective vocabularies, networks are feeble, and they tend to expend energy in debates that too often pass like ships in the night. Yet tangible needs such as better school curricula, health services, and care of AIDS orphans highlight the potential for joint efforts. The challenge is to develop standards and mechanisms for faith literacy among development institutions, so they are familiar with the actors and their work, and to promote development literacy among faith communities, so they better understand secular agencies and the means and ends of their programs.

A second major challenge is expanding the organizational capacity of the development arms of faith and interfaith groups, which are often fragmented and fragile. No systematic approach or funding is yet available to address these challenges. We hope that the experiences highlighted in this book can spur efforts to change that situation.

THE RATIONALE FOR THIS BOOK

This book brings together case studies of common engagement between faith and development institutions. It is in many respects a sequel to the World Bank 2004 publication *Mind, Heart, and Soul in the Fight against Poverty*, which also focused on faith-development partnerships. Keen interest in that volume (for example, its use in college-level courses) attests to the fact that it filled a void, and to the benefits of the case study approach. However, the book barely scratched the surface of the vast well of experiences accruing in many corners of the world. Hence this second volume.

While several other books underscore the breadth and dynamism of faith-inspired movements and community work,[10] this volume focuses on bridges between faith and development organizations. Indeed, the primary thread running through this book is partnership—one of the most common terms in today's development lexicon. The notion of partnership reflects the reality that no organization can operate in isolation in today's complex world. Indeed, it would be difficult to identify a single activity of the World Bank that does not involve some form of partnership, and that applies to virtually all other organizations that operate in the development arena. Faith-development partnerships are thus part of a much broader trend that obliges institutions to work across traditional boundaries to enhance their core competencies. The extraordinary partnership arrangements depicted here range from informal cooperation to elaborate, long-range, joint ventures, and from financing for specific faith-run programs to larger grant-making efforts by foundations.

Pinpointing specific characteristics of these faith-development partnerships is rather hazardous, given the array of arrangements and their relatively poor documentation. However, each case study reveals challenges in bridging divergent approaches and language between secular and faith organizations. For example, when the Community of Sant'Egidio, a Rome-based Catholic lay movement that tackles poverty and fosters peace, works with the World Bank to test new approaches to HIV/AIDS treatment in Mozambique, a host of differences in organizational structure and practical repercussions, for example, of reliance on volunteers, arise, even before the institutions engage in their different understandings of complex issues like human rights and reasonable approaches to sustainability.

Experiences in recent years with faith-development partnerships (and faith institution partnerships with other types of organizations, like private companies) have given rise to considerable reflection. Box 1.2

presents a set of partnership principles that aim to address some underlying challenges. The principles are based on a dialogue about partnership challenges between Agnes Abuom, a leader of the All Africa Council of Churches, and Katherine Marshall, co-author of this volume.

BOX 1.2
PRINCIPLES FOR PARTNERSHIPS

Partnership is a common term in today's development lexicon, and that marks a quiet revolution. The explosion of civil society groups over the past two decades has goaded development institutions to create an array of working arrangements with widely different groups in virtually every sector. Faith-development partnerships are part of this broader phenomenon—and present some special challenges. Explicit focus on partnership principles by participants can smooth a sometimes bumpy road.

Guiding elements for principled partnerships include the following:

Work purposefully to set goals and priorities. Different parties bring different expectations and assumptions to any joint venture; careful exploration of the reasons why each group is involved can help frame a *shared vision* that includes concrete goals.

Focus on achieving genuine consensus on both objectives and path. Too many partnership arrangements reflect superficial agreement, but under the surface lurk very different understandings. Investing in a thoughtful and nuanced statement of objectives can provide a solid foundation.

Be realistic. Projects need to start from dreams but proceed via attainable steps.

Work purposefully to make sure that a shared language is well understood by all. Careful efforts to explore the significance of the wording that

(Box continues on the following page.)

(box continued)

expresses the mechanisms behind partnership agreements are essential. Faith groups and their partners need to "unpack" language so that they read the same meaning into concepts and vocabulary.

Gauge each partner's capacity with discernment and humility. A huge influx of money, demands, staff, and expectations can mortally wound fragile but functioning organizations and undermine successful work by faith and civil society groups at local levels. The partnership's shared vision should be grounded in careful assessment of local capacity and infrastructure, and acknowledge the limits of all partners.

Weigh different strengths and balance of power thoughtfully. Power differences almost always complicate relationships. Partnerships are effective only when all parties have distinctive roles to play and vital niches to fill. Community groups, nongovernmental organizations, or faith communities when they work as partners in development projects cannot be equal in every sense, but they are equally vital to success. Participants need to take careful and conscious steps to ensure that the partnership values and reflects local knowledge, credibility, contacts, and savvy.

Plan mentoring and capacity building with creativity, care, and humility. The partnership's shared vision should include mentoring that specifies the distinctive skills each side will teach the other.

Make transparency meaningful and real. A well-defined written framework for financial and project management is crucial to avoid burdening local groups with inappropriate demands while also giving funders an acceptable level of accountability and oversight.

Plan carefully for navigating bumps in the road, making changes, and evaluating results. Planning for crises before they happen is far better than inventing ways to handle them when things go wrong.

(*Box continues on the following page.*)

(box continued)

Procedures for midcourse correction and face-to-face resolution of disagreements are essential to all development partnerships, especially when administrative mechanisms do not exist and the "case law" of experience is limited. Regular joint meetings—perhaps run by a neutral third party—can help participants air grievances, hammer out problems, and establish new directions without judgment.

Look objectively and without illusions to the future—especially long-term financial support—and make sustainability a real and meaningful goal. Partners need to articulate their expectations for the longer term— that is, whether they envisage an "exit strategy," continued interest in the project, or a more open-ended relationship with periodic review and adjustment. Fuzzy expectations often result in deep misunderstanding, and can sour even successful ventures. The long-term nature of development work is often appreciated far more in word than in deed. If partners are aware that the life expectancy of an engagement is finite, they must make this clear from the beginning.

Source: Adapted from a forthcoming article by Agnes Abuom and Katherine Marshall, "New Partnership Models for Faith and Development Work: Clownfish and Sea Anenomes?"

This book is above all practical and experience driven. Partly because of the scarcity of research on such efforts, the material is generally drawn from lived experience. Indeed, the book is premised on the assumption that parties all too rarely mine practical experience—which often diverges from the best-laid plans—for its lessons. But these case studies also invite more research on the vastly underexplored nexus of faith and development.

Using the lessons of practical experience, this book aims to help translate into action the ideals and principles that so strongly motivate both development and faith leaders and institutions. It takes inspiration from the prophetic commitment of world leaders expressed in the MDGs. The faith and development leaders who inspired the WFDD urged making the MDGs the foundation for their efforts. Thus the spirit of the UN's Millennium Declaration—with its clarion call to end poverty in our generation—permeates the book and the experiences that underlie it.

THE BOOK'S ORGANIZATION AND GOALS

The book is organized into four parts. Part I addresses the framework of the MDGs and broad faith-based efforts to mobilize to achieve them. Part II focuses on case studies of faith-development engagement in communities, villages, and cities. Part III looks to global and local efforts to build alliances and partnerships. Part IV focuses on societies in conflict, where faith communities play major roles in forging peace, preventing further conflict, encouraging reconciliation, and rebuilding torn societies.

In selecting these case studies, our primary purpose has been to make an extensive but poorly understood body of experience more accessible. This experience forms part of an important global trend toward "many to many"—that is, to enlist multiple actors and organizations in development work.[11] The book's fundamental goal is to enable the resulting ideas and experience to shed light on best practices, and thus to improve policies and programs so that they yield better and more lasting results.

With today's focus on strategies that encourage diverse activities to add up to a larger whole, the important but often fragmented work of faith organizations presents special challenges. Thus this book also suggests avenues for surmounting the pitfalls of "separate and diverse," while continuing to harvest the extraordinary virtues and value of development work inspired by faith.

NOTES

1. Examples of a rethinking among leading figures are Madeline Albright, 2007, *The Mighty and the Almighty: Reflections on America, God, and World Affairs* (New York: Harper Perennial), and President Clinton's 2006 speech at the Tanenbaum Center for Religious Understanding (June 15, available at http://www.tanenbaum.org/lectures/2006_Clinton.pdf).

2. For information on this innovative process, see http://www.tripartiteinterfaith forum.org/.

3. See especially Pope Paul VI, March 26, 1967, *Populorum Progressio,* an encyclical that provided a detailed commentary on virtually every facet of development policy. Available at http://www.vatican.va/holy_father/paul_vi/encyclicals/ documents/hf_p-vi_enc_26031967_populorum_en.html.

4. For a description and analysis of the Washington consensus see http://www. cid.harvard.edu/cidtrade/issues/washington.html.

5. See "Learning with Jubilee: World Bank Engagement with the Jubilee 2000 Debt Campaign," chapter 3, in Katherine Marshall and Lucy Keough, 2004, *Mind, Heart, and Soul in the Fight against Poverty* (Washington, DC: World Bank).

6. The WFDD Website, http://www.wfdd.org.uk, includes a variety of documents detailing the organization's history and work.

7. For a detailed account of these arguments, see Katherine Marshall, 2005, "Faith and Development: Rethinking Development Debates," available at http://www.worldbank.org/developmentdialogue/.

8. Two books describe the meetings and the substantive agenda that emerged from them: Katherine Marshall and Richard Marsh, 2003, *Millennium Challenges for Faith and Development Leaders* (Washington, DC: World Bank); and Katherine Marshall and Lucy Keough, 2005, *Finding Global Balance* (Washington, DC: World Bank).

9. Available at http://wfdd.org.uk/documents/publications/poverty_development_ english.pdf.

10. This book can be read in parallel with two other books that focus on the work of faith institutions on development, and that grew out of the experience of the WFDD: Wendy Tyndale, 2006, *Visions of Development: Faith-Based Initiatives* (Aldershot, Hampshire, UK: Ashgate); and Makarand Paranjape, ed., 2005, *Dharma and Development: The Future of Survival* (Delhi: Samvad India Foundation).

11. Carol Lancaster, 2007, *Foreign Aid: Diplomacy, Development, Domestic Politics* (Chicago: University of Chicago Press).

PART **I**

Partners on Millennium Challenges

Introduction

The Millennium Development Goals play several central roles in global affairs. First and perhaps most important, they represent a covenant binding all nations in a clearly stated moral imperative and commitment to fighting poverty.

Second, the MDGs set priorities for action. Third, they establish a framework for accountability by defining measurable targets and setting deadlines for meeting them. Fourth, they address the cost of achieving the goals—and thus provide additional markers for assessing progress.

Finally, the MDGs imply an allocation of responsibilities—above all, between richer and poorer countries, but also, in various iterations and refinements of the framework, between national and global communities. Overall, the MDGs define an architecture for socioeconomic development, and demand a heroic, multifaceted, global partnership to respond to the challenges.

So what prompted the MDGs—today a touchstone in development circles, posted on bulletin boards in many institutions and the subject of numerous speeches and conferences? In September 2000, the Millennium Summit of world political leaders made poverty a global priority, and the summit's prophetic Millennium Declaration committed nations to taking significant steps to address that priority:[1]

> We will spare no effort to free our fellow men, women and children from the abject and dehumanizing conditions of extreme poverty, to which more than a billion of them are currently

subjected. We are committed to making the right to development a reality for everyone and to freeing the entire human race from want....We resolve therefore to create an environment—at the national and global levels alike—which is conducive to development and to the elimination of poverty.

Success in meeting these objectives depends, *inter alia*, on good governance within each country. It also depends on good governance at the international level and on transparency in the financial, monetary and trading systems. We are committed to an open, equitable, rule-based, predictable and non-discriminatory multilateral trading and financial systems. We are concerned about the obstacles developing countries face in mobilizing the resources needed to finance their sustained development. We will therefore make every effort to ensure the success of the High-level International and Intergovernmental Event on Financing for Development, to be held in 2001.

We also undertake to address the special needs of the least developed countries. In this context, we welcome the Third United Nations Conference on the Least Developed Countries to be held in May 2001 and will endeavour to ensure its success.... We are also determined to deal comprehensively and effectively with the debt problems of low- and middle-income developing countries, through various national and international measures designed to make their debt sustainable in the long term.

After the summit, the principles that the leaders agreed on were refined into the detailed, quantified framework known as the MDGs, with eight goals and specific targets broken down by country, and even regions within countries. With a target date of 2015, the MDGs invite evaluations, and 2005 marked the first major international stock-taking effort.

The Millennium Summit immediately followed a gathering—the first at the United Nations—of leaders of the world's religions, who also focused sharply on global inequities and the urgent need to tackle them. This faith summit highlighted many of the specific topics that the national leaders then addressed.[2] Thus the millennium commitments link spiritual ideas and institutions with secular ones.

In the ensuing years, the interest of faith leaders and communities in the MDGs has grown, including both the specific goals and the framework for accountability. The following excerpt from a sermon by Canon John L. Peterson tying the MDGs to an urgent call for peace and justice illustrates the power of faith interpretations of the MDG framework:[3]

> The eight Millennium Development Goals are a good beginning.
>
> Truly we will know no peace until we eradicate the oppression of extreme poverty and hunger.
>
> Truly we will know no peace until universal primary education is achieved.
>
> Truly we will know no peace until gender equality and women are empowered.
>
> Truly we will know no peace until child mortality is reduced.
>
> Truly we will know no peace until maternal health is improved.
>
> Truly we will know no peace until HIV and AIDS, malaria and other diseases are combated.
>
> Truly we will know no peace until environmental sustainability is ensured.
>
> Truly we will know no peace until global partnership for development is achieved.
>
> And I would like to add one more challenge. That we will know no peace until governments speak and work with those with whom they differ, and with whom they call enemies, be it the United States and Iran, or the Government of Uganda with Northern Uganda and Sudan. Until we break down those barriers, in our respective countries, how many more Archbishop Luwums are going to become martyrs around the world, because there is no peace with oppression?

The chapters in this section focus on the MDG framework and diverse faith-based and faith-secular partnerships that are tackling particular MDG dimensions.

Chapter 2 discusses broad alliances among faith institutions inspired in good measure by the MDGs. This chapter highlights the engagement of these institutions in the global MDG mobilization, and their growing use of the MDG framework as a basis for advocacy and action. This overview also highlights the intersections between the poverty and social justice work of many faith organizations, and the countless links between faith and development work.

Chapter 3 turns to HIV/AIDS. The global battle against this pandemic has sparked dialogue, capacity building, and creative partnerships that highlight the vital role of faith and faith institutions more graphically than any other issue within the MDG framework.

Chapters 4 and 5 recount faith-based collaborations on other global health challenges, including malaria. These experiences underscore the challenges that remain in realizing the potential of faith development partnerships.

Chapter 6 explores the complexities of one of the most vital challenges of the MDGs: bringing education to all. Faith communities are deeply engaged in addressing this challenge, often focusing on improving educational quality and incorporating values into school curricula.

The final two chapters explore issues that are vital to the MDG framework but not highlighted as specific goals. Chapter 7 recounts an exemplary partnership in Ghana between faith and secular partners working on waste and sanitation. Chapter 8 underscores the commitment of faith communities to ensuring decent housing for all.

NOTES

1. See http://www.un.org/millennium/declaration/ares552e.htm.

2. For a summary of the meeting, see Katherine Marshall, 2001, "Religion and Development: A Different Lens on Development Debates," *Peabody Journal of Education* 76 (3,4): 339–375.

3. Canon John L. Peterson, National Cathedral, Washington, DC, February 18, 2007.

CHAPTER 2

Faith Communities Engage the Millennium Development Goals

The Millennium Development Goals (MDGs) were crafted through meetings involving both national leaders and staff from the headquarters and specialized agencies of the UN. The simplicity of the goals and targets belies the complex processes involved in agreeing on priorities, debating what should and should not appear, and setting quantitative targets that were sufficiently inspirational yet realistic enough to encourage practical action. What has emerged is an elaborate framework that details goals and targets globally, regionally, and nationally, and in some instances even subnationally.[1]

Faith communities and the global interfaith world did not immediately enter the fray of framing targets and goals based on the declaration that emerged from the UN Millennium Summit of political leaders. The summit of world religious leaders at UN headquarters just before the Millennium Summit did address aspects of the global development agenda, including debt, poverty, water, and the environment. However,

---

This chapter draws on events and activities in which the authors were involved and includes inputs from other participants. It does not purport to offer a comprehensive picture of the diverse and dynamic engagement of faith communities in the MDG process.

the faith leaders focused more directly on peace and conflict. They also sought to highlight, albeit in broad terms, the vision that religious voices could bring to bear on urgent global challenges.[2]

This unprecedented interfaith gathering did not produce the synergy many had hoped for, given longstanding interfaith tensions combined with the intrinsic challenge of finding common ground among disparate actors. Yet since that meeting in 2000, faith groups have steadily intensified their engagement in the MDG framework, and religious actors are now poised to play even more significant roles. The major areas of engagement include national, regional, and global advocacy and mobilization around the MDGs; implementing specific programs to help fulfill them; and monitoring progress. This chapter highlights a few of the many faith-development partnerships designed to achieve the MDGs.

In their raw form, the goals are not always easy to convey, and indeed they were never intended to provide a comprehensive blueprint for action. A better analogy is a map, which provides a sense of direction and allows a wide range of actors to see themselves as contributing to a global process with one overarching goal—ending the worst forms of poverty—and which provides a central means for achieving it: scaling up policies and programs that work. The growing engagement of faith communities in the overall MDG process as well as key program areas is a hopeful portent.

GLOBAL FAITH ADVOCACY AND MOBILIZATION

Three events highlight the expanding role of faith networks in the MDG campaign, and the convening power and moral voice of faith communities. The first event—a conference at the UK Treasury in London in February 2004—was instrumental in framing an ambitious agenda for the global Year of Development in 2005 (a designation both of the UN and the G8 leaders). Later that year, the Micah Challenge, an alliance of Christian organizations, was launched at UN headquarters. And in 2006, the global assembly in Kyoto of the WCRP—one of the world's largest interfaith organizations—made the MDGs the focus of practical workshops designed to equip the more than 600 religious leaders attending that meeting to take action in their communities.

The London Conference

The conference in London was, in retrospect, a pivotal event in the extraordinary mobilization of 2005, which culminated in elaborately orchestrated events around the meeting of the G8 nations at Gleneagles, Scotland, in July 2005.[3] The London conference was the brainchild of Lord Carey of Clifton, James Wolfensohn (then president of the World Bank), Lord Griffiths of Goldman Sachs, and Gordon Brown, then UK Chancellor of the Exchequer. Only about 200 people participated, but they were noteworthy in their diversity, as they included representatives from the diplomatic corps, politics, business, faith groups, NGOs, media, the arts, and academia. The meeting's memorable speeches included an address by Brazilian President Luiz Inácio Lula Da Silva (by video).The original small group also expanded to include two remarkable specialists in communications: Live Aid leader and musician Bob Geldof, and rock group U2's lead singer Bono.

The conference's initial goals were rather modest: to bring faith and development leaders, primarily from the United Kingdom, together in active partnerships in the broad area of alleviating poverty, specifically geared to the MDGs. However, during the preparations for and during the conference—entitled Making Globalization Work for All: The Challenge of Delivering the Monterrey Consensus—a far more ambitious agenda took shape. The Monterrey Consensus referred to the special moment of global consensus and determination that emerged from the March 2002 global meeting in Mexico on Financing for Development, which probably represented the high point of optimism that a true global will to fight poverty had been forged. The London conference sought to expand and revitalize the spirit that was evident there. What stands out in retrospect is the dual focus on ensuring financing for development, and on communicating to the public and mobilizing broad support for meeting development challenges.

Several key themes emerged from the London discussions. The importance of clear, memorable "melodies" and messages cast in unambiguous terms was repeatedly underscored. The slogan "Make Poverty History", which marked the alliance that formed over the ensuing months, was one outcome, reflecting the admonition of the artistic advisors that the movement would need messages couched in no more than three words. The ambitious notion of working for the largest social mobilization in post–World War II history was also a centerpiece.

The active role of faith leaders at the conference marked an important new dimension in global discussions of the MDG challenge. Later that year, the Vatican and the World Council of Churches organized meetings that focused on the MDGs (in Rome in July 2004 and Geneva in October 2004, respectively), and the critical roles of faith groups in leading global mobilization, advocacy, and dialogue about poverty.

The Micah Challenge

During roughly the same period, a group of Christian leaders came together to form an alliance known as the Micah Challenge (though its origins date from 2001). Led by the World Evangelical Alliance and the Micah Network, a coalition of some 300 Christian organizations providing relief, development, and justice ministries throughout the world, the challenge draws inspiration from the Bible's book of Micah: "What does the LORD require of you? To do justice, and to love kindness, and to walk humbly with your God" (Micah 6:8). The challenge focuses explicitly on global poverty and frames its goals in terms of the MDGs. As the organizers put it in their statement of vision and purpose, they aim to seize a unique moment.

The Micah Challenge was launched globally on October 15, 2004, in conjunction with the UN's International Day for the Eradication of Poverty.[4] The campaign specifically aims to deepen Christian engagement with the poor, and to influence leaders of rich and poor nations alike to fulfill their public promise to achieve the MDGs. Toward that end, the challenge kicked off 11 national campaigns that year, and 15 more in 2005 and 2006. The year 2004 also saw the release of educational materials and advocacy materials designed to allow local congregations to be powerful advocates for different global events like the G8 Heads of State Meetings and UN summits.

The Micah Challenge works to strengthen the capacity of its members to mount a biblically shaped response to the needs of the poor and oppressed; to speak strongly and effectively regarding the Church's mission to proclaim and demonstrate the love of Christ to a world in need; and to convince decision makers to respect the rights of the poor and oppressed and rescue the weak and needy. The campaign aims both to change public policy and encourage Christians to participate, and intends to judge its success in that light. Organizers see the lengthy roster of organizations and individuals who have signed the Micah Call and participated in advocacy as a benchmark of its success. The campaign also aims to raise awareness of the MDGs among Christian organizations, and track their direct contributions in fulfilling them.

The Global Assembly of WCRP

It was clear by the time of the August 2006 assembly of the WCRP that the potential for significant interfaith contributions to the MDG process was large and largely untapped. A year earlier, the UN Millennium Campaign had asked WCRP to develop tools to enable the campaign to work with faith-based organizations on the MDGs. This collaboration helped make the MDGs an important focus of WCRP's assembly, which brought together the formal leadership of one of the world's most prominent interfaith organizations with other leaders and scholars from virtually every religious tradition.

The focus was apparent in the assembly's central theme of "shared security." Reiterated over and over again during the assembly, and in pre-assemblies focusing on women and youth, was the notion that there can be no true security unless it is shared by all people and all communities. That notion took the classic meaning of physical security—above all, the absence of warfare—and built from there to a much broader concept. With religious tensions running high in today's world, the focus of interfaith gatherings, including this one, tends to be on deep faith traditions of peace, and the practical roles of faith leaders and communities in making peace and building peaceful societies. However, shared security means far more than the absence of violence, and complex causal links among poverty, social injustice, inequity, anger, and violence were woven throughout the assembly. Far more than previous WCRP assemblies, this one underscored the responsibility of religious leaders and communities to engage in efforts to end poverty.

Toward this end, WCRP prepared a presentation and manual on the roles of religious institutions and leaders in implementing the MDGs.[5]

Introduced at the assembly, the "Faith in Action" toolkit—designed as a practical guide—prompted discussions of concrete avenues for advocacy and mobilization as well as moral imperatives and common purpose.

Faith communities and UN agencies alike now use the toolkit. For example, the Egypt office of the UN Development Programme has used the Arabic language version to engage religious communities around the MDGs. In South Africa, the Centre for HIV/AIDS Networking at the University of KwaZulu-Natal and WCRP organized an interfaith meeting of 75 people to focus on the MDGs, and on building collaboration between government agencies and faith-based groups to achieve them. Senior religious leaders in KwaZulu Natal also used the toolkit in choosing MDGs as a key priority.

MONITORING PROGRESS

The Africa Monitor, a group inspired and led by Winston Njongonkulu Ndungane, Anglican archbishop of Cape Town, illustrates the potential for involving faith leaders in an important aspect of the MDGs: accountability.[6] The archbishop was concerned that the monitoring mechanisms proposed during the UN's Year of Development and the Year for Africa, which UK Prime Minister Tony Blair also designated for 2005, depended largely on governments. The New Partnership for Africa's Development (NEPAD) for all its promise does not, in his view, have sufficient mechanisms to ensure that civil society's voice is clearly heard. The archbishop also shared the nagging concern of many that the end of 2005 might see a loss of focus and momentum on poverty and Africa. Above all, he wanted to ensure an authentic African voice in these challenges. Thus he launched Africa Monitor to serve as a voice for African civil society— too often a missing "fourth piece of the jigsaw," as he termed it during 2006 meetings in Washington DC. The monitor frames its purpose in moral terms: to ensure that promises are truly implemented, and that the focus remains real people.

The archbishop initially sought support from the Center for Justice and Reconciliation, based at the National Cathedral in Washington, DC, which had hosted a conference in September 2005 at which the archbishop played a leading role. He also sparked interest among leading supporters of advocacy and monitoring around the MDGs, including Debt and Trade for Africa (DATA) and the Bill and Melinda Gates Foundation.[7] Interest among these groups reflected growing awareness of the power of faith-based networks, especially in Africa, and the archbishop's personal charisma and conviction.

The archbishop formally launched Africa Monitor during events in Kigali, Rwanda in June 2006, and in London in October, by pledging to monitor progress on African development. The Kigali meeting brought together African religious leaders and marked the formal inauguration of the Interfaith Action for Peace in Africa, which included representatives from African traditional religions, Islamic leaders, Christians, Hindus, Jews, Buddhists, Bahá'ís, and Rastafarians.

COUNTRY AND REGIONAL ENGAGEMENT

The Africa Monitor links advocacy around the MDGs to faith communities and networks and the specific challenges in Africa—which in many respects represent the core of the MDGs. No faith-led counterpart has yet emerged for other regions. However, faith leaders in virtually all countries are using the MDGs as a framework for action through their individual communities and interfaith networks.

The involvement of faith communities in the MDGs and national strategies to address poverty takes quite different forms in different countries. An example is a study by the Catholic Agency for Oversees Development that estimated the costs of implementing the MDGs in Zambia. That study was designed to feed into a meeting on coordinating aid for that country in May 2005.[8] Organized through CIDSE, an international alliance of 18 Catholic development agencies based in Europe and North America, church groups lobbied individual aid-giving governments before the meeting to increase their aid.

On the other side of the world, the Cambodia MDG Campaign planned rallies and spurred mobilization around Buddhist events. These included the Kan Ben Buddhist ceremony in September 2006 and the Water Festival in November that same year.[9]

More broadly, faith advocacy is focusing on the World Bank's Poverty Reduction Strategy process, because it enlists civil society leaders as formal participants, and identifies specific areas for action and monitors progress. Active participation by faith leaders in the processes varies widely in practice, depending both on the capacity of faith groups and on receptiveness of the various governments. This is a long-term process and is wisely seen as an important vehicle where dialogue about priorities in social policy and for poverty programs can take place over time.

Small-scale, piecemeal efforts by individual congregations illustrate the potential of local faith-based engagement, as well as its improbable paths. For example, during the 2007 U.S. college basketball championships, known as "March madness," the Website of a Methodist congregation in North Carolina urged members to donate $10 to the Nothing but Nets fund each time their team lost ("your team goes for nothing but nets").[10] The church used the funds to buy bednets for families in Zambia, to prevent children from dying of malaria. This effort enlisted support from the UN Foundation, the U.S. Methodist Church, *Sports Illustrated* magazine, and the American Basketball Association.

SCALING UP

An extraordinary array of programs led by faith communities can be seen as tied to the MDGs, in ways direct and indirect. This confirms the moral and practical force behind the MDG idea, and the energy and insight of its leaders and promoters. The efforts also underscore the depth of engagement of faith communities in poverty work, which is what the MDGs are about.

Nagging questions remain, however. Can the programs that faith communities run and support fulfill the aims of the UN Millennium Summit proclaimed in September 2000? Can those programs be scaled up and replicated? Can lessons be learned, so the programs can be adapted and improved? Are the programs of different actors complementary, to minimize duplication and realize the benefits of coordination and collaboration?

The answers to many of these questions are either uncertain or negative. Too often faith-run programs do not operate at the scale needed to make a significant difference in reversing global poverty. This may be because such programs tend to focus on charitable efforts at the individual, congregation, and community levels, or because policy impediments at the national level limit the programs' reach or dampen their impact.

Monitoring and evaluation systems are also often too weak to allow small-scale faith-based efforts to serve as models for learning and redesign. Finally, coordination between the vision and insight of faith-run programs and those implied in national strategies—whether macroeconomic, sectoral, or regional—is often fragmentary and ephemeral. To fulfill the MDGs, proponents need to address these problems, and better integrate faith-based efforts with national and international programs and strategies.

FAITH PARTICIPATION IN POLICY MAKING AND PROGRAMS

The remaining chapters in this section describe dilemmas and partnerships that engage faith institutions and communities in addressing one or more of the MDGs. The leading topic is HIV/AIDS, because this is where faith and secular development partners have done the most work, and where their complementary roles may be the most compelling.

Though often historically overlooked, the role of faith communities in providing health care, both overall and in combating specific diseases like malaria, is attracting considerable attention today in global health circles. The depth of faith-based engagement in formal education also stands out, given the particular insights of a faith lens in this arena.

The link between the MDGs and the capacities of faith communities is remarkable even in more unexpected arenas, including the mundane but critical question of garbage and sanitation. Faith communities also play pivotal roles in fulfilling MDG number eight, which calls on wealthier countries to provide practical support for the MDGs, and to develop a new array of partnerships to achieve them. Faith networks span rich and poor countries, and thus offer channels for communicating and mobilizing around the moral imperative of shared security.

These chapters offer a very partial treatment of an enormously rich topic. Each target and goal within the MDG framework feeds into the interests, commitments, and direct roles of faith communities in many ways. The discussions here scratch the surface even as they illustrate the potential for investigation and action.

NOTES

1. For more on the MDGs, see http://www.un.org/millenniumgoals/.

2. For a description of the summit of religious leaders and some of the issues surrounding it, see Katherine Marshall, 2001, "Religion and Development: A Different Lens on Development Debates," *Peabody Journal of Education* 76 (3,4): 339–375.

3. The leaders of eight industrialized nations meet once a year in one of the countries.

4. For more on the origin and recent activities of the Micah Challenge, see http://www.micahchallenge.org/.

5. Religions for Peace, 2006, "Faith in Action: Working towards the Millennium Development Goals—An Action Toolkit for Religious Leaders and Communities," available at http://www.millenniumcampaign.org/.

6. The Africa Monitor Website has more information on history and objectives of the effort. See http://www.africanmonitor.org/about.

7. See http://www.data.org/.

8. See http://www.cidse.org/.

9. See http://www.millenniumcampaign.org/.

10. See http://christchurchcharlotte.org; and http://nothingbutnets.net/.

CHAPTER 3

Strategic Challenges
for Faith-Based
Health Care

Religious communities own, run, or inspire substantial parts of the health care systems in many countries. Like religious faith traditions themselves, these systems vary widely in approach and organization. However, they often stand out for their special focus on the poorest of the poor (Mother Teresa's programs, for example), as well as their superb management and cutting-edge research, although instances of badly run shoestring facilities do exist.

Debates about the purpose and intent of these faith-based facilities are gathering momentum. How strongly are they linked to proselytizing? Does theology trump science? How do these facilities reflect or advance political agendas? However, the questions should not detract from the important reality that these systems are a critical part of health delivery worldwide, accounting for perhaps 30–50 percent of the global health care landscape.

Although embedded in a larger system, faith-based health care is in some ways a world of its own—ancient in origin, and driven by profound human values and concern for people and souls. Indeed, many faith communities see caring for the sick as a profound mission not open to question. "The hospital is our cathedral," commented one prominent

This chapter draws on research and discussions by Katherine Marshall. Drafts benefited from thoughtful comments from Father Robert Vitello, Jacques Baudouy, William Lesher, Roger Sullivan, and Lincoln Chen.

Catholic cardinal during a Rome discussion in August 2006 with the author. Leaders from many faiths refer with pride to the long-term, sustainable nature of their engagement, contending: "We are part of communities, not outsiders, not parachuting in; we are not fly-by-night briefcase NGOs; we were here long before any other development partners were even born. We are here for the duration."[1] These leaders thus tend to take issue with contemporary public health experts who might, if strongly secular in bent, tend to view faith-run facilities as something of an anachronism with limited relevance for their mission of developing public health systems.

Because faith-led health systems plainly play such an important role, it stands to reason that they should be part of the global commitment to the MDGs—especially the goals that focus on expanding access to health care and alleviating poverty. However, the hard reality is that despite much common-sense rhetoric, engagement at a practical and policy level between faith-based and public institutions is often rather fractured; communication tends to be poor, and a strategic approach appears to be lacking. And lack of literacy cuts both ways: public health and development officials often have scant or distorted understanding of religion, while many religious leaders who may oversee health systems have little formal training in public health.

Many participants and observers of health care systems assume that these habits and presuppositions make sense. However, the MDG challenge calls them into question, as do intractable diseases such as HIV/AIDS, malaria, childhood diarrhea, and even avian flu. What's more, debates on health care ethics and morality are picking up steam in public policy circles, accentuating the need to rethink and redress the divide.

The central questions can be framed as follows:

- Do national, regional, and global health care projects and institutions have significant blind spots in considering the roles of faith-inspired institutions? What are the major areas of disconnect and what are the missed opportunities?
- How could more intelligent and purposeful engagement with faith-run health services enhance services for poor people and communities?
- Should participants in health care systems tackle this challenge institution by institution, or country by country, or is a regional and even

global policy approach needed? What regions deserve priority attention: Africa? The South Asia subcontinent? Latin America?

ANCIENT ROOTS

The ancient roots of religion and medicine are deeply intertwined. As early as 4,000 BC, religions identified certain deities with healing. The temples of Saturn, and later of Asclepius in Asia Minor, for example, were recognized as healing centers.

Hindu Brahmanic hospitals were established in Sri Lanka as early as 431 BC, and King Ashoka established a chain of hospitals in Hindustan about 230 BC. The Romans established hospitals (*valetudinaria*) around 100 BC, while state-supported, faith-inspired hospitals appeared in China during the first millennium AD. Various monastic orders of different faiths and in widely different regions have run a variety of facilities for the sick.

The history of Christian health care (as well as its contemporary profile) tends to be the best documented, but it is not more significant than its counterparts in other faiths, especially Islam. Muslim hospitals developed a high standard of care between the eighth and twelfth centuries. Hospitals in Baghdad in the ninth and tenth centuries—precursors of the modern hospital—employed up to 25 staff physicians and maintained separate wards for various conditions. Jewish institutions have similarly been leaders in health policy and practice in many parts of the world.

Religious organizations founded many contemporary hospitals that are more than 50 years old—partly because those groups were the only ones willing to start money-losing propositions. They were also, with just a handful of exceptions, the only institutions that reached out to rural, marginalized populations, especially outside of Europe. These institutions have been in the vanguard in caring for ethnic minorities—whom majorities, or those who held money and power, sadly often regarded as less than human.

Today the Brahma Kumaris in India run a widely acclaimed hospital at the forefront of practice and research on heart disease.[2] And the unique approach of faith traditions that place a high premium on meditation—notably Buddhism—is becoming important to medical science. In Thailand, Venerable Dr. Mettanando Bhikkhu, a Buddhist leader, is a pioneer in health systems, advocating a deeply reformed, community-based national system that emphasizes elder and hospice care.[3]

Despite this record, the global role of faith-run health facilities is hard to trace, because they have often followed complex historical paths in interacting with public health systems. This may be most significant in Africa, where countries such as Mozambique have sometimes abruptly nationalized church-run facilities, and have renegotiated church-state arrangements several times. The result is hybrid systems unique to each country. Religion in Africa is particularly dynamic, and that also affects its role in health care.

Faith-run systems now account for a significant part of health care facilities on that continent (the estimates of exactly how much reflect an extraordinarily wide range, from 30–70 percent). In conflict areas, faith-run institutions are often the only providers on the ground. Churches created the modern health systems in the region, and retain special interest even when they pass ownership to others. Church organizations continue to train many doctors and nurses, for example. They also act as guardians of quality and—they would argue—ethical concerns underpinning health policies and systems.

INFORMATION CHALLENGES

The emergence of public health systems and the burgeoning of for-profit care have brought dramatic changes to this picture. However, as noted, faith-run facilities remain a key component of the health care system in most countries. And, frankly, those institutions may well be where we would like to find ourselves or our families if we are in need, because the quality of care tends to be high, and the approach particularly humane.

One observer aptly described contemporary faith-run health systems as a galaxy. Most are decentralized, with day-to-day management—including fundraising and financial administration—located in specific institutions. The largest single faith-run system—that of the Catholic Church—includes countless kinds of facilities. Many are run by religious orders, while others are initiated directly by bishops (who have ultimate responsibility within their diocese); Catholic NGOs (such as Caritas Internationalis, a confederation of relief, development, and social service groups); and movements (such as the Community of Sant'Egidio, which is a lay Catholic group whose fundamental work is with the very poor). The mapping of these institutions is imperfect, to say the least. Catholic institutions, including the Vatican's Pontifical Council Cor Unum, the Pontifical Council on Health Care, and Caritas Internationalis, maintain large directories. However, information is often available only to those who know how to locate and read it, and there is no obvious single global repository. And analyses of how these faith-based institutions work and interface with other health institutions is weak, particularly in developing countries.

The dearth of specific information is a major impediment to defining actual and potential roles for faith-based health institutions, and even to framing policy questions. Fortunately, several efforts to map the faith-based health care landscape are under way. A noteworthy example is the African Religious Health Assets Program—a joint venture of Emory University and the University of Capetown—which is documenting health assets in Zambia and Lesotho, supported by the World Health Organization (see box 3.1). The Unions of Superiors General—composed of the heads of both male and female religious orders—are collecting information on HIV programs and services sponsored by these orders throughout the world.

BOX 3.1
MAPPING RELIGIOUS HEALTH ASSETS IN ZAMBIA AND LESOTHO:
THE IMPORTANCE OF LOCAL WISDOM

As the HIV/AIDS pandemic entered its twenty-fifth year, a coalition of researchers—working through the African Religious Health Assets Programme (ARHAP)—set out to understand more fully the contribution of religious entities to health, especially in the fight against HIV/AIDS. In mapping a broad spectrum of faith-based health assets, the researchers focused on Zambia and Lesotho, because of high national seroprevalence rates (17.0 and 23.2 percent, respectively), and because distinctive social and cultural factors could offer a

(Box continues on the following page.)

(box continued)

multitude of analytical lessons. For instance, in Zambia, Christian networks provide 30 percent of national health services, while in Lesotho that number rises to 40 percent. The researchers performed the study under contract to the World Health Organization, in cooperation with universities in South Africa and the United States.

ARHAP team members employed a distinctive research methodology they called "participatory inquiry into religious health assets, networks, and agency." In this approach, participatory workshops hosted over 350 people invited as a purposive sample of citizens and religious and health leaders. These participants discussed all facets of the pandemic and the ways in which religious entities have responded to the HIV/AIDS crisis and to broader health issues, often steering the debate toward locally pertinent topics. ARHAP then used these qualitative insights, along with quantitative analysis, to create maps of faith-based health work in various geographical areas. The researchers were especially successful in pinpointing small local groups that often escape the attention of national and regional public-sector agencies and faith organizations.

The study offers the first credible data on the contributions of the faith-based health infrastructure in Zambia and Lesotho. It is also a first attempt to map both "tangible" and "intangible" religious assets. The researchers argue that religious and cultural norms and values define the health-seeking strategies of many Africans, and that the failure of health policy makers to take into account the overarching influence of religion—and the important role of faith-based organizations (FBOs) in providing HIV treatment and care—could seriously undermine efforts to scale up health services.

The report's recommendations include a call for greater collaboration between public health agencies and faith-based organizations, especially in the following arenas:

- *Fostering faith and public health literacy,* such as by creating shared materials and offering joint training and formal courses to improve understanding between FBOs and public health agencies.

- *Encouraging respectful engagement,* such as by expanding the community workshops as used in the ARHAP study and involving more FBOs in health work, and bringing together religious and public health leaders to encourage long-term collaboration in policy making and project implementation.

- *Coordinating religious and health systems,* such as by using health mapping to identify FBOs that could scale up such services and linking them to nearby state-run hospitals, clinics, and dispensaries.

- *Pursuing further collaborative research,* such as by extending participatory mapping of both tangible and intangible health assets to other African countries and low- and middle-income regions.

An apt observation from the study sums up its ethos and conclusion: "Though often hidden from Western view, religion is so overwhelmingly significant in the African search for wellbeing, so deeply woven in the rhythms of everyday life, and so deeply entwined in African values, attitudes, perspectives and decision-making frameworks that the inability to understand religion leads to an inability to understand people's lives."[a]

a. *Source*: African Religious Health Assets Programme, October 2006, "Appreciating Assets: Understanding the Contribution of Religion to Universal Access in Africa," Report for the World Health Organization (Cape Town: ARHAP). Available at http://www.arhap.uct.ac.za/publications. php#reports.

The greatest gap concerns evaluation and analysis. While individual studies have examined the effectiveness of health care systems run by faith-based institutions, the picture is patchy at best. And systematic evaluation has rarely been a central concern of faith-inspired systems, particularly those operating under stress in poor countries.

Ritva Reinikke and Jacob Svensson's 2003 study "Working for God," which compared the effectiveness of church-run and public health institutions in Uganda, is a notable exception.[4] The study's central finding—that church-run facilities are more efficient and effective by most measures—is hardly surprising to those who have observed these facilities in action. Still, the study barely scratches the surface of questions that could be posed.

CHALLENGES FOR FAITH-RUN HEALTH CARE

Contemporary health care challenges differ radically from those of the past, when faith institutions were at the center of efforts by societies to care for the sick. Modern hospitals also present new financial, technical, and social demands. As a result, some faith institutions are rethinking their roles in direct provision of care.

For example, in many developing countries, "foreigners" have staffed and administered Catholic health care facilities for 100 years or more. Today many of these facilities have developed nursing and medical schools to train local professionals, and are turning over staffing and administration to nationals. Yet these nationals may lack contacts with outside donors whose support is needed to keep them operating.

Continued unease in relationships between faith-led institutions and governments on occasion prompts the former to fudge reports of their assets and facets of care. One large faith-based NGO retains ownership of facilities with its international rather than its national arm, to protect against seizure of assets.

At the root of many challenges to faith-based health care systems is money: How can they remain viable, especially when their core mission is to serve the poorest segments of the community? And who pays? Modern health care surely cannot, on a large scale, continue to run as a charity. Yet public funding for faith-based care is often provisional and precarious, and with crises either occurring (such as in Eritrea, where the role of faith-run hospitals faces uncertainties) or looming (such as in Uganda—see box 3.2).

BOX 3.2
UGANDA'S FAITH-BASED HEALTH PARTNERS: A WORKABLE SYSTEM CONFRONTS A CRISIS

Uganda stands out among African nations in its long-standing arrangement with Catholic, Protestant, and Islamic medical bureaus. These form part of the backbone of the country's pioneering, sector-wide approach to health care. The bureaus participate in all major policy dialogue on health through the monthly Health Policy Advisory Committee and annual Joint Review meetings. That system brings together service providers and funders, which allows faith leaders to interact systematically with both government policy makers and the international development community.

Indeed, although official documents seldom highlight the role of faith institutions in Uganda's health care system, they own and run over a third of the facilities. The faith community has been central to Uganda's remarkable cross-sector partnerships on HIV/AIDS, and Catholic Bishop Halimana chairs Uganda's AIDS Commission. The faith-run hospitals and clinics are an integral and established part of the health system and they train a large share of health sector personnel for the country.

The government supports these faith-based facilities through an annual subvention, which goes directly to district governments and thence to health care facilities. These funds cover about 35 percent of the operating costs of faith-based facilities, while user fees cover about 50 percent, and charitable contributions account for the remainder. Although the system has its hiccups, including delays in the transfer of government funds, participants describe it as working reasonably well over the past decade. Still, serious problems are brewing.

(Box continues on the following page.)

(box continued)

Although faith-run institutions provide slightly over 30 percent of the country's health care, they receive only 7 percent of the national health care budget. Like other providers, these institutions must contend with constantly rising demand and costs. Furthermore, in 2006 the government agreed to substantial salary increases for government health workers. However, the subvention directed to faith-run health care institutions did not change. The result is that their health care workers left at a significant rate, threatening some facilities with closure. Several faith-run hospitals have celebrated 100 years of operation, and with a strong track record and stronger commitment, leaders hope that they will muddle through. However, the fragility of the system, and the lack of a clear vision for its future, are facts of life.

The Catholic Medical Bureau,[a] which runs the oldest and largest part of the faith-run health system and employs some 6,000 health workers, is concerned that the government does not fully recognize the excellent performance and value of the faith-run system. The bureau also believes that the government, and by implication the international partners that support it, accords lower priority to health care today than in the past. Overall there is an air of resignation that the "muddle through" approach is likely to continue into the foreseeable future.

Source: This box is based on author discussions in Uganda August 2006. Peter Okwero, World Bank office in Kampala, also provided information and useful comments.

a. Described in Daniele Giusti, Peter Lochoro, John Odaga, and Everd Maniple, 2004, "Pro-Poor Health Services: The Catholic Health Network in Uganda," *Development Outreach* (March 2004), (Washington, DC: World Bank Institute). See http://www1.worldbank.org/devoutreach/march04/.

The theme of corruption arises constantly—on both sides. Faith leaders harbor strong views that most government systems are deeply corrupt and unreliable, while public officials often maintain that faith-led institutions lack financial skills which encourages waste and leakage. Active debates about church-state relations in some countries complicate this situation.

How can and should public health leaders and institutions engage with faith-run hospitals? Where are the boundaries in medicine between church and state? What are their respective roles? Are faith-run health systems simply part of the "not-for profit" sector, or do they need or merit special consideration?

Many faith providers would fiercely defend the premise that compassion and morality are integral to their approach. Others would argue, just as fiercely, that faith-run medicine is driven by a professional quest for excellence that cannot and should not be sharply distinguished from other health providers. On balance, the significant public service role of faith institutions seems to warrant acknowledgment, if not special focus.

THE MORALITY CONUNDRUM

Moral qualms lie at the heart of many debates about the role of faith-inspired institutions in health care, with such qualms sometimes provoking raging public exchange and sometimes quieter concern. Contemporary debates about medical ethics, for example—including bioethics, stem cell research, and policy and practice at the beginning and end of life—seem to become most intense regarding faith-run health care systems.

Many faith leaders would describe their role as providing a moral compass for health care. For example, one senior Catholic official with decades of involvement in health care objected to what he termed "moral conditionality."[5] That is, urgently needed public funding often comes with conditions that run counter to church teachings, and thus are immoral and unacceptable.[6]

However, alternative perspectives on the same moral questions can draw just as deeply on tradition and ethics. Most significant is the view that faith-run approaches breach core principles in their unwillingness to accept that women have fundamental rights to reproductive health care and freedom of choice. These critics see providing accurate and complete information to patients about their options—including access to contraception and abortion—as an ethical imperative. This view is commonly associated with women's groups, but many other advocates also promote it.

Thus different parties fight fiercely for the moral high ground, and positions become polarized, perceptions drown out facts, and emotions run high. Dialogue is often totally blocked because of the perceived force of the respective moral principles. The irony is that passionate advocates often share powerful and common concerns about the need to offer care to poor people and communities, including women who lack any prospect of asserting a meaningful notion of rights. The debate over reproductive rights helps explain why many public health experts are deeply reluctant to engage faith leaders, although that is not the only sources of tension. Health care presents ethical dilemmas at every step, and stalemate can ensue if participants are unwilling to engage in respectful dialogue.

The questions are complex enough when the area of focus is health institutions, which include hospitals, clinics, and trained health care workers. However, public health involves far more than health facilities—it also includes "health assets." Such assets include the intangible forces of community and social capital, as evidenced by the important role of faith congregations in fighting malaria and HIV/AIDS. Congregational roles may include the influence of mothers' unions, youth groups, or other means of conveying powerful messages. The African Religious Health Assets Program is striving to come to terms with this far broader and important dimension of assets.[7]

Faith institutions are powerful advocates for greater international support for health care, including through the MDGs. For example, the Website of the United States Conference of Catholic Bishops includes a wealth of materials on global health imperatives.[8] However, without clear agreement on the role of faith institutions in addressing these issues, disconnects between faith-based and secular institutions remain as numerous as connections.

The lack of analytic work also poses a serious impediment to informed exploration of potential collaborative work. Most outside funders do not find anecdotal evidence on the wonderful work of faith-based institutions sufficiently convincing. However, recognition is growing within faith-based health circles that evaluation can help them provide care to those most in need more effectively.

THE PROMISE OF PARTNERSHIPS

The HIV/AIDS pandemic has profoundly challenged institutions across the world, and one result is an impressive array of new partnerships involving faith-run health institutions. These include programs within individual countries; the large role of Catholic Relief Services and World Vision in the President's Emergency Plan for AIDS Relief (PEPFAR); support from a wide array of institutions including foundations, banks, and private companies for specific efforts such as the Sant'Egidio Drug Resource Enhancement against AIDS and Malnutrition (DREAM) program; and support for training in the basics of public health in theological institutions.

Humanitarian work is another area of active and productive engagement between deeply respected faith institutions and secular institutions. The roles of Caritas Internationalis, World Vision, and Islamic Relief in responding to the Asian tsunami, the Pakistan earthquake, the conflict in Darfur, and the Katrina catastrophe in New Orleans are only a few of many contemporary cases where faith institutions were key partners.

International institutions such as Christian Connections for International Health have supported dialogue and information sharing between faith-inspired and secular providers for years. Similar initiatives in the Muslim world include a promising initiative in the Middle East supported by the UN Development Programme, and interfaith alliances amongst faith leaders in India and South Asia more broadly. However, many standoffs between faith and secular leaders and practitioners still occur.[9]

LOOKING AHEAD

At the beginning of this chapter the following question was posed: Do national, regional, and global health care projects and institutions have significant blind spots in considering the roles of faith-inspired institutions? The answer seems to be a resounding yes. The large gaps in awareness, knowledge, and collaborative work—stemming from lack of good data, habits of mind, and ethical concerns—have profound consequences. Commitment, openness to new perspectives, and goodwill can help overcome these barriers.

Toward that end, international development institutions and donors could pursue several important activities:

• Support efforts to collect better information on faith-run health programs, assets, and policy, and integrate this information into analyses of health challenges at community, national, regional, and global levels.

- Encourage and support more evaluation of the effectiveness of faith-run systems.
- Investigate the experiences of several countries as case studies.
- Draw practical and institutional lessons from faith-based work on HIV/AIDS and in the humanitarian sphere.
- Develop faith and health literacy materials and case studies for discussion and training.
- Investigate the perspectives of faith institutions on training health workers and addressing personnel shortages.
- Convene policy-making sessions with key health care actors from both faith-based and secular worlds.
- Start with the Vatican and affiliated organizations, such as Caritas Internationalis given their large scope of activities and their interest in the topic.
- Focus on Africa, drawing on experience in other regions, especially Latin America.
- Tackle moral issues in a variety of settings, including through facilitated discussions in "safe spaces."
- Map how faith and international development institutions interact formally, such as through World Health Organization (WHO) and the Joint United Nations Programme on HIV/AIDS (UNAIDS), and in informal settings.

Given the enormous challenges facing both faith-run and national health systems, dialogue and engagement on health issues are urgent.

NOTES

1. This formulation reflects a composite drawn from numerous discussions on the topic.
2. See http://www.ghrc-abu.com/aboutus.htm.
3. See http://www.mettanando.com/main/aboutus.asp.
4. Ritva Reinikke and Jacob Svensson, 2003, "Working for God: Evaluating Service Delivery of Religious Not-for-Profit Health Care Providers in Uganda," Policy Research Working Paper 3058 (Washington, DC: World Bank, May).

5. Exchange with Father Robert Vitello, Caritas Interationalis.

6. Various Websites recount in detail U.S. debates about the role of several church-run systems in providing reproductive health services. U.S. Catholic hospitals must observe the Ethical and Religious Directives for Catholic Health Care Services established by the National Conference of Catholic Bishops. The 70 directives forbid all reproductive health services that contradict official Catholic teaching. These include tubal ligation, vasectomy, abortion, in vitro fertilization, and the prescription or dispensation of contraception—including condoms for safer sex, contraceptive counseling, and emergency contraception, even for victims of rape—unless there is evidence that fertilization has not occurred.

7. Jim Cochrane, 2005, "Reconceptualizing Religion and Public Health," *ARHAP International Colloquium*, Papers and Proceedings, July. See also African Religious Health Assets Program, 2006, "Appreciating Assets: the Contribution of Religion to Universal Access in Africa: Mapping, Understanding, Translating and Engaging Religious Health Assets in Zambia and Lesotho" (African Religious Health Assets Program under contract to WHO, November).

8. See http://www.usccb.org/sdwp/international/global1.htm.

9. Katherine Marshall and Lucy Keough, 2004, *Mind, Heart, and Soul in the Fight against Poverty* (Washington, DC: World Bank) includes some case studies of faith-development partnerships, notably in Uganda and with the Community of Sant'Egidio.

CHAPTER 4

Partnerships in Battling AIDS

The idea that religious leaders would become vital actors in the global fight against HIV/AIDS once seemed improbable. The complex issues at the heart of the transmission of HIV/AIDS—particularly those that touch on sex, sin, and sexual decision making—were approached by many religious groups with taboos or preaching. In truth, most leaders of different faiths were reluctant to enter this public policy arena for some time, and, if they did, tended to speak with condemning and thus stigmatizing voices. Faith leaders seemed particularly vulnerable to the blinders that for so long kept HIV/AIDS in the shadows of global priorities, making it a topic discussed largely by a small if passionate group of advocates.

This situation has changed dramatically in the past five years. The ferocity of the HIV/AIDS pandemic has drawn many religious leaders and groups—by insight, compassion, or the practical realities around them—to respond. The moral call to act has also led many to a change of heart, as the links between HIV/AIDS, poverty, and development have become increasingly clear. It is important to recognize and not paper over important differences in views about how to address the pandemic, many firmly associated with specific faith communities. And many religious leaders remain part of the problem, condoning stigma or ignoring HIV/AIDS in their midst. The broad picture, however, is of faith leaders and communities from widely differing traditions who have emerged not only genuinely as part of the solution, but as pioneers and true innovators in confronting the global crisis.

Presenting a comprehensive picture of what faith groups worldwide are doing to combat HIV/AIDS is difficult if not impossible because the efforts are so widespread and decentralized, and because data collection and evaluation are fragmentary and fragmented. This is often true regarding all responses to HIV/AIDS, but applies more vividly to faith institutions because their work so often falls outside public reporting systems. However, the depth and magnitude of the work of faith groups on HIV/AIDS is great. It is quite clear that religious leaders and organizations provide important services, advocacy, and highly relevant experience. Too often, regrettably, this work remains unappreciated and, partly for that reason, untapped.

Faith institutions are engaged in combating HIV/AIDS in several ways. Among the most significant is direct provision of health services, as faith institutions run many hospitals and clinics. The work of faith leaders also influences health-related behavior in ways that extend far beyond basic health facilities. Faith leaders are core members of communities. Through their organizations and presence in countless communities, faith institutions are well positioned to understand people's daily challenges. Faith communities have taken a particularly active role in caring for children, including orphans and those living with HIV/AIDS. Religious leaders often serve as moral authorities and opinion leaders in their communities and countries, and influence public opinion on the pandemic; through their communications networks and their schools, they play important roles in education and prevention.

Faith institutions have become ever more engaged in a wide array of partnerships to address HIV/AIDS within communities and countries, and internationally. Some of these efforts are denomination specific. Examples include a Catholic engagement led by Caritas Internationalis, and successive meetings within the Anglican Communion (both of bishops and of broader church institutions) to address HIV/AIDS. Ecumenical efforts include the work of the Ecumenical Advocacy Alliance and Christian Connections in Health, the global advocacy of WCRP, and numerous interfaith initiatives at national and regional levels. These partnerships embody the long-term commitment of faith leaders to their communities and social justice, and there is exciting potential for multiplying these efforts, given the vast networks of religious institutions. Faith leaders, especially, stress their sustained, long-term commitment to social justice and to their communities. They see themselves as there for the long haul, and contrast their sustained presence to what they view as the shorter-term horizons of many nongovernmental organizations and companies.

In light of the seeming success of these programs (a common judgment though it is not so far well bolstered by concrete evidence), and perhaps still more of their untapped potential, international organizations such as the World Bank and many bilateral donors have in the past few years focused significant attention on learning from and supporting these experiences. Examples include national, regional, and global meetings between these organizations and religious leaders designed to tap their experience and encourage more active advocacy; the engagement of faith communities and leaders in recent global HIV/AIDS meetings; and specific programs to encourage more systematic funding for faith organizations under global HIV/AIDS programs. The result is an increasingly explicit focus on faith institutions in the decentralized funding processes administered by many national AIDS councils, and greater interest in working directly with faith organizations or intermediaries to increase their access to resources.

This chapter reviews some of the many challenges at stake as faith institutions engage in the global battle against HIV/AIDS. The discussion reflects a broad survey, but focuses on specific areas where the authors have been directly involved. The topics include gathering information on faith-based work, embedding such efforts in national AIDS strategies, promoting advocacy, engaging faith groups in larger forums, forming faith-secular partnerships, tackling the core challenges of HIV/AIDS work, and addressing the capacity challenge. In the vast landscape of faith institutions working on HIV/AIDS, our aim is to illustrate past successes while highlighting remaining challenges and possible paths forward.

MAPPING THE TERRAIN

Information gaps regarding faith-based work on HIV/AIDS are widely recognized as an important obstacle to tapping and expanding those efforts. Several ambitious efforts to redress the situation have occurred or are under way. These efforts take several forms. The first entails detailed attempts to map faith-based work, such as through the Religious Health Assets survey, supported by the WHO (see box 3.1). Similarly, the Union of Religious Superiors, with support from Georgetown University, WHO, and UNAIDS, has undertaken a survey of HIV/AIDS work by Catholic orders. This work points to both the lack of comprehensive knowledge about faith-run health services and, more significantly, the lack of knowledge about the actual and potential community roles of faith institutions on health matters related to HIV/AIDS.

A second effort entails analyzing faith-based work on HIV/AIDS. The most prominent example is the thorough report by the Ecumenical Advocacy Alliance entitled *Scaling Up Effective Partnerships: A Guide to Working with Faith-Based Organizations in the Response to HIV and AIDS*.[1] The Global Health Council and the Catholic Medical Mission Board prepared a document with a similar purpose, entitled *Faith in Action: Examining the Role of Faith-Based Organizations in Addressing HIV/AIDS*.[2] Georgetown University's Berkley Center for Religion, Peace and World Affairs also created a "faith literacy" document that traces the broad landscape of faith organizations working on HIV/AIDS.[3]

A third effort is exemplified by a series of reports issued by Tearfund, the UK-based NGO, on how organizations such as the Global Fund to fight AIDS, Tuberculosis and Malaria[4] and the World Bank are engaging with faith organizations, and thus bringing outside evaluation to the study of faith-based work on HIV/AIDS. The titles of their reports are telling: *Many Clouds and Little Rain? The Global Fund and Local Faith-Based Responses to HIV and AIDS*, and *The Warriors and the Faithful: The World Bank MAP and Local Faith-Based Initiatives in the Fight against HIV/AIDS*.[5] Country-specific case studies by various organizations include the story of HIV/AIDS work by faith communities in Uganda, presented at the World Bank organized Shanghai Conference on scaling up poverty programs in May 2004.[6]

The weakest realm is evaluation: few studies have examined the effectiveness of faith-run programs. Much specific material on faith-based programs has a quality of advocacy—for the institution and its positions, and as a basis for fundraising. The most prominent exception to the dearth of information is the often-quoted work of Dr. Edward Green on Uganda.[7]

He documents the effectiveness of messages from many leaders—above all, faith leaders—in delaying the start of sexual activity by adolescents, and reducing the number of partners, but many agree that his findings are over-simplified in many settings because they tend to reinforce certain approaches. The extraordinary focus on these findings highlights the paucity of data on how different programs do and do not work, and therefore the pitfall of undue reliance and even distortion of what information is available.

INTEGRATING FAITH-RUN PROGRAMS INTO NATIONAL HIV/AIDS STRATEGIES

The role of faith-based HIV/AIDS programs in the broader national and international picture deserves particular focus, especially in light of growing concerns about the coordination and sustainability of the global effort. Institutions that have governments as their primary clients, including the World Bank, work primarily through national HIV/AIDS programs and argue strenuously that this is the only sensible way to assure program direction, coordination, and sustainability in an extraordinarily demanding task. However, in most countries, a variety of groups administer a patchwork of donor-supported HIV/AIDS programs, including local and international nongovernmental and faith-based organizations as well as health ministries. While important work is occurring on many levels, the overlapping and poorly articulated efforts to provide health care overall, and address HIV and AIDS in particular, are significant obstacles.

Recognition is widespread that effective strategies and coordination mechanisms are crucial, especially at national levels. Otherwise efforts can work at cross-purposes, learning from experience is limited, and scarce funds are not well allocated. The frustrating phenomenon of available funds not reaching those who need it is part of the problem of weak linkages all around. The continued raging of the pandemic, and the arrival of treatment programs that are costly and only partially accessible, have fueled mounting concerns about the sustainability of programs under way and planned.

The framework of the "Three Ones" deserves special focus (it reflects a strong consensus among partners including UNAIDS, WHO, and the

World Bank). These principles call for *one* HIV/AIDS action framework, to provide the basis for coordinating the work of all partners; *one* national AIDS coordinating authority, with a broad-based, multisector mandate; and *one* country-level monitoring and evaluation system.[8] It stands to reason that faith-run efforts should be part of this enhanced strategic and managerial focus.

Significant faith-secular partnerships around HIV/AIDS have taken shape in several countries, and the participation of respected faith leaders in many national AIDS councils is notable. However, faith-run AIDS work remains rather piecemeal and is often not well integrated into national development strategies or responses to HIV/AIDS. Faith-based work too often occurs in pockets and not countrywide, and those needing care and support may not be able to find it. Thus the route to more coherent strategies that involve faith partners more effectively stretches ahead.

EMPHASIZING ADVOCACY AND MESSAGES

Another core challenge is the need for better communication on approaches to HIV/AIDS prevention. Though often touted as a comprehensive "save all" of HIV/AIDS prevention, the ABC model (for "abstinence," "be faithful," and "use condoms") leaves some uneasy. ABC grew into prominence in Uganda in the 1990s, and is emphasized in the U.S. government HIV/AIDS program launched by President George W. Bush—the President's Emergency Plan for AIDS Relief (PEPFAR). To counter what they see as partial and potentially stigmatizing aspects of the ABC focus, some religious leaders are developing their own prevention messages.

In 2006, the African Network of Religious Leaders Living With or Personally Affected by HIV and AIDS developed a strategy around the acronym SAVE that aims to be more comprehensive. SAVE stands for "safer practices," "available medications," "voluntary counseling," and "testing and empowerment through education."[9] There are many actual and potential formulations. The message is that groups that include religious leaders and institutions, which are integral to the moral fabric of most societies, need to debate clearly how their communications around HIV/AIDS are perceived and to improve them over time.

Recognition among the major development organizations of both the actual and potential roles of faith-based institutions in advocacy and messaging is mixed—and ranges from purposeful engagement to veiled skepticism or even hostility. Some secular organizations are particularly hesitant to work with specific faith institutions and groups (and vice versa), because they anticipate conflicts over issues like proselytizing and behavioral change and especially the role of condoms in the hierarchy of program options, where different communities hold widely divergent views. For some faith communities these issues pose fundamental ethical principles from which they cannot diverge, while for many in the development world the faith-inspired focus on abstinence, for example, can be seen as unrealistic and even undermining a more comprehensive public health strategy for curbing HIV/AIDS transmission.

There is a marked contrast between the almost instantaneous faith-based response to the December 2004 tsunami and the often slow response to what some term the "silent tsunami" of HIV/AIDS. And the demands of the HIV/AIDS pandemic seem to stretch long into an indefinite future. Starting someone on treatment implies a commitment to keeping that person on medication for his or her lifetime, and stop-and-go orphan care measures are a recipe for disaster. This picture underscores the continuing need for forceful and effective advocacy for global support for HIV/AIDS so that it can indeed be sustained. Here faith leaders have proved extraordinarily effective. Particularly in the United States, the role of evangelical faith leaders especially in moving political leaders to direct funding to HIV/AIDS is extraordinary.

The network of faith and development leaders that met under the aegis of the WFDD in Canterbury in October 2002 and in Dublin in January 2005 thus has great potential as a force for leadership and willingness to address both advocacy and difficult issues. At both meetings, representatives of the world's religions came together with members of the international development community, philanthropists, the private sector, and the arts to discuss the MDGs and how these groups might better work together to realize them. HIV/AIDS was a central focus of both meetings, and the impetus for new multisector partnerships was visibly stronger as a result.[10]

An illustration of a link forged as a result of the actions of this network is a series of dialogue events engaging Canon Gideon Byamugisha, the

Ugandan Anglican priest who came to prominence as one of the first religious leaders to be open about being HIV positive. Canon Gideon's interventions at the Canterbury meeting galvanized listeners to reflect on what they could themselves do, whether in India or across Africa. The network of those present at the WFDD-sponsored meetings has actively promoted a dialogue on how women are involved in the epidemic, compassionate approaches to HIV/AIDS-discordant couples, and other issues. In Canon Gideon's words, "History will judge: there was a preventable disease that killed millions. Who were the leaders at that time? Dialogue alone can generate the right concepts and help us see the answers."[11] Much work remains to be done in generating the right concepts, building on the work that has been done, and finding better ways forward.

ENGAGING FAITH LEADERS IN NATIONAL, REGIONAL, AND GLOBAL FORUMS

International institutions and governments, as well as religious leaders themselves, are increasingly recognizing the important role the latter must play in combating HIV/AIDS. While there have been many longstanding and extraordinary religious activists on HIV/AIDS—notably Canon Gideon—many others are joining the response later. Recognition is also growing of the importance of mobilizing faith and interfaith networks to fight HIV/AIDS, and of publicly acknowledging their roles.

Religious groups are increasingly making their presence known at international HIV/AIDS gatherings and demanding a place in international policy making and advocacy. Faith groups have taken active roles at each of the biannual global AIDS meetings, such as in Bangkok in 2004 and Toronto in 2006.

Religious voices are also increasingly heard at regional meetings. An example is the 14th International Conference on HIV/AIDS and Sexually Transmitted Infections in Africa, held in Nigeria in 2005. Before the meeting, the Pan African Christian AIDS Network (PACANet) met with Catholic Relief Services, Christian Connections for International Health, and the Catholic Secretariat of Nigeria to discuss and proclaim the role of Christian stakeholders in combating HIV/AIDS. Institutions such as

UNAIDS and the World Bank participated in the meeting to learn from and engage with Christian practitioners.

The Middle East has also seen an effort to engage faith leaders with secular HIV/AIDS programs. In December 2005, the United Nations Development Programme (UNDP), UNAIDS, and Family Health International, in coordination with Egypt's National AIDS Programme, the Egyptian Ministry of Endowment, and the National Council for Childhood and Motherhood, helped bring together 80 Christian and Muslim religious leaders from Arab countries. This group adopted the remarkable Cairo Declaration of Religious Leaders in the Arab Region in Response to the HIV/AIDS Epidemic.[12] Out of this initiative emerged a regional Religious Leaders Steering Committee, as well as Muslim and Christian HIV/AIDS response kits with information on transmission of HIV/AIDS, prevention, care, stigma, and discrimination. Among the many dissemination efforts was a session at the World Economic Forum Middle East meeting in Sharm el Sheikh in May 2006. UNDP convened a follow-up meeting in March 2007.[13] In April 2007, UNAIDS and the Regional Program on AIDS in Arab States organized workshops to train male and female faith leaders in launching an HIV/AIDS campaign.

Another effort by faith leaders has focused on joining the challenging effort to address HIV/AIDS in India—paralleling work by UNICEF and UNAIDS that has also seen faith leader engagement as a vital part of the HIV/AIDS battle. A December 2004 meeting of faith leaders in Delhi marked the first discussion of AIDS-related issues by many attendees, and they were clearly moved by the encounter. This meeting was closely coordinated with NACO, India's national HIV/AIDS organization, and the private Amity Foundation, and also included international and national partners, students, representatives of the military, NGOs, the public sector, and business. A high point was a declaration expressing the determination by faith leaders to act together against the pandemic in India.

This was the first opportunity for many prominent religious leaders to discuss HIV/AIDS with each other. Virtually all of India's major faith communities participated, and particularly noteworthy was the engagement of Sri Sri Ravi Shankar and Swami Agnivesh. Other faith participants included Dr. B.K. Modi, Rev. Vincent Concessao, the Catholic archbishop of Delhi, Dr. Ipe Joseph of the India National Council of Churches,

Archarya Dr. Sadhvi Sadhana Jain, Giani Bhai Ranjit Singh, Dr. Swami Satyamji, Maulana Sultan Ahmad Islahi Saheb, and Mrs. Farida Vehidi.

Many of these leaders are part of a national and international "network of networks," and each leader spoke about the importance of partnerships in combating HIV/AIDS. The most prominent theme was the need to focus on spiritual values to combat the corrosive effects of many facets of modernization. The willingness of these leaders to speak frankly about sex, the role of sex workers, and drug abuse stood in marked contrast to several other international interfaith gatherings, and many participants remarked on the call to action.

This meeting illustrated the very different strands that go into effective responses to HIV/AIDS and the faith leader engagement. Dr. Quraishi, then director general of NACO, gave a thoughtful and informed presentation on Islam and HIV/AIDS. Participants from different regions—notably the Community of Sant'Egidio, a Catholic lay organization—shared their experiences in fighting HIV/AIDS in Africa. A number of Indian institutions made presentations, including two singers from Calcutta who highlighted the critical role of the arts in fighting HIV/AIDS.

The keen interest in this meeting, both in India and globally, reflected the consensus that involving faith leaders and communities in the fight against HIV/AIDS in India is critical. Regional workshops and a second major interfaith meeting followed this initial meeting—though the work of maintaining the network and ensuring that its members fulfill their promises and are accountable to each other will prove difficult in a country where HIV/AIDS still remains somewhat hidden as a leading social issue for many religious leaders. Nonetheless, the meetings have raised consciousness among faith leaders about the gravity and nature of the HIV/AIDS threat and sparked concrete planning, such as in mobilizing youth.

FORMING INNOVATIVE SECULAR-FAITH PARTNERSHIPS

One of the rare silver linings of the HIV/AIDS pandemic is the deep sense of commitment it has generated in both faith and development worlds, which is leading to powerful advocacy for innovative and sustainable programs. An example is the role of the Community of Sant'Egidio in highlighting the human rights and social justice dimensions of the pandemic, based on that group's lived experience, especially in Mozambique but now in other African countries.[14]

Sant'Egidio's DREAM program also makes a frontal effort to tackle the urgent need to expand successful programs. Sant'Egidio began to offer treatment in Mozambique early in 2002, and has now extended the DREAM program to Malawi, Tanzania, Kenya, Guinea, Guinea-Bissau, Nigeria, Angola, and the Democratic Republic of Congo. The program provides broad-based support for people affected by HIV/AIDS in the context of comprehensive treatment. Besides providing drugs free to eligible patients, the program includes diagnostics, strategies to assure adherence to treatment, monitoring for potential drug resistance, support from trained personnel, and treatment for diseases that coexist with HIV infection, including malaria, tuberculosis, other sexually transmitted diseases, and malnutrition.

In Mozambique, where the DREAM program is most fully realized, Sant'Egidio now manages 10 day hospitals. DREAM is implemented entirely within the framework of the Mozambican health system, and is a critical part of the country's HIV/AIDS response. Complementing other programs, it is housed within public hospitals and maternity wards, reflecting the fact that the government of Mozambique is the primary partner. The program relies on Mozambican medical professionals and a team of rotating Italian volunteers.

However, the need in Mozambique alone is vastly greater than the program can serve, and funding for continued treatment is not secured. The lack of Mozambican doctors is a primary impediment to scaling up. Thus, while some have seen the program as the gold standard, this assessment seems accurate only insofar as Sant'Egidio focuses on providing individuals a level of treatment that the Italian founders of Sant'Egidio might want for themselves. Services provided in Mozambique, though of high quality, are far from luxurious, and focus on essential treatment.

To help sustain the DREAM program, Sant'Egidio joined an alliance grounded in the Treatment Acceleration Program (TAP), which is funded by International Development Association (IDA) grants, and thus involves pilot partnerships between governments, the World Bank, and civil society. Beyond this pilot effort, Sant'Egidio and the World Bank remain committed to making treatment widely available—Sant'Egidio through on-the-ground services and remarkable advocacy, including yearly DREAM conferences bringing together international development agencies with African health ministers and DREAM practitioners, and the Bank through its work in helping countries build sustainable HIV/AIDS strategies.

TACKLING THE CORE CHALLENGES OF HIV/AIDS WORK

Coordinating development assistance inevitably poses challenges, but work on HIV/AIDS presents particular tests. All actors need to be constantly apprised of the latest information and what other actors are doing. Protocols, costs, and "best practice" lessons learned change rapidly, and funding challenges are dynamic and complex. Yet, as noted, coordination channels are far from optimal.

To help faith communities understand and navigate IDA-funded Multi-country AIDS Projects (or MAP Projects, a core part of the World Bank's HIV/AIDS response), the Bank organized two workshops, the first in Addis Ababa in 2003, the second in Accra in 2004, explicitly directed to interfaith teams working in a total of 16 African countries. The target audience also included national AIDS councils from participating countries, as well as representatives from the Global Fund, UNAIDS, interfaith organizations, and key bilateral agencies. The highly productive workshops serve as a reference point on the engagement needed to address numerous practical challenges. The workshops also helped demonstrate the critical importance of faith groups in fighting HIV/AIDS.

The workshops specifically highlighted 10 challenges, some common to a broad range of civil society groups, and others more specific to faith institutions:

Scaling up: In the face of enormous needs and visible suffering of individuals and communities, faith leaders have reacted with a blend of energy, desperation, and purpose. The core message was the urgent need to use all means to remove obstacles to action so that programs can expand as quickly and efficiently as possible.

Sustainability: The response to HIV/AIDS is often and aptly characterized as a marathon, underscoring the need for stamina, good pacing, and a long-term view. Other concerns—born of long experience—include the unpredictability, impenetrability, and short time horizons many perceive among funding partners, both national and international. Faith leaders are torn between their sense of urgency and great unease about launching programs that raise expectations, especially those that offer support for orphans, without firm financing commitments, and even assurances that donors' past tendencies to chop and change will not apply. These faith leaders stress the need for procedures and relationships that allow for bold, flexible, and responsible action.

Trust: With many—especially small—institutions largely unfamiliar with monitoring and reporting systems, tensions surface around standard donor requirements. Part of the challenge is that faith institutions and communities often and proudly base their relationships on trust. However, HIV/AIDS programs must build not only on shared values and a sense of purpose but also on proven excellence, adaptability, and administrative transparency. This calls for rather different procedures in most situations.

Leadership and community roles: Leadership is a critical element in changing people's attitudes and behavior. Strategies need to focus on "fire from above"—guidance by national and faith leaders—and "fire from below"—action at the community level. Interfaith efforts can help harness these multiple sources of energy to face the enormous challenge of the pandemic.

Nuts and bolts: Procurement, financing, and reporting and monitoring are essential ingredients of successful programs. If practitioners lack respect for these instruments—regarding them as needless bureaucracy—and a determination to make them work well, the implications will be disastrous.

Capacity: The need to expand HIV/AIDS programs presents institutions created for other purposes with novel challenges. A first priority is to use existing capacity and systems built over time more effectively, thereby expanding these programs in positive new directions. Building capacity through training, external support, and sharing among institutions is also critical.

Information: Teams working on HIV/AIDS at the local level are hungry for information, especially about what works and what does not. Using the diverse information channels and networks of faith institutions creatively and well is one option.

"Covenant": Faith communities care deeply about "speaking truth to power" and fulfilling their scripture-based commitments. This spills over into their expectations of partnerships, that they will entail true engagement to live up to promises and "keep the word."

Special aspects of faith institutions: Faith communities working on HIV/AIDS often confront essentially the same problems as civil society institutions, but some are more specific to the former. The complexity of the world of faith, and its unique vocabulary, experiences, priorities, history, and geography, present special challenges. For example, in Ethiopia, a specific challenge is to inform and mobilize the very large body of clerical personnel: one estimate puts the number of clergy of the Ethiopian Orthodox Church at some 500,000, and the number of Islamic imams at some 150,000 (and that is only part of the religious spectrum).

Special faith partnerships: International interfaith organizations working on HIV/AIDS are often not well known at the local level, and their work may seem to overlap. Better mechanisms are needed to inform institutions better about the activities of others and to enhance cooperative efforts.

BOOSTING THE FAITH-BASED CAPACITY TO RESPOND

Capacity is perhaps the more commonly cited impediment to more far-ranging and effective roles for faith organizations in the global HIV/AIDS strategy. Whatever the hopes and potential of faith leaders and institutions to deliver both messages and programs, many clearly lack the needed capacity to scale up existing programs and engage in new areas.

This is particularly true for the numerous small-scale faith groups that have taken on HIV/AIDS work. These groups lack infrastructure, personnel, and funding to expand and even continue this work. These capacity problems often present a vicious circle, wherein poor capacity hampers efforts to secure funding, which might enable the organizations to build greater capacity. For many faith institutions, scaling up HIV/AIDS programs calls for fundamental shifts in their roles. Groups that take on orphan care and support families living with HIV/AIDS, for example, confront unfamiliar challenges and the need for rapid increases in scale commensurate with enormous demand.

In 2006 the World Bank undertook preliminary mapping of the role of faith leaders and institutions in Mozambique's HIV/AIDS strategy.[15] A central finding was that faith leaders are key actors in the fight against HIV/AIDS, but that realizing their significant potential will require more capacity, recognition, and inclusion in the country's HIV/AIDS strategy.

Religious organizations play central roles in Mozambique. They co-administer some of the country's most reputable public hospitals, and run one of the few medical schools. As noted, Sant'Egidio administers a major HIV/AIDS treatment program, and many other religious groups and faith-based organizations engage in care, treatment, and support for people with HIV/AIDS, as well as in education and prevention.

Mozambique's government and development partners increasingly recognize this involvement. Government leaders and the National AIDS Council look to faith communities for leadership in responding to HIV/AIDS. UNAIDS supports a Programme Acceleration Fund to develop capacity among faith-based institutions. Several bilateral partners, notably the United States, focus explicitly on the role of faith institutions, and major foundation and private-sector partners are exploring new forms of partnership.

However, while faith organizations are very much involved in working on HIV/AIDS, their entry into this realm is rather recent and small scale. Examples of their interventions include local programs to assist orphans, home-based care, and publishing booklets on HIV/AIDS for congregations. Many faith groups want to work on HIV/AIDS but lack the wherewithal, and the established networks, to know how and where to begin. To reach their communities more effectively, faith institutions need to build their capacity to address HIV/AIDS-related problems by training personnel and developing programmatic strategies. Efforts by other actors to engage faith communities also need to be grounded in a well-tailored approach to addressing these capacity challenges.

Many other countries share Mozambique's HIV/AIDS challenges. The pandemic clearly needs far stronger leadership at all levels, and faith communities are no exception. The untapped potential of existing faith programs provides many opportunities. Key first steps might include convening local discussions and organizing workshops to train volunteers and staff members on the nuts and bolts of action. National leaders and international funders also need to consider faith communities an integral part of programs and strategies—with their contributions ranging from advocacy and prevention to the care of the sick and their families and communities.

NOTES

1. See http://www.e-alliance.ch/media/media-6695.pdf.

2. See http://www.globalhealth.org/images/pdf/faith_in_action/cover.pdf.

3. See http://berkleycenter.georgetown.edu/.

4. For more information see http://www.theglobalfund.org/en/.

5. See http://tilz.tearfund.org/ for copies of all the Tearfund reports.

6. See http://info.worldbank.org/etools/reducingpoverty/case-Uganda-Conquering HIV-AIDS.html.

7. Edward C. Green, 2003, *Rethinking AIDS Prevention: Learning from Successes in Developing Countries* (Westport, CT: Praeger).

8. For more on the "Three Ones," see http://www.who.int/3by5/newsitem9/en/index.html.

9. *Medical News Today*, March 30, 2006 "African Religious Group Announces New Group to Fight HIV/AIDS, Meant to Replace ABC." See http://www.medicalnewstoday.com/medicalnews.php?newsid=40521.

10. Katherine Marshall and Lucy Keough, 2005, *Finding Global Balance: Common Ground Between the Worlds of Development and Faith* (Washington, DC: World Bank).

11. Katherine Marshall and Richard Marsh, eds., 2003, *Millennium Challenges for Development and Faith Institutions* (Washington, DC: World Bank).

12. United Nations Development Programme, 2005, "Egyptian Religious Leaders Convene to Break the Silence on HIV/AIDS." See http://www.undp.org/.

13. UNDP, March 30, 2007, "Global Challenges: Bahrain Launches Campaign to Involve Religious Leaders in Fight Against HIV/AIDS." See http://www.undp.org/.

14. For more information on the Sant'Egidio DREAM program, see the Sant'Egidio's Website (with references to publications), http://santegidio.org/eng/index.html. A summary of the program is in Katherine Marshall and Lucy Keough, 2004, *Mind, Heart, and Soul in the Fight against Poverty* (Washington, DC: World Bank), chapter 10, pp. 125–34; and Katherine Marshall and Lucy Keough, April 2006, "HIV/AIDS—Getting Results: Mozambique's Battle against HIV/AIDS and the DREAM Project" (Washington, DC: World Bank).

15. Lucy Keough and Marisa Van Saanen, 2007, "Faith Leaders and Institutions in Mozambique's HIV/AIDS Strategy" (Washington, DC: World Bank).

CHAPTER 5

Together Against Malaria

Faith-Led Community
Mobilization in Mozambique

We have much to learn about how community-based interfaith resources can be deployed to meet social and health challenges. Despite the long track record of faith-based health and social programs, intentional and systematic engagement of interfaith resources for large-scale community mobilization and impact is an untapped opportunity—and a not-to-be-underestimated challenge.

This chapter describes an ambitious campaign initiated by Mozambique's interfaith community to mobilize congregations and communities against malaria. Launched in early 2006, the campaign has received support from many quarters, among them the U.S. President's Initiative for Malaria, the Washington National Cathedral, and the government of Mozambique. The initiative promises to serve as a test case of how

---

This chapter was written by Jean Duff, Managing Director of the Center for Global Justice and Reconciliation (CGJR), Washington National Cathedral, Washington, DC. The chapter summarizes the progress of the Inter-Religious Campaign against Malaria in Mozambique (IRCMM), a program supported by CGJR. The center's Director is the Reverend Canon John L. Peterson. CGJR's mission includes programs that support interfaith collaboration for justice. Efforts to fight malaria and other CGJR programs are part of the cathedral's overall endeavor to help heal a broken world. Contact the author at jduff@cathedral.org.

partnerships across divides of sector, geography, and belief can tackle an intractable public health challenge.

THE CHALLENGE

Pastor Rick Warren of the evangelical Saddleback Church in the United States, speaking at the Time Global Health Summit in November 2005, called attention to the untapped potential of the faith community on the ground:

> In many countries, the only infrastructure is the local church or mosque or synagogue.... That is the untapped resource in the global fight against disease.... What if we were able to mobilize this infrastructure and use houses of worship as distribution centers to advance the fight against the global health crises that affect all of us?[1]

The question for practitioners is: how can local faith-based infrastructure be made accessible to partners in health and social programs, and how it can be deployed effectively?

In answer to the first challenge, faith-based infrastructure clearly has the potential to be widely accessible to support health and social programs, as houses of worship exist in remote areas even where government agencies do not. However, this pervasive presence also defines the challenge: scattered houses of worship and faith leaders do not an infrastructure make! Because most faiths and denominations are part of complex hierarchical structures which have few working links among them, a different style and focus of local and national leadership is needed to bring these dispersed interfaith facilities into a coherent health focused system. International faith leaders also can play important roles in supporting in-country faith leaders in such efforts.

In answer to the second challenge, this remarkable interfaith infrastructure can become effective if its leadership, capacity, resources, ability to work as partners with government and NGOs, and accountability are all enhanced. Training can enable faith and lay leaders alike to build the specific skills they need to address social and health challenges, so that they are better positioned to collaborate with secular partners. Overall, faith-based infrastructure need to be intentionally organized, developed, and supported if it is to be widely available to partners in health and social programs, if is to be effective, and if it is to have a sustainable impact.

THE WASHINGTON NATIONAL CATHEDRAL AND INTERFAITH ACTIVISTS IN MOZAMBIQUE

The Center for Global Justice and Reconciliation (CGJR) at the Washington National Cathedral was established to fight global poverty and enhance global justice. A central aim is to amplify the impact of the religious community on global health and social challenges through interfaith collaboration, forging partnerships with secular organizations, and scaling up effective programs. The Millennium Development Goals (MDGs) frame the center's priorities, which include combating malaria and empowering women.

A pivotal program is the center's partnership in an ambitious program to mobilize the faith community in Mozambique against malaria. This program—known as the Inter-Religious Campaign against Malaria in Mozambique (IRCMM)—aims to reach every faith leader in the country with information about how to control and prevent malaria, so these leaders in turn can educate and mobilize their congregations.

Although it is preventable and treatable, malaria remains one of the leading causes of death in Africa. Statistics for Mozambique alone paint a grim picture of debilitation and loss of life. Malaria is responsible for:

- 6 million reported cases each year
- 44 percent of all outpatient hospital admissions and 65 percent of all pediatric hospital admissions each year
- 40,000 deaths a year among children under age five
- a high-risk population of 3.6 million children under age five, and 900,000 pregnant women
- year-round transmission, peaking from December through April

Many of Mozambique's institutions and development partners have long worked to address the constant malaria threat. In the past two years, the various leaders working on malaria have stepped up their pace sharply in the context of a renewed global focus on this disease. Several multilateral and philanthropic donors have provided funding to Mozambique's health ministry, and are working together to support a comprehensive national malaria control and prevention program.

The Global Fund to Fight AIDS, TB, and Malaria awarded a grant of US$28 million to Mozambique in 2006. The fund is directing most of this financing to the Lubombo Spatial Development Initiative, a multicountry malaria control project based in southern Mozambique that received two US$21 million grants from the fund.

The Bill and Melinda Gates Foundation is also deeply engaged in Mozambique, its investment efforts focused on developing malaria vaccines. The World Bank, too, has long supported Mozambique's health sector, and the next phase of its support focuses on the government's anti-malaria initiatives. For its part, the U.S. government has allocated US$17 million per year to Mozambique for three years under the President's Malaria Initiative.

The Ministry of Health administers the overall national malaria control program. The faith community has developed its IRCMM in close collaboration with the ministry. The collective goal is to extend the impact of all interventions.

THE INTER-RELIGIOUS CAMPAIGN AGAINST MALARIA IN MOZAMBIQUE

Represented by 11 leaders, Mozambique's faith community formally launched the IRCMM in April 2006. The campaign is grounded on the premise that faith leaders are uniquely positioned to mobilize people against malaria, given their long-standing role as activists, community educators, and advocates against malaria. This leadership group offers several advantages:

- They are where the government is not.
- They are among the country's most trusted leaders and teachers.
- They can mobilize entire communities to achieve the large-scale action required to make a significant impact, and they have a history of effective collaboration across different faiths.

Faith leaders involved in IRCMM have long been prominent national and regional spokespeople in the fight against malaria. For example, Anglican Bishop Dinis Sengulane, president of the Christian Council of Mozambique, is also president of the facilitators group for Roll Back Malaria in Mozambique (see box 5.1). The country's faith communities also have a long history of collaborating on humanitarian relief, post–civil war reconstruction, and provision of health services.

BOX 5.1
GLOBAL PARTNERSHIPS AGAINST MALARIA

Malaria, an ancient and deadly killer, disproportionately affects the poor, causing more than 1 million deaths and up to 500 million clinical cases each year.[a] An African child dies every 30 seconds from the disease, a death in most cases preventable and treatable. The international community has pledged that there will be no more complacency in addressing malaria. A complex array of initiatives, alliances, and financing vehicles—either specific to the disease, or including it within larger programs—is taking shape to carry this global commitment forward. Efforts of faith communities need to fit within this overall picture.

International partnerships include the Global Fund to Fight AIDS, Tuberculosis, and Malaria; the World Bank's Global Strategy and Booster Program; Malaria No More; and the Roll Back Malaria Partnership.[b] The latter is a 90-member organization that includes the Global Fund, the U.S. Agency for International Development, and the Bill and Melinda Gates Foundation. Major bilateral initiatives include the U.S. Presidential Malaria Initiative.

The World Bank launched its booster program in 2006 to accelerate progress against malaria in Africa, and committed US$500 million to a three-year intensive first phase.[c] By mid 2007, the program included approved funding for four projects, in the Democratic Republic of Congo (US$30 million), Eritrea (US$2 million), Niger (US$10 million), and Zambia (US$20 million). The goal is to protect

(Box continues on the following page.)

(box continued)

80 percent of the at-risk population by 2010, and to treat 80 percent of malaria patients with effective medicines within one day of the onset of symptoms.

In most malaria-prone countries, numerous actors are already engaged in confronting the disease. NGOs, private companies, faith leaders and faith-based organizations, movie stars, and student groups play key roles in raising awareness of malaria and providing direct support for preventing and treating it. The intent is that all actors will work within national control programs to meet malaria-reduction targets—and particularly to curb child deaths.

Faith organizations are involved in many of these efforts, but so far a coherent approach from national and global faith institutions is lacking. However, the potential to mobilize faith networks to educate people on how to prevent and treat malaria is significant.

a. See http://web.worldbank.org/.

b. For more on the Roll Back Malaria Partnership, see http://www.rbm. who.int/.

c. World Bank, April 24, 2006, "World Bank Intensifies Anti-Malaria Effort in Africa," press release. See http://web.worldbank.org/.

The interfaith profile of IRCMM's founding membership is broad and deep. Board members include Archbishop Francisco Chimoio and the Rev. Horatio Simbine of the Roman Catholic Church; Mrs. Jaintilal Prafulta of the Hindu community; Bishop Joao Somane Machado of the United Methodist Church; the Rev. Dinis Matsolo of the Christian Council of Mozambique;[2] Sheikh Abdul Karim, Imam Ali Mecusserima, of the Islamic Council of Mozambique and and Mr. Hassan Makda of the Islamic Congress of Mozambique; Mr. Sabapathy Alagiah of the Bahá'í community; Bishop Dinis Sengulane of the Anglican Church; the Rev. Antonio Chicolo of Assemblies of God; and Pastor Miguel Simoque of the Seventh-day Adventist Church.

To mobilize resources for the campaign against malaria, Anglican Bishop Dinis Sengulane, Islamic Congress Chair Hassan Makda, and

Methodist Bishop Joao Machado commissioned a Working Group to Support IRCMM, headquartered in Washington, DC. This group includes representatives of the Anglican, Methodist, Seventh-day Adventist, and Catholic churches, as well as media experts and advisors from the National Institutes of Health, the Centers for Disease Control and Prevention, the World Bank, the UN Foundation, and USAID. The Working Group is staffed by CGJR, which also provides technical support to IRCMM directly.

Besides raising funds, members of the Working Group provide technical and programmatic support to IRCMM. For example, the Seventh–day Adventist Church produced *Together Against Malaria*, a documentary about the campaign.[3] CGJR is an integral partner of IRCMM, providing technical, programmatic, human, and financial resources designed to enable the interfaith community to wipe out malaria in Mozambique.

The faith-based Adventist Development and Relief Agency (ADRA) has supported a range of community-level primary health programs in both development and relief contexts for more than 30 years. ADRA has worked in Mozambique since 1987, providing emergency food distribution in partnership with USAID during the last few years of the war and its immediate aftermath. ADRA has since participated in various development and emergency relief activities in the provinces of Gaza, Inhambane, and Zambezia, funded by USAID, the European Union, AusAID (the Australian government), the Irish government, and the Mozambican government.

ADRA submitted a funding proposal for IRCMM to USAID in September 2006, which in April 2007 the agency indicated it would fund. The proposal sets out as its campaign aim: "to decrease malaria morbidity and mortality across the population, with priority given to high-risk groups of pregnant women and children under five years of age."[4] The core strategies to achieve this goal include educating the interfaith community about how to prevent and treat malaria, and assisting them to mobilize congregations and communities to pursue these practices; and building a sustainable infrastructure that will continue to provide health education, training, and community mobilization after USAID funding ends.

The three partners—IRCMM, CGJR, and ADRA—agreed to launch Together against Malaria (TAM) in Zambezia, the nation's most populated province, home to some 3.8 million people. There, the faith community is being mobilized to work with the Ministry of Health to reach more than

1.6 million people directly and 2.6 million indirectly. The partners will focus on reducing malaria morbidity and mortality by scaling up prevention and treatment efforts in faith communities, especially among pregnant women and children under five years of age.

CREATING A SUSTAINABLE INTERFAITH INFRASTRUCTURE

Faith leaders estimate that the province of Zambezia is home to at least 2000 imams and Christian pastors, as well as many indigenous faith leaders. To tap this infrastructure, IRCMM is developing a train-the-trainers campaign, whereby TAM staff and national Muslim and Christian leaders will train key provincial faith leaders with support from technical experts from the WHO, the international Malaria Consortium, and others. These provincial leaders will then be equipped to model best practices in malaria control and prevention in their own families, and to train other faith leaders in 10 of the 17 districts of Zambezia.

District faith leaders will then mobilize their congregations against malaria by continuously educating people on malaria prevention and control. To maximize the impact of these interventions, district training will occur in parallel with the rollout of the Ministry of Health's Indoor Residual Spraying program, and with a project to distribute long-lasting insecticide-treated bednets. Overall, TAM aims to achieve the following:

- Reach about 340,000 at-risk citizens of Zambezia through congregation-based training, outreach, and support.
- Reach 1.6 million people directly through trained faith leaders, who will use interactive messages to convey information on malaria prevention and the importance of early and effective treatment.
- Train 270 faith leaders (of which 30 will be trainers of trainers) to mobilize their congregations and communities in their congregations and with local health care resources.
- Establish an identified, quantified, and sustainable local infrastructure in Zambezia that mobilizes communities against malaria.

TAM is built around the understanding that solid information and greater capacity are two vital elements of a successful campaign to combat malaria. Thus a first step is for IRCMM staff to work with local faith leaders and national organizations such as the Christian Council of Mozambique to map the assets of religious actors in Zambezia, and to create a database to support IRCMM, TAM, and other health and social initiatives.

A second major premise is the existing weakness of the administrative faith-based infrastructure. TAM will thus establish or strengthen District Inter-Religious Councils as a locus for collaboration against malaria. As the capacity of these councils develops, they will enable the faith sector to respond to a variety of health and social needs. In addition coordinating mechanisms between the faith and health sectors will be established at provincial and district levels.

In a subsequent phase of the TAM program leaders will link these local malaria networks with other faith leaders and provinces in Mozambique, extending the impact of TAM. Many of these lay leaders will be women, drawn from various faith communities: geography, not religious denomination, will be the organizing principle.

The TAM program recognizes that partnerships between faith communities and public authorities, including ministry of health officials, are critical to long-term success. The training programs will therefore enhance faith leaders' ability to advocate on behalf of high-risk members of their communities, and to gain access to public health resources. Forging these links is a major responsibility of the interfaith council.

There is widespread agreement that a mobilized faith community can help improve public health by changing people's behavior, but much is still unknown about how best to foster and leverage that impact. TAM provides an ideal opportunity for a planned case study to discover and document answers that can inform future public health initiatives in Mozambique, as well as other large-scale interfaith collaborations to improve health and social welfare.

NOTES

1. See http://www.time.com/time/2005/globalhealth/transcripts/110105warre npc.pdf.
2. CCM is an ecumenical organization linking 22 mainline and African indigenous Protestant churches, plus the Bible Society and Scripture Union, representing about 3.5 million Mozambicans.
3. To view the video, see http://www.togetheragainstmalaria.org.
4. Quoted from project submission from ADRA to USAID, 2007.

6

Education, Values, and Global Citizenship
Centro Magis and
the Council of 100

Two notable international ventures are focusing on the links between religion and teaching, educational quality and values, and efforts to build peaceful, equitable societies. The first—a partnership between Fe y Alegría, a grass-roots educational movement born over 50 years ago, a business-inspired foundation, and a catalytic intermediary— aims to enhance the quality and reach of a Jesuit-run school system that now operates in 17 Latin American countries. The second, an initiative of the World Economic Forum launched in 2003, highlights the critical importance of education, including religious schools, in overcoming social conflict and building social cohesion. Both ventures reflect the urgent need to support intercultural dialogue and build cross-cultural social capital to ensure peaceful coexistence within and among dynamic and plural societies.

This account draws on discussions with the institutions involved and AVINA Foundation, Centro Magis, and the Federation of Fe y Alegría documents, and benefited particularly from inputs and comments from Emily Fintel, of AVINA. See Katherine Marshall and Lucy Keough, 2004, *Mind, Heart, and Soul in the Fight against Poverty* (Washington, DC: World Bank), for more on the genesis of the Magis/AVINA partnership.

EDUCATION FOR CHANGE IN LATIN AMERICA

Maybe this spark will become a wildfire; it is only a seed, needing soil in which to multiply.

Father José María Vélaz, founder of Fe y Alegría

Fe y Alegría was born in 1955 in a poor neighborhood in Caracas, Venezuela, as a partnership among Jesuit priests, university students, and families. Their mission was to combine high-quality education for children who were beyond the reach of the existing public school system with community mobilization.

Fe y Alegría worked in Venezuela alone in its early years, its approach shaped by the philosophy and charisma of its founder, Father José María Vélaz. Then, in 1964, nearly 10 years after its birth, Fe y Alegría crossed borders and began operating in Ecuador, and then shortly thereafter in Panama and Peru. In 1970, as national Fe y Alegría programs consolidated and grew in size, the organization held its first international assembly. This marked the beginning of a conscious process of joint reflection between the Jesuit Order and Fe y Alegría, which would focus on the development of a distinctive and in many respects unique Fe y Alegría theory of and approach to social change. From the early 1980s to the mid-1990s, Fe y Alegría became more international and more institutionalized. Still, a decade ago, Fe y Alegría was marked by the independence of its national members and the sheer complexity of its efforts to link countries and communities. Nonetheless, by 1999 Fe y Alegría had developed ambitious plans to strengthen the movement and to build bridges with other international organizations.

Today Fe y Alegría's educational programs reach close to 1.3 million students in 17 Latin American countries. National programs differ quite markedly, reflecting the specific conditions and challenges of the individual country but also the differing historic roles the Jesuit education system has played. Some programs focus more on primary or secondary education, for example, while others give more emphasis to vocational or adult education or radio-based literacy training. Fe y Alegría's "international federation,"[1] based in the Dominican Republic, with a branch in Spain, has grown from running annual assemblies to devising a proactive and far-ranging program to support the national units. The federation is considering a far-ranging initiative to expand Fe y Alegría to Africa.

As leaders of a highly decentralized grassroots movement, Fe y Alegría originally stuck close to its roots in communities, determined to work with and on behalf of poor communities, primarily through their schools. While some school and national leaders espoused revolutionary social change, pragmatism and working within existing systems emerged as the name of the game. Schools could not run solely on revolutionary fervor. Thus, from the movement's earliest days, national units pursued compacts with governments to ensure stable funding—especially in countries where governments would undertake to pay teacher salaries—while still allowing sufficient management autonomy for Fe y Alegría schools to retain their unique character. The relationship with the Society of Jesus (the Jesuits) has been close, complex, and dynamic. The central Jesuit organization originally held Fe y Alegría at some distance, but today it is a core project of the Order and an object of pride in Latin America and globally.

Fe y Alegría is thus an international organization with strong community roots—one that is not easy to pigeonhole. Fe y Alegría describes itself as a movement, and its identity is deeply shaped by its close contact with communities and its focus on social transformation. The group sees itself as part of the public sector, yet it also prides itself on independence from governmental authority. Grounded in espoused values of justice, participation, and solidarity, Fe y Alegría maintains that its mission begins "where the asphalt ends"—that is, where the poorest people live.

Although Fe y Alegría is well known and respected across Latin America, those who have encountered it have often been left with a sense of potential not fully realized. Who knew more than Fe y Alegría about the real problems of children, parents, teachers, and communities? Who understood better why children dropped out of school, and why youth could not make the transition from schools to jobs and family? Yet Fe y Alegría was rarely present during high-level policy discussions about how best to tackle poverty and devise educational strategies and programs.

Enter Stephan Schmidheiny, a visionary philanthropist, and Brizio Biondi-Morra, then director of AVINA, the foundation that Schmidheiny established.[2] Both were highly successful business leaders who were pioneers in the ethics and social responsibilities of private companies and the business sector. Both men also share a deep concern for the development path in Latin America. Serendipity united them with Xavier Gorostiaga and Luis Ugalde, Latin American Jesuit leaders with a similar strategic vision and values. Intensive exchanges with these leaders convinced Schmidheiny and Biondi-Morra of the untapped potential of Fe y Alegría, and the benefits of collaborating with the Jesuit Order in a systematic fashion across Latin America.[3]

A new partnership took form. Its centerpiece is Centro Magis, launched in 2000, whose mission is to build partnerships with the wide-ranging educational and social initiatives that the Jesuit Order leads or supports across Latin America.[4] For example, Centro Magis works with the Latin American Jesuit university network AUSJAL, and on community development efforts with more than 100 Jesuit-led organizations.[5] However, Centro Magis has focused primarily on Fe y Alegría.

The creation of Magis Americas—a U.S.-based nonprofit that aims to advance equitable, sustainable, and environmentally sound development throughout Latin America and the Caribbean—added a new partner to the group.[6] Magis Americas supports education and community development in the poorest areas of the region through partnerships between U.S. groups and a vibrant network of Jesuit-led social action groups, as well as other Catholic orders.

This variable geometry of relationships emphasizes several goals. These include moving (a) from quantity to quality; (b) from schooling to education; (c) from promoting individuals to enabling communities to participate in a global society; (d) from a collection of schools to an international educational network; and (e) from classrooms to public action. Of particular interest, given the roots of the Magis initiative, is its explicit aim of creating links that will heighten the private sector's consciousness of its social responsibilities. Fe y Alegría holds that "education is not only a private good owned by the educated person, it is also a social good that benefits the whole of society and arises from the rights of all its members."[7]

The Magis partnership has supported the development of a strategic plan for Fe y Alegría and a wide range of programs. Some are fairly classic strategies for improving information systems, financial management, and teacher training, and for tapping Fe y Alegría's regional network to identify and disseminate best practices. The strategic plan and programs also reflect the Jesuit orientation of the Magis effort, focusing on values and ethics as fundamental elements of the educational enterprise. The ethical approach to education is thus a feature both of teacher training programs and of strategic reflections across the system and in "best practice" curriculum modules.

All told, the strategic programs of the Fe y Alegría Federation illustrate the movement's scope:

- Developing methods for measuring educational quality and fostering an institutional culture that focuses on evaluation. Evaluation efforts are under way in some 450 schools.
- Building stronger links between schools and employers, and education and jobs. This focuses on curriculum development, teacher training, partnerships between educators and the private sector, support for technological innovation, and specific programs for people excluded from the labor market.
- Making greater and better use of computers in education. This entails linking schools to national and regional information networks, installing computers in classrooms, training teachers, and establishing e-learning communities. The federation is working to create a platform for distance training for teachers.
- Extending the reach of radio and other distance learning. This builds on existing radio-based Fe y Alegría networks in Bolivia, Venezuela, and Ecuador.
- Using strategic planning to improve the management and sustainability of each national Fe y Alegría program. This entails a new guide to the Fe y Alegría project cycle, developing computer programs to support project management, developing software and training in fundraising and accounting, elaborating an ethical code, and strengthening internal organization and communication.
- Using best practices by building a culture of sharing among educators and developing techniques for learning from experience.
- Training both teachers and management teams.

- Supporting advocacy to inform public opinion on education, and lobbying for better national and international educational policies.
- Refining the social objectives of the Fe y Alegría Federation, thus providing training in values at the individual and community level, and building the identity and spiritual aspects of the Fe y Alegría movement.

Centro Magis and Fe y Alegría aim to expand in several new directions. These include more intensive work at the preschool level, and with disabled children and adults; and greater focus on the "new poor" (who have come on hard times after living in relative prosperity), and adults who face exclusion from labor markets. Fe y Alegría also envisages new initiatives in civic values, governance and democracy, and the environment, and is considering expanding to Uruguay and Mexico as well as Africa. Distance learning (including a university-level seminar on poverty) is part of the Magis program.

AVINA's dynamic partnership with Centro Magis has evolved significantly. AVINA serves as a key financial partner and a member of the Magis board. Aside from financial support, AVINA initially saw its major contribution as helping to strengthen Fe y Alegría by encouraging an "entrepreneurial focus." The transformation of the federation from a hand-to-mouth, under-resourced organization to one that emphasizes strategic planning and programs is a tribute to this partnership.

AVINA sees a future wherein Centro Magis and Fe y Alegría diversify their funding, and Magis Americas heightens its public advocacy and builds alliances beyond the Jesuit community. AVINA also aims to facilitate partnerships between Centro Magis and Magis Americas and other Jesuit-led organizations in Latin America and the Caribbean, especially Jesuit-run social action programs. AVINA is especially interested in building entrepreneurship networks and enhancing socioeconomic development in poor communities—thereby linking the social transformation interests of the Jesuit Order with AVINA's emphasis on social entrepreneurs and networks. AVINA sees its relationship with Centro Magis and Magis Americas as holding rich potential for building new continent-wide partnerships and spurring systemic change.

EDUCATION AND RELATIONS BETWEEN WESTERN AND ISLAMIC NATIONS

Following the terrorist attacks of September 11, 2001, the World Economic Forum[8] (a global independent organization "committed to improving the state of the world") launched a new and quite distinctive initiative, forming the Council of 100 (or C-100). This multisectoral group of roughly 100 leaders, drawn from five sectors (business, politic, religion, media, and civil society) was given the mandate to address tensions and challenges in West-Islamic relations.[9] The group recognized that education emerged time and time again as *the* central avenue for long-term solutions to these challenges. An education group therefore was established with two aims: to help define a specific group of educational priorities that might bear on the challenge of improving West-Islamic relations, and to support the development of specific programs to bring best practice to scale.

Education emerged as the priority for several reasons. First, struggling educational systems present a fundamental obstacle to socioeconomic development in many majority-Muslim countries. Poor education undermines competitiveness, leads to high unemployment, and contributes to migration pressures. Second, women have significantly less access to education in many Muslim-majority countries, and face a variety of specific challenges within schools. This has far-ranging effects on families, civic institutions, and labor markets. These are broader challenges for leaders from all sectors. But the C-100 has focused more sharply on a set of issues that tend to figure less prominently in global and regional discussions about education, but which are at the crux of intercultural relations and peaceful and respectful societies. It has identified, within the framework of the broad challenges for educational reform and development, a priority agenda of issues that have the potential to help in building peaceful, multicultural societies.

The C-100 has focused on teaching by religious organizations and about religion as one of the pivotal elements that belongs in national and international educational strategy discussions. This is true in many countries, but has particular significance in societies with plural populations which are undergoing dynamic change. This in turn highlights the roles that religious leaders can play in dialogue about education policies. Also important is what is transmitted in the faith institutions that train future religious leaders. The content of curricula and attitudes of teachers across all schools also deserve attention viewed through the lens of West Islamic relations. There is great potential for grounding young people in values that build respect and resolve conflicts, though best practice in this area has been little explored. Poorly designed curricula also have the with potential to exacerbate existing intergroup tensions. Extracurricular activities for youth are seen as offering special opportunities to build bridges across cultures and countries. Business and the media also play critical roles, and developing the capacity of emerging leaders in those fields to address intercultural relations openly and creatively is crucial.

A facet of education that emerged as a lightning rod in C-100 discussions is the role of the Islamic schools often referred to as madrasas. The term is inexact, because in Arab-speaking countries *madrasa* is Arabic for school, and implies no particular link to religion. In non–Arabic-speaking countries, schools run by Islamic authorities are often called madrasas because they teach in Arabic. The perception that Islamic schools provide only rote learning of the Koran, and convey largely negative views of non-Muslim cultures, is widespread but tells only a piece of the story. In fact, Islamic schools vary widely within and between countries, ranging from part-time religious instruction to fully articulated systems encompassing preschool to higher education, and from under-resourced, poor-quality institutions to outstanding centers of learning. Still, information on Islamic schooling systems, including even basic enrollment figures, is patchy, and even less is known about their quality.

The C-100 has focused on the need to better understand how Islamic school systems work overall and in individual countries, and the factors that contribute to parents' decisions to enroll their children in Islamic schools even when public education is accessible. Many parents appear to have greater confidence that their children will learn core values in religious schools than in public schools, where the underlying value system is often obscure. The Carnegie Endowment is exploring support for a scholarly stocktaking of the state of knowledge and agenda of issues.

What students learn about their own and other faiths has particular relevance to intercultural harmony. Yet many public school systems have eschewed teaching about religion, even in history and geography classes, which contributes to major knowledge gaps and limits intercultural understanding in many societies.[10] Others present the subject in ways that are clearly biased toward one particular group. The concept of cultural literacy and competence is a centerpiece of today's efforts to reintroduce teaching about different religions into public schools. Thus the C-100's second priority is to identify and disseminate best practices and models of excellence for such teaching in different settings.

The C-100 experience suggests three important lessons. First, reforming educational systems and practices to meet the particular needs of plural, dynamic, and modernizing societies is emerging as a central policy issue in countries as diverse as Ireland and Indonesia, Qatar and the United States, Senegal and India. Each society, and even each community, will respond somewhat differently, but in each case thoughtful teaching about the culture and religious history and practice of different communities is an essential grounding. In this dynamic field, there is considerable merit in harvesting best-practice experience in different settings with a focus on identifying models of excellence.

Second, the challenges include clarifying and adapting the social role of religious schools, enhancing their quality, and engaging them in the dialogue about how to build respect among communities. Exploration of this important yet sensitive topic has barely begun. Chapter 11 describes the promise of engagement with Pakistan's madrasas but more work is needed to expand dialogue, information gathering, and engangement. More broadly, the issue of values belongs more centrally on educational agendas. New efforts are needed to encourage an active and open exploration by teachers and students of their own community's values and their links to religious and secular traditions. And third, these challenges extend far beyond educators to include private companies, secular civil society organizations, public authorities, the media, and religious leaders. Finding effective solutions clearly depends on how well they work together.

NOTES

1. See http://www.feyalegria.org/images/office/69110103108105115104455150671111101034669100117999799105243110801111121171089711 4_441.doc.

2. For more on Schmidheiny and links between business and philanthropic objectives, see his personal Website: http://www.stephanschmidheiny.net. For more on AVINA, see www.avina.net/.

3. The Catholic Encyclopedia has a good brief introduction to the Jesuit Order, with references to more in-depth material. See http://www.newadvent.org/cathen/14081a.htm. The Jesuit portal is at http://www.sjweb.info/.

4. Centro Magis works across Latin America from its base at Andres Bello University in Caracas. See http://www.centromagis.net/.

5. For more information on the Association of Jesuit-Linked Latin American Universities, see http://www.ausjal.org/.

6. For the Magis Americas Website, see http://www.magisamericas.org/.

7. Presentation by Federation of Fe y Alegría at Magis Americas meeting, San Jose, California, March 15, 2007.

8. See http://www.weforum.org/.

9. Chapter 23 deals covers the C-100 itself in greater depth.

10. For a vivid description of the sharp deterioration in knowledge about religion in the United States, see Stephen Prothero, 2007, *Religious Literacy: What Every American Needs to Know, and Doesn't* (San Francisco: HarperSanFrancisco).

CHAPTER

7

Ghana's Interfaith Initiative to Manage Waste and Care for the Environment

An unusual interfaith initiative in Ghana is addressing the very practical problem of garbage collection and sanitation. According to its founders, the Inter-Faith Waste Management Initiative (IFAWAMI) aims "to contribute to a national crusade against filth and the issue of waste management in Ghana."[1] IFAWAMI entails an ambitious and eminently practical plan to build new forms of cooperation that enhance the health and welfare of the whole community.

IFAWAMI came about in response to mounting evidence that the growth of Ghana's population, especially in cities, was overwhelming the management capacity of local authorities. Ghana has authorized a host of laws and regulations designed to deal with waste, but their ineffectiveness is evident in the face of a rapidly growing and very visible trash problem. An important recognition took root that the government alone could not solve the problem—that it must be a shared responsibility of all Ghanaians.

This chapter is based on materials prepared by IFAWAMI, the interfaith group responsible for the project. Kafu Kofi Tsikata, a communications specialist in the World Bank's Ghana office who is facilitating the initiative, provided assistance and helpful comments.

What is notable about IFAWAMI is that both leadership and practical support to address a civic problem have come from Ghana's religious communities, which have joined together in a seemingly improbable partnership with the World Bank. They have been inspired by not only a successful project in Manchester, United Kingdom, that involved local authorities and faith groups, but also by Ghanaian concerns and realities. The religious coalition explains its role in both pragmatic and religious terms: "It has become clear that all hands need to be on board if improving waste management is to be effectively tackled from all angles.... It is a common belief that cuts across all recognized religions that man is to relate responsibly to the environment which is a major gift from God."[2]

ROOTS OF THE RESPONSE

The backdrop to the initiative is Ghana's strong religious ethos and organization. The vast majority of Ghanaians (94 percent, according to the 2000 Population and Housing Census) report that they belong to one religion or another. Religious leaders are respected and freedom of worship is assured, with considerable and growing religious pluralism (an estimated 69 percent of the population is Christian, and 16 percent Muslim, with the remaining population belonging to traditional and other faiths). Religions have traditionally played active roles in providing services, notably health care and education, but modern-day efforts offered no particular precedent for the sanitation program.

Discussions about what faith communities might do to help the sanitation crisis began in 2005, as public concerns about uncollected garbage and poor sanitation mounted. The problem was far from simple, and its numerous elements quickly became apparent. Solid waste includes domestic refuse as well as commercial and institutional waste, construction debris, and rubbish from sweep sweeping. Mountains of filth and garbage clutter streets, choke gutters, and endanger the food sold by nearby street vendors. Plastic bags are everywhere, including on beaches, and street children sleep in garbage. The problem extends to basic sanitation, including the presence and effectiveness (or absence thereof) of home latrines. The situation contributes to the risk of disease, including cholera, typhoid, and malaria. Yet elected political leaders and bureaucrats hesitated to enforce regulations for fear of electoral consequences. And the problem is far from purely technical, as it reflects people's attitudes, mindset, beliefs, and behavior. It was from this angle that Ghana's faith leaders entered the picture.

The World Bank office in Ghana, under the purview of an outreach program known as the Development Dialogue Series, organized a meeting in 2005 with local faith groups and the Waste Authority of Accra to discuss a possible response. A relatively small amount of discretionary funding under the communications budget of the Bank's country director brought together a diverse group that included representatives of all the religious bodies in Ghana.

The challenge to the interfaith group was framed in graphic terms as "a menace of filth and waste which is destroying our beautiful nation. If no remedies are found immediately to stem this problem, our beloved nation will, with time, be engulfed with all kinds of disease and sicknesses."[3] The focus on dialogue allowed consensus to form that an Inter-Faith Waste Management Initiative (IFAWAMI) should champion an action program. IFAWAMI's birth was spurred by the approach of the Golden Jubilee celebration of Ghana's independence, an upcoming African Union Summit, and a conference of finance ministers. In 2008, Ghana will host the CAN 2008, the All-Africa Confederation of Football, and wishes to be a worthy host of these important events.

This group prepared a solid three-year project proposal in 2006, and formally launched the nationwide program in late 2006. It will encompass cities, peri-urban areas, and rural areas, and rely on both religious leaders and technical experts from the public sector.

IFAWAMI is chaired by Rev. Dr. Paul K. Fynn, who heads the Christian Council of Ghana and the Lutheran mission in Ghana. Under his leadership, a technical committee has developed the initial concept into a practical plan. That committee consisted of the Rev. Dr. Nathan Iddrisu Samwini, a minister of the Methodist Church Ghana, with advanced degrees in theology and Islamic Studies; Mrs. Rosemary Mills-Tettey, vice chair of the National Spiritual Assembly of the Bahá'ís of Ghana; and a practicing architect in Accra; Dr. Musheibu Mohammed-Alfa, a food safety expert working with the Ghana Food and Drugs Board since 2003, and head of its Food Inspectorate Department; and Mr. Lukman Y. Salifu, a former World Bank sanitation expert and now CEO of WasteCare Associates. The World Bank office in Accra facilitated the dialogue and planning.

IFAWAMI calls for the government to discharge its responsibilities, citizens to take an active part, and the private sector to engage. The initiative is establishing a national secretariat to ensure coordination and followup, and has committed itself to both encouraging interfaith cooperation and engaging with other nongovernmental groups, such as the Girl Guides and the Boy Scouts.

THE PROGRAM

The overall program is a creative blend of technical waste management—including waste reduction, reuse, recycling, and recovery initiatives—with promotion of home latrine facilities and community-based advocacy.

IFAWAMI will play several key roles in the three-year multisectoral program. These include advocacy cum inspiration, monitoring and oversight, and direct action to mobilize communities. The core idea is to change behavior through example and persuasion. This will be furthered by a strong and united religious voice on proper waste management practices, appropriate to Ghana, in tandem with an effort to ensure that agencies responsible for managing waste have adequate resources. The IFAWAMI segments of the program will cost just over US$2 million (sources of funding were still under discussion at the time of writing).

Practical interventions will be designed as strategic demonstrations. Proposals that bridge the faith and technical worlds include training artisans and small-scale builders linked to faith-based groups on improved latrine technology options.

The advocacy component aims to harness interfaith collaboration to promote visible public efforts, such as community cleanup campaigns. An education component will incorporate information on waste management into basic school curricula, including the teaching of faith-run schools, and into adult education programs. The group aims to establish waste management clubs in 150 mission (that is, church-run) schools based on the IFAWAMI philosophy, and to give pep talks on environmental and sanitation concerns in schools.

A communication component involves preaching in churches and mosques as well as extensive media dissemination through press contacts, printed materials, and film documentaries. IFAWAMI plans to sponsor announcements, advertisements, debates, talk shows, interviews, and even dramas on waste management on radio and television. An illustration is a public rally led by a group of imams, which drew crowds in the thousands. A core group of religious leaders are promoting articles on waste management, and circulate information on the importance for religious bodies of participating in national policy making and implementing best practices. Specific proposals include producing a brochure on waste management that includes scriptural passages and spiritual principles such as the oneness of humankind, the importance of treating others as you would like to be treated, economic justice, moderation, cleanliness, and collaboration.

LESSONS BEYOND GHANA

Solid waste management and irresponsible use of natural resources constitute a serious problem in many developing countries. Ghana's emerging creative coalition of faith groups working with technical leaders in the public sector at both national and local levels offers an important model. It is significant as an illustration of unusual paths for transmission of innovative ideas that this concept transited from Manchester, United Kingdom, thanks partly to work there by the Alliance for Religions and Conservation (the UK–based organization that works to engage faith communities in conservation work[4]) with support from the World Bank and the government of Norway, and that Zambia is already exploring a similar program.

NOTES

1. IFAWAMI communiqué, Accra, Ghana, November 14, 2005.
2. Ibid.
3. Ibid.
4. See http://www.arcworld.org/.

CHAPTER

New Alliances to Tackle the Housing Dimensions of Poverty

Decent shelter plays a central role in combating poverty, as inadequate housing is both a symptom and a cause of desperate poverty. Homelessness in many senses is the ultimate manifestation of the failures of social and economic systems to meet human needs, and to offer people the chance to lead a life with dignity. Concerns about and approaches to housing have ancient origins. Religious teaching and practice are important parts of the evolution of housing policies over time in many countries, as virtually every faith tradition includes stories and admonitions about welcoming strangers and offering people a decent place to live.

Today faith-based organizations are working worldwide to overcome practical obstacles to a lack of housing. However, there is no coherent "mapping" of their activities or assessment of their aggregate impact. Anecdotal evidence suggests that most faith-based housing programs address immediate needs by providing temporary shelter or helping build homes. However, faith institutions do not typically address the array of

This chapter draws on discussions at the Berkley Center for Religion, Peace, and World Affairs at Georgetown University on December 4, 2006, and on materials prepared by Habitat for Humanity International, especially Steven Weir, vice president for strategy at Habitat for Humanity, and Dani Elias El Tayar, Habitat for Humanity Country Director, Lebanon. Tom Jones, Habitat for Humanity special ambassador, provided useful comments on a draft.

93

policy issues that modern housing typically involves. Thus the potential for mobilizing faith engagement in housing needs has yet to be fully realized.

More broadly, the role of decent shelter in the architecture of the MDGs is less clear than that for other problems. What is part of the MDG framework in effect centers on the challenges presented by slum communities, especially in large cities. However, housing per se does not benefit from the quantified accountability structure that comes along with the MDGs.

This chapter describes efforts to address that gap—especially through alliances that link faith-based and secular development institutions in tackling housing. These accounts build on an interfaith meeting at Georgetown University's Berkley Center for Religion, Peace, and World Affairs in Washington, DC, in December 2006, and draws on the interfaith experiences of Habitat for Humanity International, a leading faith-inspired organization dedicated to shelter.[1]

THE CHALLENGE

For virtually all faiths, the importance of working for social justice lies at the very core of beliefs, and is a binding drive within each community. Each tradition professes a moral imperative to care for the poor, and providing shelter for poor people and communities is a central aspect of long-standing faith teaching and practice. Because the highest moral values call faiths to this work, decent housing worldwide has emerged as a priority for those working on poverty and through interfaith alliances.

The challenge is how to translate the ideals, teachings, and historical practice of faith traditions into a modern context. Providing shelter as part of disaster relief is a relatively straightforward proposition. In Sri Lanka and Aceh, Indonesia, after the tsunami of 2004, the number of new houses needed and then actually built could be readily measured and progress monitored. Similarly, when a house burns down, the community can respond and rebuild.

However, with a majority of the world's population living today in cities and towns, housing policies present challenges that go well beyond community-based building. Key elements include establishing land tenure and security, providing financing, forming policy, and setting and monitoring standards. The need for social cohesion and sound community relations in plural urban societies complicates these issues. They must addressed if the basic challenge of scale—that is, assuring decent housing for all—is to be achieved.

Faith communities such as the National Council of Churches of Christ and Sojourners are venturing into national advocacy in the United States, but no comparable global faith voice has yet appeared. It is thus noteworthy that Habitat for Humanity International—one of the world's largest voluntary organizations, and an institution deeply tied to faith traditions—is seeking to enlarge its engagement in the policy arena, to complement its work in mobilizing volunteers to build individual homes.

The absence of an explicit focus on adequate shelter in the MDGs is something of a concern to some advocates for poor communities, because it means that the discipline and framework of concrete goals must be created in a different context. Nonetheless, there is little disagreement in either faith or development circles that shelter should be a central focus of debates about global poverty and programs to combat it. Stable, decent housing can improve health and education, promote stronger communities, and enable people to accumulate wealth—helping guarantee access to basic services and offering hope for the future.

An exploratory December 2006 forum organized jointly by Habitat for Humanity and Georgetown's Berkley Center identified a range of potential areas where faith and interfaith engagement offers promise for the housing challenge:

- *Community-level shelter programs*: Encouraging community and grassroots gatherings worldwide to focus on housing as a core issue
- *Knowledge and information*: Filling large gaps in knowledge about what is working and what is not, including specific instruments and approaches
- *Advocacy*: Promoting interfaith advocacy for decent housing, touching on land tenure, the structure of financial markets, government regulations, livable communities, and access to financing for poor people, among other issues
- *Research*: Investigating the strong relationship between housing and other priority social issues and programs
- *Partnerships with leading international development agencies*: Encouraging joint work between organizations such as the World Bank and UN Habitat that focus on human settlements

APPLYING PRINCIPLES IN PRACTICE

Today's faith-based housing programs fall roughly into three categories. The first is hands-on work: faith communities come together to provide support for poor communities in normal times and when disaster strikes. There are countless examples across the world of such support—whether it involves building with hammers and nails or providing financial resources from a greater distance.

Second, faith communities lend a prophetic voice to advocacy efforts that focus on housing, as religious leaders and communities urge public authorities and the community at large to address the need for shelter. Again innumerable examples of such advocacy occur across different regions and faith communities, and touch the full gamut of problems, from the regulatory framework for building and financing through discrimination based on religion that plays out in housing markets and situations.

A third area of involvement is intentional efforts to combine the goal of providing decent housing with the broader social objectives of strengthening communities and fostering peace. In these efforts, faith communities come together to provide both direct support and advocacy. This practical focus on resolving tangible common concerns helps participants overcome historical and theological differences. Though this is a less typical area of action, many examples nonetheless arise all over the world, especially as communities come together to overcome common barriers.

The following short accounts of Habitat for Humanity ventures in the Philippines and Lebanon illustrate both what is happening and the potential that such interfaith approaches offers.

INTERFAITH COMMUNITY ACTION IN THE PHILIPPINES

A Philippines experience that illustrates the power and potential of interfaith work with housing as its focus is a Habitat for Humanity program in Mindanao. This is an area in the southern Philippines with long-standing and seemingly intractable tensions dividing Muslims and Christians, manifested in frequent armed conflict and other intercommunal violence. An interfaith housing program has proved successful in both providing much-needed shelter and helping overcome ancient hostilities. The core objective of Habitat for Humanity's program has been and remains peace.

Habitat for Humanity's affiliate in the Philippines set out deliberately to contribute to peace-building efforts through its housing construction programs. The organization began with consultations with various governmental and nongovernmental groups. What emerged was a "Peace Build" program that entailed, in its initial phase, the construction of 200 housing units for families that had lost their homes. In another area of Mindanao, a Peace Build project benefited rebel returnees by mobilizing volunteers locally and from other municipalities to help build houses. Regional and municipal governments fully supported the program.

Although the program involved a complex partnership between very different organizations, its practical details were fairly simple. According to the model, the mayor enters into an agreement with the Habitat for Humanity Philippines organization, which stipulates the roles and responsibilities of each party. The municipal government takes charge of road and site development, provides technical support during house construction, and facilitates other community development needs.

Habitat for Humanity, meanwhile, selects and educates qualified families, constructs the houses and turns them over to the families, and coordinates with governmental and nongovernmental agencies to achieve truly holistic community development. In this case, the UN Multi Donor Program provided funding for the Sustainable Integrated Area Development Program, including water systems. Notre Dame University provided training designed to help build a "culture of peace"; and Balik Kalipay, a Christian college, provided training on sustainable agriculture. The projects enlisted the support of local parishes as well as local governments.

The program was closely tied to the process of negotiating and building peace, and a peace covenant setting out the framework of the Peace Build program strengthened those ties. This agreement, formalized on August 8, 2001, attracted an impressive array of signatories, including Col. Bobby Calleja of the Armed Forces of the Philippines and Kumander Nasser Sambutol of the Moro National Liberation Front. Other signatories included representatives of the provincial, municipal, and barangay governments; an array of leaders from the Catholic Church and the United

Church of Christ of the Philippines, as well as the local imam; home partners (who work with families during the building process); the secretary of the National Department of Social Welfare and Development; representatives of the Peace Panel; the former Miss Universe; and the president of the Philippine Habitat for Humanity affiliate.

The program's results were immediate and tangible, and Habitat for Humanity reported significant shifts in attitude among the beneficiaries. For example, Danganan Sagadan, a Muslim farmer who contributed a plot of land to the Habitat for Humanity program, was asked if its Christian identity conflicted in any way with his Islamic faith and values. He replied that building a house "has nothing to do with religion, but is rather an exhibit of brotherhood among men, because Muslim and Christian alike can now own the same kind of houses." Mr. Sagadan's family was one of many victims of atrocities in the area, and in 1999 his house was strafed by unidentified armed men. He was determined, though, not to leave his land, which his forebears had tilled, and which he hoped his children's children would continue tilling. He saw real hope for the future in community programs to build an elementary school nearby, a water system, and a light and power connection—and, of course, in prospects for peace.

Another partner in the Peace Build program, Patotin Akong, lived alone with his three children, because his wife had worked as an overseas contract worker in Saudi Arabia since 1998. Today the family lives in a new home built by the community. The family has vivid memories of when they were evacuated from their home time and time again because of fighting. Life was like a game of hide and seek: "once bullets come they must hide carefully for safety." The new home gave them new perspectives and new hope. Mr. Akong's wife sends money for house payments and ideas for curtains and kitchen utensils. Mr. Akong shares his dreams for peace within what he hopes will be a model community: "We hope that this new community will slowly erase the bad memory of fear, anger, and hatred in children because if they [the children] forget those pains then peace will blossom in this land."

Habitat for Humanity has worked to draw lessons from the experience in Mindanao, because the organization knows full well that peace building is not an easy task: everyone's contribution in rebuilding lives and pointing communities toward peace is vital. Important lessons include attention to detail in consultations before the start of the program, and in the memorandum of understanding. The active involvement of NGOs operating in the area filled gaps. Technological innovations—including the use of interlocking concrete blocks—reduced construction costs by 31 percent while ensuring durability. A repair and renovations program allowed some of the lowest-income families that could not afford to completely rebuild to benefit from the Habitat program.

Habitat for Humanity's "sweat equity" requirement differentiates its housing programs from most others. Home partners must complete at least 400 hours of work on their own and others' houses. This imparts technical skills to the home partners, and develops cohesiveness as they work together and help each other. Habitat for Humanity's "save and build" program is another innovation: families must save 33 percent of the cost of their house, and present a record of those savings in the form of a bank passbook. This teaches the family the habit of saving, and Habitat encourages group saving.

The Peace Build program offers several broader lessons:

"We know the solution to the problem, but who will take the first step?" The barangay of Lower Pagangan, municipality of Aleosan, in Cotabato province served as an entrance and exit for rebels and soldiers hunting each other. It is a place where nobody dared to tread. The nearest elementary school, which is kilometers away, is accessible only by walking, as there are no roads. House construction for 15 families brought a different perspective—not only for those who benefited directly, but for the whole community. Many other developments followed, including a preschool program. The Muslim and Christian families demonstrate what it is to live in harmony. In short, taking the first step was all-important.

"Start from where they are and what they have." An important feature of the program was that families were not uprooted. When they returned after the war, families began cultivating the plots they owned, and they built their houses there.

"Work with local people and local partners." Creation of the Aleosan Habitat for Humanity Task Force facilitated the successful implementation of the Peace Build program. Task force members were committed and active and willingly attended regular meetings, while leaders lived in the area. Thus the program relied on local groups.

"Pay attention to the role of women." In the Peace Build program, women played an important role. Most Christian and Muslim women attended meetings and participated in consultations. They asked questions about details of house design and appearance, and volunteered to help during construction. Their broad roles in managing households, farms, and other income-generating projects became apparent, and they regarded the project as an opportunity to create a better, more peaceful community.

"Prepare both communities and plans well." Social preparation and community organizing is vital, and the processes need to be clearly defined. This is time consuming and takes resources but the payoff is great both in short-term results, and above all in sustainability.

"Partnership is important." Explore all avenues for partnership with governmental agencies, NGOs, faith groups, home partners, and all other parties operating in an area. The Habitat program was part of a broader plan for the community, and was well tied to barangay and municipal development efforts. This smoothed paths.

"Do not neglect the paper." Thorough documentation of all experiences and processes, and effective monitoring and evaluation, helps participants apply lessons to other projects.

INTERFAITH DREAMS IN LEBANON

Habitat for Humanity's work in Lebanon provides a classic example of the goal of providing decent housing tied to broader social objectives of strengthening communities and fostering peace.

Two decades of civil war, foreign military occupation, and armed resistance movements in Lebanon wreaked massive havoc on the country's infrastructure, economy, and social fabric. World Bank estimates suggest that 25 percent of Lebanon's housing stock was destroyed in the violence, and hundreds of thousands of people were displaced. The protracted violence not only destroyed homes, but also shattered the fragile Lebanese social mosaic. Civic values eroded as most families lost loved ones to death, disability, or disappearance. Southern Lebanon, once known for diversity and peaceful coexistence, splintered into bitter factions.

Government post-war grants proved inadequate to rebuild homes, and were often distributed inequitably, only deepening sectarian divisions. Community spirit remains a casualty of war. Without the chance to rebuild, communities remain fractured.

At the same time, the gap between the affordable housing supply and the demand in Lebanon continues to widen. With the end of the civil war, and especially since the 2000 Israeli withdrawal from southern Lebanon, families are slowly returning to their communities—many to discover that there are not enough safe, secure homes, and that they cannot afford to rebuild. People are forced to live in damaged or deteriorating buildings, sometimes with inadequate sewage systems, sometimes crowded into houses too small for burgeoning families, sometimes with repairs half-finished from lack of funds.

There is a traditional Lebanese cultural value of mutual help in villages (referred to in Arabic as *aouni*—when the entire village turns out to help build a neighbor's home). Due to social fragmentation during the civil war and the impact of modernity and urbanization, aouni had become a rarely practiced, but fondly remembered, thing of the past. Habitat for Humanity in Lebanon worked to revitalize this cultural value through the incorporation of mutual help components into program design, such as the following:

Engaging inclusive leadership. Key for long-term sustainability and socio-economic impact of the program are the local committees managing the program in each cluster of villages. These local leaders are volunteers who exemplify the values needed to rebuild civil society. They must also reflect the diversity of race, religion, gender, socioeconomic class, ethnicity, tribe, color, and physical disability of the community served, to ensure that equity and unity are preserved in the distribution of resources. The training and support these volunteers receive help to restore civil society.

Promoting unity through volunteerism. One of the simplest but most powerful elements of the program was its community volunteer work days. Homeowners, neighbors, and visiting volunteers alike have joined together to build across sectarian lines, helping to restore relationships fractured by war. Habitat Lebanon and its partners have held public celebrations after these volunteer work days with several hundreds participating, including local villagers, corporate employees, national youth clubs, and expatriate visitors—joyful expressions of unity not always seen in a still-fractured country.

Selecting families in need without discrimination. Habitat Lebanon insisted that family selection be equitable, with no sectarian discrimination, and based only on (a) housing need, (b) ability to repay a no-profit loan, and (c) willingness to partner. Families served are proportionate to the displaced persons from four ethnic groups in the villages where Habitat works, including Maronite and Catholic Christians, and Shiite and Sunni Muslims.

An example of aouni at work is the story of a family that fled during the civil war, then was welcomed back into the neighborhood by people who were once their enemies. Twenty years after fleeing their home, a group of volunteers—Muslims and Christians from Lebaa and the surrounding villages—worked all day to transform the family house and erase the scars that marked it. Habitat Lebanon National Director Dani El Tayar said that "it was as if the whole community was welcoming them back with open arms, inviting them to come home. It was reconciliation in action, both on a personal and community level."

NOTES

1. For information about Habitat for Humanity, a nonprofit, ecumenical Christian organization that works worldwide, see their rich Website at http://www.habitat.org/. Some information about these case studies is available there but the stories presented here are largely based on exchanges with Habitat leaders.

II

Faith Communities In Action

Introduction

Two major insights have shaped much recent thinking among development practitioners. First, social and economic endeavors—whether they entail identifying clean water sources, launching a child vaccination scheme, or working to end female genital cutting—rarely, if ever, succeed without the active engagement of communities. Second, social capital—rich and dense networks linking different actors within communities—plays a pivotal role in social and economic change. Yet although consultation, participation, and empowerment have become sine qua nons of development work, practitioners too rarely acknowledge the central role of faith institutions and leaders in many communities, and in building social capital across cultures, socioeconomic divides, and even continents.

Churches, synagogues, mosques, and temples serve not only as places of worship but as community centers where friends, family, and neighbors come together. These institutions not only celebrate marriages and host other key initiation rites, but often keep birth and death records. Because people's everyday lives play out in congregations, they are often keenly aware of members' financial, emotional, and spiritual health. Indeed, significant social progress and development work can emerge from the intimacy of local religious organizations.

Pastors and imams, of course, are central players in these endeavors, but some faith groups organize beyond the formal hierarchies to care for the sick or people otherwise struggling, in the community and beyond. Faith-based mothers' and youth groups are often essential. These faith-based organizations and congregations may function independently or link locally, nationally, and even globally to larger organizations and social movements. They may range from a group of concerned citizens opening a Baptist home for children to Nahdlatul Ulama, the world's largest Muslim association, which focuses on reproductive health and education in Indonesia.[1]

While religious institutions are mortal, subject to the same flaws as any other organizations, they retain a place of privilege and trust within many communities. Faith leaders have a vested interest in communities not only because of their calling, but also because they live in those very same places, rather than simply passing through as visitors or outside consultants.

Indeed, people often rate religious leaders and organizations as the most trusted members of their communities.[2] In 2006, for example, the Gallup World Poll asked residents of 19 sub-Saharan countries to rank eight social and political institutions. In each African country, religious organizations ranked first (76 percent), followed by military (61 percent) and financial institutions (55 percent). In Latin America, where the Catholic Church has played a critical role in social policy for hundreds of years, the Latinobarómetro surveys yield similar results.[3]

In South Asia, faith leaders and religious life are so interwoven into the culture that drawing distinctions between secular and faith-based efforts can be difficult (in marked contrast to Europe, for example). The United States, too, has seen a resurgence of interest in faith-based community development; these practitioners often reach out to the poorest and most vulnerable people, who otherwise would fall through government safety nets.

The chapters in this section focus on the initiatives and movements inspired by people of faith to address the challenges and problems around them. In most of these cases, faith is only part of the story, and its contribution varies from community to community. Still, this handful of accounts suggests lessons that apply to faith-driven community development in almost every country.

Chapter 9 tells the story of Tostan, an organization based in Senegal that works throughout West Africa.[4] Tostan—which means *breakthrough* in the language of the Wolof of Senegal and the Gambia—is a nonprofit, nongovernmental organization that incorporated in the United States in 1991. Its mission is to contribute to the dignity of Africans by developing and implementing an informal, participatory educational program in national languages. Tostan provides citizens with the knowledge base and skills to become confident actors in the social transformation and economic development of their communities. A guiding principle of the Tostan method is the African tradition of ensuring the participation and respectful consultation of all affected by any potential decisions and policies. Villagers themselves determine their future goals, and the obstacles they must overcome to achieve them. The Tostan process entails consulting with local religious leaders; the American Jewish World Service, among others, has helped fund this process.

Chapter 10 focuses on Sri Lanka's largest social movement: the Sarvodaya Shramadana Movement, a Buddhist and Gandhian organization with a presence in some 15,000 villages and 1,500 staff throughout the country.[5] Founded in 1958 by Dr. A.T. Ariyaratne, a high school teacher who inspired his students to contribute to community development, Sarvodaya works across ethnic and religious lines with a range of partners, and encourages communities to participate actively in building and sustaining development. The Sarvodaya movement was a first-line responder to the Asian tsunami of 2005, relying on its vast and comprehensive network throughout Sri Lanka. And it remains an important actor in sustaining recovery efforts, as well as in resolving conflicts and building peace.

Chapter 11 shows how the International Center for Religion and Diplomacy (ICRD)[6]—based in Washington, DC, and founded on the belief that religion is the missing dimension of foreign policy—has partnered with the Institute for Policy Studies, an Islamabad-based think tank, to reform madrasas in Pakistan. In collaboration with the Institute for Policy Studies and other Pakistani religious and civic organizations, ICRD has been working with madrasa administrators, oversight boards, and senior faculty to improve education and moral guidance for students by offering teacher-training workshops. This unique effort aims to address educational quality and national and international security simultaneously through the madrasa system.

Chapter 12 explores prospective partnerships of Kenya's Coptic Church Mission, which has responded to public health challenges by establishing hospitals and HIV/AIDS clinics and emphasizing prevention and community support.[7] The Coptic Church is rooted in a philosophy that people come to know Jesus Christ through compassionate care that serves their needs. The Church's Hope Center in Nairobi, which focuses on HIV/AIDS, has drawn funding from the (U.S.) President's Emergency Plan for AIDS Relief (PEPFAR).

Chapter 13 addresses local and international faith-based responses to poverty based in the United States. Some of these efforts are longstanding, while others are rather recent. This chapter focuses in particular on efforts aimed at fighting poverty and HIV/AIDS in Africa.[8] Two boxes illustrate first, the combination of advocacy mobilization and hands-on work that is exemplified by Bread for the World, and second the extraordinary appeal of an artist, Bono, to faith-inspired communities in the U.S. heartland states, around the issue of HIV/AIDS.

NOTES

1. See Christopher Candland and Siti Nurjanah, February 9–11, 2004, "Women's Empowerment through Islamic Organizations: The Role of Indonesia's Nahdlatul Ulama in Transforming the Government's Birth Control Program into a Family Welfare Program," case study prepared for the WFDD workshop in New Delhi. See http://www.wfdd.org.uk/.

2. See "Africans' Confidence in Institutions," http://www.gallupworldpoll.com/.

3. See "Latinobarómetro Report, 1995–2005: A Decade of Public Opinión," http://www.latinobarometro.org/.

4. For more on Tostan, see http://www.tostan.org/.

5. For more on the Sarvodaya Shramadana Movement, see http://www.sarvo daya.org/.

6. For more on the International Center for Religion and Diplomacy, see http://www.icrd.org/.

7. See http://www.copticmission.org/.

8. See White House Office of Faith-Based and Community Initiatives, http://www.whitehouse.gov/government/fbci/.

CHAPTER 9

Shifting Community Attitudes

The Tostan Story in West Africa

Values, religion, and faith are very much linked with motivation and behavioral change. In many societies, religious teaching plays a significant role in molding people's values and ideas about how they should conduct their lives. Cultural practices develop over time in communities, and complex relationships evolve between such practices and the teachings of various faith leaders and traditions. This applies to all faith traditions, from the largest world religions to local and traditional faiths. Gender relations, initiation practices, sex and marriage, and reproductive health are all arenas where cultural values interplay with religious teachings as significant factors in decision making.

While cultures clearly do change, and are deeply affected by modernization, there are abundant stories of change efforts that have not worked,

The World Faiths Development Dialogue and the World Bank Development Dialogue have followed Tostan's work in West Africa over several years. This chapter draws especially on "Women's Health and Human Rights in Africa," a presentation by Malick Diagne and Molly Melching of Tostan, at Bank headquarters in 2006, and other resources on Tostan's work. Molly Melching provided helpful comments on the draft of this chapter.

and that have backfired and produced unexpected consequences. With the passage of time, people may realize that discarded practices contain more merit than earlier supposed, and communities may close ranks to reject government or outside inducements to change. Individuals and communities are divided on which traditions are worthy of preservation and which should be questioned, debated, and altered. In short, efforts to induce cultural change and "shift community behaviors" need to be undertaken with care.

The widespread practice known as female genital mutilation (FGM), or female genital cutting (FGC), illustrates well the dilemmas involved in trying to change a practice that has been considered ingrained in certain cultures. Change has over time been slow and difficult, and many communities and individuals have resisted efforts to induce it, including both prohibition and persuasion. However, a long-standing program in West Africa, developed over a 25-year period by Tostan, a nonprofit NGO, offers an inspirational story of how change can be achieved when communities are fully engaged. The role of religious leaders in the partnership has been vitally important.

TOSTAN

Tostan is a remarkable example of an organization that truly lives its core value of empowering communities to make their own decisions about economic and social change.[1] Tostan is based in Senegal, and was founded by an American woman, Molly Melching, who attended the University of Dakar, then served as a Peace Corps volunteer in Senegal in the 1970s. Over the years, several international organizations and agencies such as UNICEF, the Bill and Melinda Gates Foundation, the American Jewish World Service, the Swedish International Development Agency, the U.S. Agency for International Development, the Wallace Research Foundation, the Wallace Global Fund, and many other donors have supported Tostan, because of their commitment to its mission and in recognition of its carefully tested and articulated approach to social change.

Tostan—which means *breakthrough* in the Wolof language of Senegal and the Gambia—was incorporated in the United States in 1991. Tostan's mission is to contribute to the dignity of Africans by developing and implementing a nonformal, participatory educational program in national languages.

Although Tostan is often solely associated with efforts to end FGC, its mandate is actually much larger: its goal is to empower African communities socially and economically through a human rights–based program that enables them to lead their own development in a sustainable way. In each village where it works, Tostan holds classes for 25 adults and 25 adolescents, each of whom adopts and teaches a learner outside the class. Key features of the participatory empowerment approach are:

- It aims to be holistic—that is, not based on a single development issue, but rather a process that works under the premise that social and economic issues are interrelated.
- It aims to be learner-centered—involving participants through modern and traditional techniques, including theater, games, and song.
- It aims to be participatory—involving all constituencies: men, women, adolescents, and religious and traditional leaders.
- It aims to be respectful—based on a tradition of consultation, dialogue, negotiation, and mediation.

In this model, Tostan trains facilitators from local communities who in turn implement the participatory nonformal education sessions with community members, helping them identify goals, challenges, and steps they can take to fulfill their vision for a better future.

The Tostan approach includes sessions on democracy, human rights and responsibilities, problem solving, hygiene, health, math, literacy, and management skills.

Participants have begun small businesses and income-generating activities after gaining skills through the Tostan program.[2]

ADDRESSING FEMALE GENITAL CUTTING

FGC is the issue for which Tostan is best known. The practice has attracted passionate debate and study because it is widely seen, especially among feminist groups, as the epitome of a cruel practice that affects young and vulnerable girls. It has also, falsely, been closely associated with the Islamic faith, because it is most commonly though by no means universally concentrated in Muslim communities.

Anthropologists and Islamic scholars and teachers alike see FGC as transmitted and preserved by cultural tradition, and many eminent Muslim scholars have sought to make clear that it is not in any fashion a religious obligation or recommendation. The topic is highly sensitive. Those who condemn or seek to change the practice are often caught off balance by angry rejections of their interventions by women and men from affected communities, who argue above all that outsiders cannot understand the complex motivations behind a practice embedded in their culture and, some argue, their faith.

Despite the sensitivity, and because it is seen as so harmful to the health of girls and women and as a basic infringement on their human rights, many development programs have sought to work in partnership with a wide range of groups to bring about change. Among these, the World Bank has engaged in a Donors Working Group on Female Genital Mutilation and Cutting, and several World Bank–supported projects in African countries such as Somalia include measures to address this challenge. In one instance, in Burkina Faso, enforcement of the Burkinabé law against FGC was part of a reform program supported by the International Monetary Fund and the World Bank.

Among a wide array of programs where few are successful and many more show limited results, the work of Tostan stands out. In explaining the group's success, Molly Melching, Tostan's founder and executive director, focuses on the importance of probing deeply into the reasons why societies do change harmful cultural practices. She highlights the work of Dr. Gerry Mackie, who studied social change in China, and links his findings to an approach to change that Tostan has applied in West Africa.

The practice of foot binding was widespread in China only a century ago, and was plainly very painful for women and resistant to outside pressure to change. Why, the study asked, have such social conventions persisted so stubbornly? Why have they proved so difficult to change? Why would women who have undergone the painful process of foot binding then insist on it for their daughters?

The key link between these phenomena and the core of both practices is the marriageability of girls, which explains why the practices are widespread within communities, why they persist over generations, and why even those who oppose them believe they must practice them. Melching related a story of a mother who, despite the death of her first daughter from FGC, went ahead and had her second daughter cut. The mother plainly felt she had no choice but to protect her daughter's future, defined within her community as ensuring that girls are marriageable. This explains why, in the case of both foot binding in China and FGC in Africa, women have perpetuated and defended the practice: they care deeply about the future of their daughters. Because of this strong community involvement in sustaining the practice, change must involve the community as a whole, in an explicit and open way that changes the norms and rules of the game. In China, the remarkable sequel is that the practice of foot-binding disappeared across that huge country in less than a generation, as the norms within communities changed and "tipped" so that bound feet, by common agreement and will, were no longer seen as a prerequisite for social acceptance and marriage.

Since the start of the Tostan program, more than 2,000 villages have publicly declared their commitment to abandon FGC. Tostan stresses that the community, not the NGO, makes this decision. In brief, in many villages, participants identify health as a human rights issue, a key to development, and see FGC as one of the barriers to women's health. Subsequent discussions lead the community to come to the natural conclusion that it needs to include their intra-marrying communities in this decision and collectively abandon the practice. A key premise of the program, and reason for its success, is the idea that social transformation can happen only on a larger scale, and that it requires collective, not individual, change.

PUBLIC DECLARATIONS AND COMMUNITY ENGAGEMENT

During a public declaration—a unique outcome of Tostan's program—a group of intra-marrying communities formally announces its pledge to abandon FGC for the sake of girls' human right to health and bodily integrity. A public declaration can occur only after the following components are in place:

- Participants share what they are learning and deciding with other individuals, with their families, and with their intra-marrying communities.
- Participants involve religious and traditional leaders and seek the support of local government.
- Participating villages hold inter-village meetings and establish pilot committees.
- The meetings include members of the same ethnic groups and intra-marrying communities.
- Representatives from other regions and countries are often invited to participate, including religious leaders and other influential personalities.
- Participants pursue extensive media coverage of their efforts, especially in local languages, in order to inform others that the practice is changing on a large scale.

Highlighting the importance of the public declaration is the finding that in some African communities, attitudes to FGC have changed but behaviors have not. Social convention theory explains why holding negative opinions of FGC does not necessarily lead people to abandon the practice—no one family can give up the practice alone. Gerry Mackie likens it to changing a convention of driving on one side of the street to the other: such a change can happen only when everyone agrees to it at the same time.

Other strategies that have typically been used to try to eliminate FGC and the reasons for their failure to bring lasting change include the following:

- *Propaganda and prohibition*: Harsh propaganda is disrespectful and ineffective; prohibition with criminal penalties can have broad impact, but without consistent effect.
- *Focus on religious leaders*: Religious command is not the cause of the practice.

- *Modernization:* This does not succeed because it does not lead to collective abandonment.
- *Compensate the cutter:* This approach has not succeeded because cutters do not cause the practice; they merely service demand for it.
- *Alternative initiation rites:* In most groups, FGC is not associated with initiation rites.[3]

Melching concludes that a rapid and universal end to FGC is possible with the appropriate strategy and effort through a human rights–based community empowerment program, organized diffusion of new information by the people themselves to locally connected communities, and a convention shift promoted through a public declaration.

When asked about challenges Tostan has faced, Malick Diagne, Deputy Director of Tostan, and Melching describe opposition from some extremely conservative religious leaders and nationalistic groups who viewed Tostan's efforts with suspicion. Diagne and Melching have dealt with hostility by being patient and keeping dialogue and communication open with all groups. At the same time, other religious leaders have been instrumental in helping to change social conventions, and Melching stresses the importance of gaining the respect and trust of local faith leaders as a prerequisite to gaining credibility within communities.

Also noteworthy is Malick Diagne's unique perspective as a man working on women's health issues. He notes the role that men play in perpetuating FGC and child marriage. He frankly acknowledges that oftentimes it is masculinity and men's insecurity that reinforces harmful practices such as FGC and child marriage, which protect girls' virginity and marriageability. These are clearly sensitive issues, well entrenched in many cultures and societies.

The Tostan story illustrates the power of bringing together community members in a creative and intensive program of nonformal education that serves as a catalyst for change. Communities prioritize their own needs and make decisions about their futures. This is a difficult process, provoking challenges from both those resistant to change and outside groups. However, the process reinforces the notion that communities can benefit and develop from the wisdom of their own people, and that partnerships between communities and external catalysts can be extremely powerful.

NOTES

1. See http://www.tostan.org/.

2. World Bank, 1998, "Senagalese Women Remake Their Culture," *Indigenous Knowledge Notes* No. 3 (Washington, DC: World Bank). See http://siteresources. worldbank.org/EXTINDKNOWLEDGE/Resources/iknt3.pdf. For a full description of Tostan's educational methodology, see http://www.tostan.org.

3. Gerry Mackie, 1996, "Ending Footbinding and Infibulation: A Convention Account," *American Sociological Review* 61(6), 999–1017.

CHAPTER

10

Grassroots Matters
Sarvodaya, the Tsunami, and Development in Sri Lanka

The Asian tsunami of 2004 struck with a mighty and devastating force. Sri Lanka was declared a national disaster, with the storm causing widespread destruction along the country's eastern, southern, and western coast. More than 100,000 houses were damaged, and a million people affected—of a total population of just 19 million.

Although the tsunami did not discriminate upscale resorts from poor coastal towns, the storm clearly hurt coastal fishermen and poor and vulnerable populations disproportionately. Cardinal Theodore McCarrick, then archbishop of Washington, DC, described the awesome power of the water shortly after visiting Sri Lanka: "The waves came in with such power that the light-fitting clothes that so many people were wearing were ripped right off of them."[1] The images from post-tsunami Sri Lanka were disturbing and stark, revealing all too much death and destruction.

The country's post-tsunami experiences offer some powerful lessons about partnerships. A key lesson is that no organization or entity could go it alone. Knowledgeable grassroots groups, experienced in community development, have the potential to reach deep into affected communities.

This chapter benefits from a 2004 visit by Marisa Van Saanen to Sarvodaya's headquarters just before the tsunami, and meetings at that time with Dr. A.T. Ariyaratne, Dr. Vinya Ariyaratne, and several other staff members. Peter Harrold (World Bank) gave helpful comments.

This potential is multiplied if it is linked effectively with the many organizations that mobilize to bring expertise and resources to bear after a disaster.

A damage and needs assessment by the World Bank, prepared in early 2005 with the Asian Development Bank and the Japan Bank for International Cooperation, estimated the total financing needed for Sri Lanka's recovery and reconstruction at US$1.5–1.6 billion.[2] Relief and reconstruction would require mobilizing a wide array of external partners as well as private resources, including both individuals and local and international organizations. At the outset, however, outsiders did not fully appreciate the potential energy of Sri Lanka's community-based organizations, or the wisdom of their strategic approach for meeting the relief challenge.

The World Bank itself provided about US$150 million to support tsunami-specific relief and the country's reconstruction and recovery program. Of this, US$75 million would help fund an immediate response, while another US$75 million in emergency credits and grants would help rebuild damaged houses, restore livelihoods, and reactivate basic services in devastated areas.

The Bank channeled its funding through Sri Lanka's Task Force for Rebuilding the Nation (TAFREN), the statutory authority responsible for the overall implementation and monitoring of the country's disaster management program. TAFREN routed international development assistance funds to national and district government agencies. Beyond the Bank, a variety of other partners worked separately and together to respond to a crisis of horrifying proportions. The programs are still continuing, as endeavor to rebuild their lives.

After the tsunami, the world beyond Sri Lanka became more aware of a group long known to those interested in community development and social movements: the Lanka Jathika Sarvodaya Shramadana Sangamaya Movement (Sarvodaya).[3] Established in 1958 by a high school teacher who wanted to encourage his students to work in poor communities, Sarvodaya today is an impressively organized movement reaching some 15,000 villages throughout Sri Lanka with a permanent staff of 1,500. When the tsunami struck, Sri Lanka's development partners, including the World Bank (which had a previous relationship with Sarvodaya), and policy makers found themselves looking with new eyes to Sarvodaya, as the organization was clearly poised to help with immediate relief, as well as reconstruction and the long path of community development ahead.

The unusual value of Sarvodaya—a Gandhian and Buddhist-inspired organization—soon became apparent. The group was on the scene first, and was able to penetrate deeply into the problems facing affected communities. Residents even of areas that had recently seen armed conflict welcomed the group, and the international organizations that flocked to Sri Lanka also turned to Sarvodaya. And the group knew what it was doing, and so was immediately effective. However, this interchange was not without challenges, and the Sarvodaya experience thus offers useful lessons for responding to future disasters.

INTRODUCING SARVODAYA

> We build the road and the road builds us.
> —Sarvodaya's motto

Sarvodaya began in the mid-1950s when a group of teachers in Colombo, Sri Lanka, including Dr. A.T. Ariyaratne, Sarvodaya's founder, organized *shramadana* work camps, which enabled students to help poor communities mobilize around basic development projects. From the outset, the group's underlying philosophy focused less on economic development than on the potential of Sarvodaya to act as a catalyst for communities to develop themselves. This effort to mobilize villages to address their own needs happens organically: Sarvodaya has always been and remains Sri Lankan, though Sarvodaya groups do now operate in other countries in support of the work in Sri Lanka. The key actors are the villagers, now supported by a secretariat and paid staff.

From the beginning, Sarvodaya saw its work not as charity but as a movement toward a more enlightened society. This movement caught on quickly and grew rapidly, with 100 villages involved in 1967, 1,000 in 1974, 6,000 in 1983, 10,000 in 2004, and 15,000 by early 2007. Sarvodaya's founders envision reaching 4 million people.

Sarvodaya claims that it never enters a village without an invitation. After receiving one, Sarvodaya brings a wide range of social, economic, and technological programs. As a first step, Sarvodaya helps the village outline its own goals for development—whether related to health care, education, or technological advance. Sarvodaya then helps organize work camps, with the able-bodied providing physical labor, chefs cooking dinners for the workers, and everyone participating in social and morale-building activities. Sarvodaya's secretariat in Moratuwa provides financial and technical support. At a certain stage of basic development, Sarvodaya then transitions the village to receive financial services through Sarvodaya Economic Enterprise Development Services (SEEDS), a microfinance bank founded in 1998. Some 3,000 Sarvodaya villages now use SEEDS, which also offers financial services and capacity building.

In pursuing such a broad geographical and sectoral reach, Sarvodaya relies on a well-articulated development model. Within each village, and within the Sarvodaya movement, organizational structure is clear and consistent, as is the expected five-state process through which villages move:

- After a village requests Sarvodaya's help, the group organizes *shramadana* camps and family get-togethers where villagers discuss community needs and priorities and assess local capacity.
- Sarvodaya forms functional groups and offers leadership training programs, based on villagers' expressed needs and priorities. These programs may target mothers, youth, elders, and children. Sarvodaya may also establish child development centers, preschools, community kitchens, and village libraries.
- To create economic and employment opportunities, the village joins the SEEDS banking program.
- The village moves toward self-management, self-finance, and self-reliance, as Sarvodaya helps promote income-generating activities to build a sustainable community.
- Self-financing continues to the point of surplus, so the village can share some profits with other communities. This final stage is termed *grama swarajya* (village self-governance), and clearly echoes the Gandhian model of sustainability.

The group's "organizational linkage" approach connects villages to local, district, and national government agencies. Overall, the goal is to eradicate poverty and fulfill 10 basic human needs: access to primary health care; cultural and spiritual sustenance; a simple house to live in;

basic clothing; simple and nourishing food; a basic energy supply; a clean and adequate supply of water; simple communications facilities; a well-rounded education; and a clean and beautiful environment.

The formal name of the movement helps explain its work and philosophy. *Shrama* means "energy" or "labor," while *dana* means "giving away." *Shramadana* is thus the sharing of energy or labor. *Sarvodaya* means "embracing everything," while *udaya* means "awakening." Sarvodaya's vision is to create a society with no poverty but also no affluence—to generate a nonviolent revolution towards the creation of a Sarvodaya Social Order which will ensure the total awakening of human personalities, human families, village communities, urban communities, national communities, and the world community. Economic and social development are seen not only as ends in themselves, but also as a means to spiritual awakening at the personal, community, country, and global levels.

Dr. A.T. Ariyaratne explained his philosophy thus:

> The economic life of a human being cannot be separated from his total life and living. *Buddha Dhamma* looks at life as a whole. In fact the entire living world is treated as a whole in Buddha's teachings. Without this holistic understanding of life it is difficult for humans to follow the path of happiness. Economics is only a fragment of life and living. Therefore moral and social implications of economic activity cannot be considered apart from economics. [4]

Sarvodaya keeps these Buddhist principles at the center of its work. Some Buddhist scholars therefore think of Sarvodaya as Buddhism in action, or engaged Buddhism. Yet Sarvodaya also speaks of itself as an organization for all Sri Lankans, regardless of their religion or ethnic group. What is less clear is how this philosophy plays out on the ground, and how Sarvodaya is perceived by various communities in a conflict-torn country.

LINKING PEACE AND COMMUNITY BUILDING

Visitors to Sarvodaya's headquarters are often struck by the diversity of its work. The headquarters include a Child Education Center, where innovative education practices are devised and tested, a women's entrepreneurial center, a home for disabled girls, and an orphanage. The headquarters also includes the Vishva Niketan International Peace Center, the site of individual and community mediation. The center displays photos of the day when all prisoners from the local jail were brought there for meditation, while another photo shows Sarvodaya members leading meditation at the jail. SEEDS headquarters is nearby, while community branches are found throughout the country. The passion and devotion of staff members throughout the Sarvodaya organization is easy to sense.

Sarvodaya is clearly the best-known NGO in Sri Lanka, and has received support from numerous individuals, organizations, and foreign governments. Dr. A.T. Ariyaratne and Dr. Vinya Ariyaratne (A.T. Aryiratne's son and Sarvodaya's present director) have consulted with the World Bank on Sri Lanka's development, through informal consultations in Colombo as well as small, discrete partnership projects.[5]

Sarovodya strives to share its model of development well beyond Sri Lanka. Father and son often speak to foreign audiences, and they are well connected to networks of interfaith leaders and development leaders. Sarvodaya USA aims to learn from and support the work of the movement worldwide, while also facilitating the use of its holistic vision for community development in the United States.

Dr. Vinya Ariyaratne recently launched an initiative—in partnership with the Asia Pacific Leadership Forum and associated with UNAIDS—to mobilize religious leaders to support HIV/AIDS prevention, control, and care. HIV prevalence in Sri Lanka is low (although the prevalence of other sexually transmitted diseases is high), and stigma around HIV/AIDS is intense. Therefore, engaging leaders of various faiths to champion HIV/AIDS issues offers great potential. This initiative drew on Dr. Vinya Ariyaratne's work with Buddhist monks on the same issues in 1995–96, supported by the WHO.

POST-TSUNAMI SRI LANKA

When the tsunami struck, international attention focused sharply on Sri Lanka. How could this small island country respond to the devastation? Donors worldwide were eager to send funds and volunteers and find ways to help with the relief and rebuilding.

In Sri Lanka, development and community organizations rallied to areas that represented their priorities. In February 2006, looking to the work ahead in rebuilding Sri Lanka, Peter Harrold, then World Bank country director, said "The need is to create a strong foundation for a longer-term reconstruction and recovery effort that ensures equity between regions and ethnic groups."[6] The World Bank's primary role in creating that foundation was in providing a financing package to the Sri Lankan government for recovery and rebuilding. The Bank focused on funding housing, roads, water supply, other infrastructure, livelihood, and capacity building, while other development partners financed health and education needs.

A needs assessment exercise in Sri Lanka identified several guiding principles for recovery and reconstruction:

- Allocation of resources both domestic and international should be strictly guided by identified needs and local priorities, without discrimination on the basis of political, religious, ethnic, or gender considerations.
- Reconstruction activities should be carried out by the appropriate level of government, with an emphasis on decentralization where feasible.
- Communities should be empowered to make their own decisions during recovery.
- Decision making and implementation should emphasize communication and transparency.
- Reconstruction should avoid rebuilding in areas vulnerable to natural hazards.
- Participants should rely on a coordinated approach, to prevent duplication of activities.

What was unusual and offered great hope in the immediate post-tsunami period was the willingness of all development partners and key stakeholders, including the Liberation Tigers of Tamil Eelam (Tamil Tigers), a separatist group, to work closely with the government to develop district-based reconstruction plans. Communities would identify those who should receive support, and housing grants would be distributed across the country in line with damage estimates.

Through a variety of funding streams and partnerships, Sarvodaya was called into action. The group was well positioned to respond, not only because of its long history of building village networks, but also because it had conducted disaster management briefings with district coordinators just weeks before the storm, after news of an approaching cyclone.

Hours after the tsunami, Sarvodaya began to receive financial support from Sri Lankans, the private sector, Sarvodaya branches in the United States, the Netherlands, Belgium, Germany, and foundations such as the Novartis Foundation of Switzerland and the Arigatou Foundation of Japan. Sarvodaya was thus able to immediately distribute food and clothes to survivors, and organize medical care and welfare camps for many who had lost their homes. These services reached all 14 affected districts and about 40,000 displaced families.

Within days of the tsunami, Sarvodaya moved to another level of response, reconstituting family units, providing counseling by personnel trained to deal with trauma, and offering continuous medical care, especially to pregnant mothers and children. Services also included cleaning wells, disinfecting temporary residences, organizing programs for preschool and school children, and finding meaningful work for adults in exchange for food and cash. Sarvodaya offered to care for all orphaned primary school children through referrals from the state childcare agency, and collected information on the degree of damage to families and communities.

Sarvodaya's on-the-ground experience was immediately useful not only to direct beneficiaries but to the multitude of other organizations trying to respond. Within days, Sarvodaya drew up a qualitative assessment of settlement camps and circulated it to relief organizations, among them UN agencies based in Sri Lanka. This was an important resource. Dr. A. T. Ariyaratne also visited all the affected districts soon after the tsunami, even meeting with Tamil Tiger leaders in the north to discuss rehabilitation. Dr. Vinya Ariyaratne participated in discussions with Kofi Annan, the secretary general of the UN, and James Wolfensohn, then president of the World Bank. The Sarvodaya Website became a clearinghouse for information on the tsunami, as Google, Apple, Nortel, and U2 linked to the site, and the group received international media coverage as a result.

As the immediate crisis receded, Sarvodaya continued its relief efforts at the same time that it worked to implement several medium- to long-term programs that would help restore economic activities in the affected areas. Sarvodaya commissioned a National Re-Awakening Council, which established a number of priority areas, including women, children, and orphans; water and sanitation; health and preventive care; camp and community management; housing resettlement; livelihood support; documentation and legal assistance; environmental management; communications; disaster management and mitigation; and integrated village development.[7]

Sarvodaya also initiated talks among tsunami-affected communities in the south and the east, with the support of a US$5,000 grant from the World Bank, resulting in *Post Tsunami Voice of the Community Leaders*.[8] This report detailed how the actions of decision makers, assistance providers, and aid recipients have affected the post-tsunami situation in Sri Lanka's east and south.

LEARNING FROM THE DISASTER

Numerous media have reported that the tsunami response was not as efficient and effective as it might have been; certainly the scale of the tsunami surprised and overwhelmed most systems. Rehabilitation work in the midst of such chaos and devastation has provided much experience on which to reflect and improve, and Sarvodaya has articulated key lessons for future disaster preparedness:[9]

Lack of coordination: Much greater effort is needed to coordinate responses to a disaster. Many organizations arrived in Sri Lanka with supplies, funds, and human resources, and the more successful partnered with local groups that knew the landscape well. In Sarvodaya's view, less successful projects proceeded independently of local groups; these projects were often unsustainable, and groups left with money still in the bank. Some organizations also ventured outside their areas of expertise, and were unable to deliver results effectively.

"Spend, spend, spend": Sarvodaya argues that an educational process is needed to convince donors and responding organizations to create projects with long-term impact. Donors place too much emphasis on

spending money quickly, and overlook more lasting results. Many groups also encountered staff poaching (though Sarvodaya did not to any significant degree), as international NGOs offering big salaries lured staff members from local NGOs just when the latter needed them most.

Allocation of land: Finding land for resettlement was very difficult. Sarvodaya worked around this by relying on government-allocated land as well as private land offered through religious organizations.

Lost opportunities for reconciliation: Sarvodaya feels that Sri Lanka as a whole failed to use the tsunami disaster as a catalyst for peace, and that peace-building efforts have deteriorated as priorities have refocused.

Attitudes among recipients: Aid and relief efforts often emphasized a culture of "neediness and expectation" over self-help and self-reliance, with the result that some recipients have become dependent on aid. Sarvodaya tried to avoid this by incorporating its philosophy of self-help and self-reliance into all its post-tsunami programs.

Lack of labor, materials, and transfer of funds: Labor and materials were in short supply, and problems in transferring funds also occurred. Sarvodaya found that its own systems for releasing funds from headquarters to affected districts were too slow, and has since acted to speed its financial flows.

THE ROAD AHEAD

The tsunami made it glaringly clear that a wide range of partners are critically needed after a disaster. However, governmental and nongovernmental initiatives were not well coordinated, and formal development processes sometimes squeezed out the voices of affected communities. The World Bank's Independent Evaluation Group sponsored a conference in April 2006 to examine the Bank's work in the wake of catastrophic events. The panel included Dr. Vinya Ariyaratne, and many of Sarvodaya's lessons learned were themes of the day, including quick donor spending on unsustainable projects and the need for more community participation.

There is much interest in learning from the immediate response to the crisis, and in improving efforts to rebuild affected communities. One small answer is the Webhamuva project, implemented by Learning Initiatives on Reforms for Network Economies (LIRNEasia) in partnership with Sarvodaya, and funded by the World Bank's small grants program. The project builds on a traditional form of community participation in the tsunami-affected villages under Sarvodaya. This is the *pavul hamuva,* or family gathering, where camp dwellers gather to share what is on their minds. LIRNEAsia's research showed that a key problem with post-tsunami reconstruction and rehabilitation was failure to consult affected individuals in meaningful ways. The Webhamuva project aims to bring the voices of villagers to the Web, so NGOs and governments can see what is working and what is not.

In this island country, development occurs through externally supported investment as well as the more organic Sarvodaya model. The latter underscores that collaboration is clearly necessary, and efforts to ensure that it occurs are still much needed.

NOTES

1. Katherine Marshall and Lucy Keough, 2005, *Finding Global Balance: Common Ground Between the Worlds of Development and Faith* (Washington, DC: World Bank).

2. World Bank, February 24, 2005, "World Bank's Support to Sri Lanka's Tsunami Recovery Reaches $US150 Million," press release.

3. Resources on Sarvodaya include Joanna Macy, 1985, *Dharma and Development: Religion as a Resource in the Sarvodaya Self-Help Movement,* revised ed. (Bloomfield, CT: Kumarian Press). See also Christopher Candland, 2000, "Faith and Social Capital: Religion and Community Development in South Asia," *Policy Sciences Journal* 33 (December): 3–4.

4. Drawn from A.T. Ariyaratne, 1999, *Schumacher Lectures on Buddhist Economics* (Sarvodaya Vishva Lekha). See http://www.sarvodayausa.org/buddhist economics.php.

5. For example, in December 2002, SEEDS became a participating credit institution under the World Bank–sponsored Renewable Energy for Rural Economic Development project. See the Website of the UNDP's Equator Initiative: http://www.tve.org/ho/doc.cfm?aid=1675&lang=English. See also a note on the visit of Praful Patel, World Bank vice president for South Asia, at http://www.seeds.lk/PDF/World_Bank.pdf.

6. World Bank, February 24, 2005, "World Bank's Support to Sri Lanka's Tsunami Recovery Reaches $US150 Million," press release.

7. For the post-tsunami report of April 2006, see http://www.sarvodaya.org/tsunami/latest-report-april-2006/.

8. See Research Consultancy Bureau, October 2005, *Post-Tsunami Voice of the Community Leaders—The Report*, prepared for Sarvodaya, at http://siteresources.worldbank.org/NEWS/Resources/srilankareport.pdf. See also World Bank, November 21, 2005, "A Buddhist Priest Offers Refuge to Tsunami Victims," at http://web.worldbank.org/WBSITE/EXTERNAL/NEWS/0,,contentMDK:20730364~pagePK:64257043~piPK:437376~theSitePK:4607,00.html.

9. For Sarvodaya's "Lesson's Learned from the Tsunami," see http://www.sarvodaya.org/tsunami/lessons-learned/.

11

Madrasa Challenges and Reforms in Pakistan

Since September 11, 2001, a host of newly framed policy issues—many of which link religion with social and economic development—have catapulted onto global agendas. In this context, complex questions about the roles that religious institutions play in education, and appropriate teaching about religion in schools, have taken on new dimensions. Discussions on the topic have highlighted important gaps in knowledge about religious schools and approaches to education across the Islamic world. These schools are known to vary widely in content and quality within and between countries. However, understanding and analysis of how the institutions actually work, and how they are evolving, is patchy at best.

The madrasa educational system in Pakistan has attracted particular attention from Pakistani and global leaders alike, largely because of concerns that these schools are directly implicated in fostering extremist attitudes that extend far beyond Pakistan itself.[1] In response, an extraordinary program of reform from within has engaged Muslim educators across Pakistan, drawing on Islamic history and beliefs to enhance madrasa curriculums.[2] The program aims to foster peaceful coexistence among diverse groups and encourage greater adherence to Islamic principles of

This chapter draws on materials from the International Center for Religion and Diplomacy (ICRD) and on presentations by Douglas Johnston, President, ICRD, and colleagues. Douglas Johnston and Azhar Hussain provided helpful comments on the draft.

tolerance and human rights, with an emphasis on how past Islamic civilizations upheld these values. And the program appears to work where others have failed, showing promise of overcoming considerable obstacles.

The path to the project seems an improbable one, in part because of persistent images and reports of hostile attitudes toward the secular West in general, and the United States in particular, in Pakistan's madrasas. But a complex background and dynamic is at work. During the 1980s, Western strategists saw Pakistan's religious schools as part of a strategic response to regional conflicts with the Soviet Union, and they received official financial support. But by the mid-1990s, with the rise of the Taliban in Afghanistan and mounting tensions involving Islamic countries, Pakistan's Islamic educational institutions began to appear less benign.[3]

The scope of the challenge is hotly contested, with estimates of the share of students enrolled in religious educational institutions ranging from less than 1 percent to 33 percent.[4] More than 9,000 religious schools are registered with the Pakistani government, with many more operating unofficially. One reason for the confusion is definition; another is the pace of change, since religious schools on a significant scale are a relatively recent phenomenon. Part of the reason for their rapid growth is a negative one, involving weaknesses in the state education system.

Recognizing a priority need to reform the madrasa system, the Pakistani government's approach, especially since 2001 and 2002, has focused on new forms of regulation of the schools and creation of exemplary institutions. But these measures have achieved limited success. This is partly because weaknesses in the national educational system are spurring rapid growth of a wide range of private educational institutions, but also because the regulatory approach does not address key concerns about values and quality that have long been central to Islamic religious education.

ORIGINS OF ICRD

Against this backdrop, the International Center for Religion and Diplomacy (ICRD)—based in Washington, DC, and founded on the belief that religion is the "missing dimension" of foreign policy—was invited in 2002 to work in partnership with the Institute for Policy Studies, an Islamabad-based think tank, in reforming Pakistani madrasas. The invitation appears to have been inspired by ICRD's long-standing reputation as a fair-minded, religiously inspired institution, and it speaks volumes considering the wariness of many Islamic leaders toward the United States.

ICRD thus began a unique effort to address education and security issues through the madrasa system. In partnership with the Institute for Policy Studies and other Pakistani religious and civic organizations, ICRD has worked with madrasa administrators, oversight boards, and senior faculty to provide a better education and improved moral guidance for their students by conducting teacher-training workshops. These workshops encourage expansion of madrasa curriculums to include scientific and social disciplines, with a special emphasis on religious tolerance and human rights (particularly women's rights), and the adoption of pedagogical techniques that promote critical thinking skills. The workshops also equip newly trained teachers with the skills to train other madrasa leaders.

A recent article describes the program as "depicting reform not as a concession to the secular west but as a return to Islamic principles of tolerance and scholarship."[5] This description conveys a critical element of the program, which begins by celebrating the past glories of Islamic education. The current aim is to reach madrasas in every province of Pakistan, including the more conflict-prone northern areas. Strikingly, the ICRD has successfully engaged madrasa leaders from each of the five sects that sponsor religious schools—Wahhabi, Deobandi, Barelvi, Jamat-i-Islami, and Shia—and from each of Pakistan's four provinces.

HOW THE PROGRAM WORKS

ICRD initially focused on a series of workshops, beginning with a two-week event that addressed Islam and Contemporary Thought, for madrasa leaders from the five sects. Next, they hosted five one-day seminars for private sector and public sector participants in key cities across the country on future educational strategies, followed by a series of 10-day teacher-training workshops. Nearly 200 madrasas and 460 madrasa administrators and teachers participated in the first phase of training workshops.

The program then moved on to 10 one-day outreach seminars in selected madrasas, designed to help previously uninvolved leaders understand the need for change and the advantages of working together to achieve it. This laid the groundwork for teacher-training workshops on separate tracks among the harder-line Deobandi and Wahhabi madrasa leaders. Thus the program has focused increasingly on the more conservative madrasas, while emphasizing pedagogic techniques that encourage far more active engagement than is traditional in madrasas.

ICRD's approach encourages madrasa leaders to reflect on their own values and goals, and to explore ways they can work together to uphold the principles of Islam and provide improved moral guidance for their students and communities. The initial sessions of the 10-day workshops explore the role of madrasas in the Middle Ages, when Islam was at its peak, with workshop facilitators emphasizing early approaches to education and governance that promoted tolerance and coexistence among different religions and minorities.

Subsequent sessions focus on human relationships and the role of the teacher, student, and madrasa in providing a balanced education. Topics include ethics and responsibilities, attitudes in the classroom, how to establish a teaching environment conducive to learning, and comparative teaching methods. The final sessions provide participants opportunities to learn from one another and from nontraditional speakers who expose them to new ways of teaching and learning.

Such activities challenge deep-seated biases commonly held by madrasa administrators and teachers, such as those built on the premise that modernity and the influence of women will somehow sabotage their ability to be effective Muslim leaders. Some of the workshop sessions have included presentations to the all-male audiences by two female Pakistani scholars, as well as Western scholars.

The positive response to the program is striking, and there are promising indications that the workshops can lead to helpful shifts in attitude and a greater willingness to discuss the role of religious institutions in propagating a culture of intolerance. Madrasa instructors have asked for further training in conflict-resolution skills, which will enable them to reach out in peace to other sects and other countries. They have requested that similar educational programs be conducted in their home madrasas for all their teaching staff. Finally, they have come to recognize that children should be treated with respect, and are now reflecting on how human rights affect performance in the classroom.

Evidently, a key element in the development and success of the program has been the ability to gain the trust of madrasa leaders and overcome their deep-seated suspicions and resistance to modernization, which they have heretofore rejected as inherently Western. Success in "winning hearts and minds" has laid the groundwork for the next phase, which entails "training the trainer" workshops. These workshops aim to produce master trainers who can work with previously uninvolved madrasa leaders on their own, significantly expanding participation in the program.

MEDIUM-TERM GOALS

A central medium-term goal is to expand madrasa curriculums to include scientific and social disciplines. Thus it is significant that the training workshops have not only exposed madrasa instructors to contemporary disciplines and ideas on religious tolerance and human rights, but also helped to overcome the negative attitude of many madrasa leaders toward modernization.

Speakers at the workshops work to make the case compelling for why madrasa curriculums should cover a wider spectrum of disciplines, include modern subjects and texts, return to the Islamic intellectual tradition of searching for deeper meaning and encouraging reflective interpretation, and move beyond sectarian differences. Specific topics addressed in workshop sessions include issues in medical science; rights and roles of women; conflict and peace: the role of religion; interfaith dialogue; history and politics; globalization; modern Western thought; economics; the Internet; contemporary issues and the need for research in madrasas; and the role of social institutions.

By the time these workshops conclude, madrasa administrators themselves are advocating for madrasa education to be harmonized with contemporary needs, and to balance better religious and contemporary subjects. In discussing these issues in small groups during the workshops, madrasa leaders have proposed adding courses on subjects such as

English, Arabic, mathematics, economics, computers/information technology, ethics, comparative religious studies, Western thought, and public speaking to madrasa curriculums, or considering them for special study programs, and reviewing Islamic injunctions in view of contemporary medical discoveries. Several madrasas have already asked ICRD to assist them in modernizing their curriculums and pedagogy on a pilot basis.

The next phase of curriculum reform will involve initiation of a Best Practices (in Islamic Education) Scholarship Program, which will select a small group of influential madrasa administrators and board members from all five sects to conduct research on the best practices in religious school curriculums in Pakistan and other parts of the world. This program will culminate in a Curriculum Enhancement Conference, which will present scholars' findings to madrasa oversight boards and selected others to promote systemic reform. An Inter-Sectarian Curriculum Reform Committee will use the conference recommendations, in turn, to develop several alternative curriculums that can serve as models for madrasa leaders. Current planning calls for the madrasa reform process to involve various stakeholders, including government officials wherever possible.

A second medium-term objective is to incorporate changes in pedagogy that will support the development of critical thinking skills. To this end, the training workshops have been exposing madrasa instructors to modern pedagogical techniques and theories of child development and child psychology, often for the first time in their lives.

The workshops themselves are participatory and interactive, giving participants experience in small-group discussion, critical thinking, and problem solving. Workshop sessions have explored topics such as educational objectives, educational psychology, methods of teaching, technical education, concepts of punishment, co-curricular activities, contemporary requirements, and the benefits of critical thinking and analytical abilities.

After completing the workshops, a significant number of the madrasa leaders have requested further training in pedagogical techniques for their staff, and are identifying problem areas in their current teaching methods. For example, in a system where madrasa students may be severely punished, madrasa leaders who have undergone ICRD's training now recognize the psychological damage that can result from such harsh practices, and are accepting the need for a more humane teaching style. Toward this end, they are requesting training in areas such as moral education, educational psychology, lesson planning, new pedagogical techniques, and community relations.

Third, the program aims to develop a related training program for teachers. ICRD has already conducted its first master training workshop, for Deobandi madrasa leaders from Balochistan. The Deobandis represent the most hard-line and most powerful sect that sponsors madrasas, and Balochistan is one of Pakistan's most radical provinces. Additional master training workshops will bring together madrasa administrators and senior faculty from all five sects. Madrasa leaders trained as teacher trainers will, in turn, work with administrators and senior faculty of madrasas not previously involved in the reform process.

ICRD's approach has enabled madrasas to view the reform effort as their own, not something imposed from the outside. The ICRD model is succeeding because madrasa leaders themselves are recognizing the benefits of reform and assuming significant ownership of the process. After participating in workshops, madrasa leaders exhibit greater self-reflection, and are able to evaluate their own institutions from a broader perspective. As a result, some madrasas have begun exploring ways to bring local public school teachers in as volunteers to teach courses in math, English, and social studies during the evening hours.

The approach is also inspiring madrasa leaders to expand their horizons by drawing on the past accomplishments of Islam. In the training workshops, madrasa leaders reflect on Islamic values that relate to peace and tolerance, and the role these core values played when Islam was at its peak a thousand years ago. The key to the success of these early Islamic societies was their ability to tap the diverse talents of their populations, exemplified by the religious tolerance established in Moorish Spain. Presentation topics have included the role of the madrasas in early Islamic education, Islamic educational curricula and modern-day requirements, the teaching of religious and ethnic tolerance in early Islamic educational systems, and modern-day failures of Islamic countries and educational systems. For many madrasa leaders, this has been their first opportunity to discuss Islamic principles, education, and philosophy with educators from other sects, and to reflect on the past successes of Islamic education in a diverse academic setting. This has provided a nonthreatening way for madrasa administrators to challenge themselves by drawing comparisons with what has gone before.

THE IMPACT OF THE PROGRAM

ICRD's project director provides a telling account of the program's impact. During a recent workshop, one madrasa leader told the following story. In his remote area of Balochistan, where tribal traditions are dominant, a girl secretly made a telephone call to a boy she had met from a neighboring village. When this was discovered, tribal leaders decided they must be punished—the boy's nose and ears were to be cut off, and the girl, her sister, her mother, and the boy's mother were to be killed. Such punishments are not uncommon, but this time something was different. The madrasa leader, a respected member of the community, had previously attended an ICRD training workshop, and had spent time reflecting on the discussions relating to human rights.

"After my experience in that workshop," he said, "I felt I needed to challenge this on religious grounds." He went to the tribal leaders who had pronounced the punishment, and by pointing out that nothing in the Qur'an prohibits a woman from talking to a man, and by emphasizing the principles of forgiveness in the Qur'an, he was able to resolve the matter without anyone being harmed. Coming from an environment where people often use aggressive speech to make demands of others, this madrasa leader indicated that his workshop experience had also taught him new ways to facilitate dialogue with those with different points of view—to ask and discuss rather than demand. By using these skills, he was able to promote human rights on a personal level, and to use Islamic principles to override tribal custom. Four lives were saved, and a new precedent has been set for the village—one that could conceivably grow over time.

Other comments on the program also speak to its impact:

> *We feel motivated to think in innovative and creative ways. We have started looking at ourselves and our system. We have learned here how to plan things for a better future ... what was our past ... how are we*

faring today and what kind of planning do we need to do for the future? We have learned here that we need to help bring changes in our environment and our society.

The importance of getting contemporary education has become all the more clear in our minds, thanks to this program. I personally feel it is essential to start teaching modern subjects in our madrasas.

We need to change ourselves in many respects for the sake of reaching reconciliation in the society.

—Comments on 10-day workshops
by madrasa teachers in Karachi

A RESPECTFUL AND INCLUSIVE APPROACH

Historical wounds, injustices, and repression have created a victim mentality among many madrasa leaders that has effectively isolated them from much of the outside world. Fearful that new ideas and interactions with others may lead to a loss of their religious and cultural identity, many instinctively reject modernization and the concept of coexistence with "others."

Conditioned by decades of such fears, madrasa teachers and administrators have internalized these feelings to the point where opposing others and living in conflict have become an integral part of their identity. The strong negative biases toward other sects and cultures taught in the madrasas tend to perpetuate an atmosphere of violence, as these ideas are passed on to students and their communities.

Animosity toward the United States and the West, which runs deep in Pakistan, exacerbates the extremism and violence. During the Soviet invasion of Afghanistan, the United States armed Muslim fighters and provided textbooks to madrasas that glorified violence, to encourage the fighters to repel the "infidel" invaders. Many of today's madrasa administrators and teachers fought against the Soviets, and they are still willing to put their lives on the line to preserve their Islamic way of life. This time, however, the enemy of Muslim identity is not the former Soviet Union but the United States. Feeling used, abandoned, and betrayed by America after the Soviets were expelled, Pakistani madrasa leaders harbor great distrust and hostility toward the United States.

The madrasas view themselves as the sole institutions left to safeguard the identity of Muslims. Fearing secularization and a loss of identity, many religious leaders are convinced that if they do not confront modernism, their way of life will be destroyed by Western decadence. Classrooms across the Muslim world have thus become a major battleground in combating Western ideals.

The negative association between modernization and secularization leads to deep resistance to reform, particularly if such reform is perceived as imposed from the outside. This is why ICRD's reform efforts have found success where so many others have failed. Rather than attempt to secularize madrasas or impose foreign values, ICRD encourages people to live up to their own laudable religious values. It is by appealing to Islamic values that one can most effectively stimulate madrasa leaders to embrace change and implement lasting reform. Engaged in a respectful and inclusive manner, Pakistani madrasa leaders accept responsibility for changing the culture of intolerance that the madrasas have helped perpetuate.

NOTES

1. The term *madrasa* is confusing because in Arabic it simply means *school*, and is used in different ways in different countries. In Pakistan and other non–Arabic-speaking countries, madrasa refers to schools run by Islamic religious authorities. The plural of madrasa is "madaris," though for ease of understanding the common term madrasas is used in this text.

2. In "Reforming Pakistan's Dens of Terror," Nicholas Schmidle concludes that "a small-scale indigenous effort to reform the religious schools could be making more progress than the combined forces of the American, British and Pakistani governments" (January 2007). See http://www.truthdig.com/report/item/20070122_nicholas_schmidle_reforming_pakistans_dens_of_terror/.

3. For a description of this evolution, see Christopher Candland, 2005, "Pakistan's Recent Experience in Reforming Islamic Education," in *Education Reform in Pakistan: Building for the Future*, edited by Robert Hathaway (Washington, DC: Woodrow Wilson International Center for Scholars).

4. Ibid.

5. Sydney Freedberg, Jr., December 6, 2006, "After Musharraf," *National Journal.*

12

Integrating HIV/AIDS Care, Treatment, and Support

The Coptic Orthodox Church in Africa

The ravages of HIV/AIDS have inspired many faith communities to help people who are suffering. Faith communities also have been inspired to advocate—that is, to elicit local, national, and global responses to what they see as an existential threat. The Coptic Orthodox Church in Kenya has taken up both challenges: to provide meaningful and well-run services to those affected by the pandemic, and to make clear why each and every citizen of the world should make HIV/AIDS his or her responsibility. This chapter describes the development of a comprehensive effort by the Coptic Orthodox Church to combat HIV/AIDS, and explores how this initiative is integrated into the broader spiritual and humanitarian activities of the Coptic Church in Africa.

This chapter was written by Nadia Kist, MPA, senior program manager, Mission of the Coptic Orthodox Church in Kenya. Bishop Paul and a team from the Church, including Nadia Kist, presented their work on health and HIV/AIDS at the World Bank in January 2007.

THE CHALLENGES

The 2005 UNAIDS report estimated that almost 40 million people are living with HIV/AIDS. The disease is disproportionately concentrated in Africa: inhabited by only 10 percent of the world's population, the continent accounts for 63 percent of all HIV infections. This percentage translates to an astounding 24.7 million individuals. There is promise in the declining prevalence of HIV/AIDS in countries like Kenya, Uganda, and Zimbabwe. However, the fact that 2.8 million adults and children were reportedly infected in 2005 tells aid workers and the global community that the urgency of halting the spread of HIV/AIDS is as great as ever.

In the 20-plus years that the virus has been known, it has had a devastating impact, particularly in the developing world, where a lack of health care and other infrastructure and services has significantly delayed an effective response. HIV is not solely a public health concern: its effects cut across every sector of human life, from the household to the national level. The economic, political, sociocultural, and medical challenges demand an integrated, multisectoral response to address this wide-ranging devastation. The sociocultural context of African communities is another important consideration underpinning initiatives that address HIV/AIDS through faith-based approaches.

Africa's faith organizations are well placed to have a significant effect on HIV/AIDS because they reach so many households—and because of their value and importance in African culture, and their mandate to serve actively those in need. However, until recently, many faith communities delayed or minimized their involvement in this scourge, or avoided it altogether. Because HIV/AIDS entails issues of sexuality and morality, many faith-based institutions were silent about the presence of the virus among their congregants. Other institutions spoke out in ways that tended to exacerbate stigmatization and propagated inaccurate perceptions of what the disease entailed.

Discussions of HIV/AIDS within faith-based institutions are still taking shape, as the impact on followers continues to grow in size and complexity. However, previous stances of silence and judgment are evolving toward a far greater acceptance of the reality of HIV/AIDS, and into provision of social services to people who are vulnerable to the compounded effects of

HIV/AIDS and poverty. At first only rare institutions were willing to combat the virus with the kind of multifaceted and nonprejudicial interventions that are critical to saving lives. But the mandate of communities of faith is clear: as advocates of service, impartiality, and love, they stand among the few institutions that can provide truly holistic HIV/AIDS care at the grassroots level.

THE COPTIC ORTHODOX MISSION

The Coptic Mission in Africa is committed to mitigating the impact of HIV/AIDS by providing comprehensive, high-quality services and advocating for greater involvement by the faith community. Supported by various donors, the mission works closely with health ministries, and also helps train other faith-based service providers. The Coptic story is thus one that provides a window into a multi-layered response to HIV/AIDS.

The Mission started work in 1976. An arm of the Orthodox Christian Church, with origins in Alexandria, Egypt, and headquarters in Nairobi, Kenya, the Mission is active in seven African countries: Burundi, the Democratic Republic of Congo, Kenya, Nigeria, Tanzania, Uganda, and Zambia. Under the leadership of H.G. Bishop Paul Yowakim, the mission integrates its Christian witness—which it sees as critical to restoring the human condition—into development work. The mission realizes this vision through programs and services that foster spiritual development, build capacity, alleviate poverty, provide medical relief, and promote child welfare.

The Mission's work in Kenya sparked an early awareness of HIV/AIDS. In the mid-1990s, the Mission saw a sudden increase in illness and death within both urban and rural congregations, rising demand for social services to help meet funeral costs, and a growing number of orphans and widows seeking assistance. At a time when it was taboo even to mention the word AIDS, Coptic recognized the severity of the situation as it lost members of its congregations and clergy.

Denial might have been an easier option, especially given that some of the Church's own leaders had died. However, Coptic began to speak openly about the virus and to educate its leaders and congregations about HIV/AIDS, in an effort to break the silence that was killing its people.

The Mission arguably performs its most influential work on HIV/AIDS through its medical mission and the work of the Coptic Hospital in Nairobi. The hospital was established in 1994, reflecting the Mission's commitment to address perhaps the most prominent need of the people of Kenya: their inability to gain access to or afford qualified medical care. It was out of this hospital that Coptic's response to HIV took its integrated form.

Right from the start, the hospital faced pressures from an overwhelming number of HIV-related illnesses among both inpatients and outpatients. By the late 1990s, some 85 percent of all inpatient cases had been hospitalized for HIV-related illnesses. At that time, HIV-positive individuals had few treatment options, because of the limited availability and exorbitant cost of antiretroviral therapy (ART). For most, the only alternative was end-of-life care. The hospital administration and staff, composed mainly of medical missionaries, also recognized a considerable gap in medical knowledge about HIV/AIDS in the region, which was resulting in improper and inadequate care.

Compelled by the needs bombarding the hospital, Coptic began a dramatic course of action designed to change the face of HIV-related medical care in Kenya. In 2002, they pioneered the sale of generic ART drugs nationally by launching a low-cost program in the hospital's pharmacy. Filling more than 3,000 prescriptions each month, the hospital gave thousands of HIV-positive Kenyans a tangible opportunity to live a longer and better-quality life.

The drug program highlighted the inadequate medical knowledge about HIV/AIDS in the region. Coptic therefore started the Hope Clinic, a subsidized facility catering to the medical, psychological, laboratory, and pharmacological needs of HIV-positive individuals. Launched in February 2004, the Hope Clinic operated out of three offices with four staff members, who tended to an average of five patients per day. However, as demand for services rose, and a lack of financial resources created barriers to ART for many (even at subsidized rates), the hospital began to explore options that would allow it to offer a free and comprehensive model of care.

In October 2005, the Coptic Hospital launched the Hope Center for Infectious Diseases, an expanded version of the Hope Clinic. Supported primarily through PEPFAR, the Hope Center offers integrated care that includes voluntary counseling and testing, clinical HIV/AIDS management, ART and treatment for opportunistic infections, laboratory investigations, general counseling, adherence counseling for ART, peer-support counseling, nutritional counseling and supplements, social work services, prenatal care and delivery, prevention of mother-to-child transmission, screening for cervical cancer, and tuberculosis and pediatric care. Using protocols established with infectious disease specialists from the University of Washington, the center offers a counseling-intensive program that determines both people's eligibility for care and their psychological readiness to adhere to long-term treatment.

After just one year, the Hope Center opened within two additional Coptic medical facilities in underserved areas in Kenya, supported by PEPFAR, and at the Coptic Hospital in Lusaka, Zambia, supported by the Global Fund. Across the four sites, Coptic relies on an interdisciplinary team of nearly 100 doctors, nurses, counselors, nutritionists, pharmacists, social workers, peer counselors, and information management personnel to deliver care to more than 8,000 patients—nearly 4,500 of whom are on ART. The high levels of adherence to treatment (93 percent) attest to the program's success. About 120 individuals start life-extending ART each month—75 percent new to treatment, who would not otherwise have access to care. Coptic has thus quickly established itself as a leader in HIV/AIDS services.

Besides clinical treatment, the mission works to foster HIV/AIDS awareness, break down stigma, and cultivate community involvement through a multinational AIDS Community Training (ACT) program in remote areas, supported by Bread for the World–Germany. Launched in January 2006, ACT in its first year conducted hundreds of specialized trainings, seminars, and campaigns. Diverse audiences ranged from multinational corporations to community-based groups to slum dwellers, and the seminars covered topics such as voluntary counseling and testing, HIV/AIDS virology, transmission and prevention, adherence to treatment, positive living, support for people living with HIV/AIDS, and home-based care.

In 2007 this program evolved into a "treatment literacy program" in three countries where the Coptic Mission is active: Kenya, Tanzania, and Zambia. This program has shifted its focus towards a targeted objective of encouraging more people to be tested for HIV and raising awareness of the availability and benefits of ART. The outreach program has been sensitive in delivering messages tailored to the most pressing issues facing communities, which have included the need for treatment for other STIs and TB as well as awareness that HIV transmission can be connected to rape and domestic violence. Through its various training initiatives, Coptic has helped build the capacity of other providers—particularly faith-based organizations—to offer integrated services with skill and sensitivity to people living with HIV/AIDS.

Coptic's innovative work, and the intentional growth and diversification of its HIV/AIDS programs, has garnered recognition. In 2007, the European Union, through the Finnish government, honored the Coptic Mission as the most competent church serving African communities. The hospital in Nairobi received the 2006 Afya Award as the most compassionate and qualified medical institution in Kenya.

Coptic's work has been effective and consistent because it is driven more by internal attributes rather than by external pressures. These include:

- An intuitive understanding of the contextual realities of HIV/AIDS for local communities, including knowledge and service gaps that need to be addressed immediately.
- A sense of urgency that propels action and fosters an organizational culture that responds to needs as they surface.
- Awareness of the Mission's strengths and limitations, coupled with a willingness to collaborate with diverse partners to build capacity and make programs more effective. Coptic is determined not to operate as a stand-alone entity.
- An understanding of the need for interfaith dialogue to break down stigma, discrimination, and ignorance, as a foundation for involving religious organizations in HIV/AIDS work.
- Commitment to sharing its expertise with other practitioners and organizations, especially those that are faith-based, to raise standards for HIV/AIDS services and make them more widely available.

Coptic Mission's dedication to offering services never depends on people's religious affiliation, or their adherence to the Church's values. Rather, the mission takes great care to preserve its spiritual identity and actively express undiscriminating love by serving the most neglected and marginalized.

CHAPTER 13

Alliances for Development

Case Studies from the United States

A n extraordinarily broad array of faith-inspired institutions contributes to development. These institutions range from those that are directly involved in communities on virtually every problem imaginable, to others that primarily advocate for specific policy issues, from foreign aid to trade, hunger, environment, and beyond (box 13.1). That this work is significant and potentially powerful is increasingly recognized, though the broad landscape and specific impact are quite poorly understood, especially within the development community. While many of these institutions are transnational, with some organizations truly defying national borders, the vast majority are rooted in communities and nations.

Religious leaders and institutions in the United States have long played varied roles in international relations and the fight against global poverty. Many such efforts began with disaster relief and then increasingly focused on development. This work builds on long-standing efforts by U.S. faith groups of all kinds to promote social change. Indeed, the United States

---

This chapter is based on the authors' participation in the events described, and their engagement with leaders of both Church World Service and Saddleback Church.

BOX 13.1
BREAD FOR THE WORLD: A CHRISTIAN CITIZENS' MOVEMENT TO END HUNGER

Faith organizations can play a central role in inspiring and leading action on issues of wide public concern. Many term this the prophetic role of faith. In the contemporary United States, few can rival the voice and energy of Bread for the World, a citizens' group inspired by its Christian faith to lead the cause to end hunger.

Bread for the World was born of a small group of Catholics and Protestants, meeting under the leadership of Rev. Arthur Simon in the early 1970s, to reflect on how to mobilize people of faith to affect U.S. policies related to domestic and world hunger. In the spring of 1974, the group decided to test its ideas, and by the end of that year 500 people had joined the movement.

Today, with nearly 58,000 members, Bread for the World is a nationwide movement and advocacy group seeking justice for the world's hungry. The group's network, led since 1991 by Rev. David Beckmann (a former World Bank staff member), includes 3,000 churches and mobilizes a quarter of a million constituent letters to Congress each year. The related Bread for the World Institute is a research and education center with the same goals.

The Bread for the World Website sets out the challenge: "Hunger is one problem we can actually solve. But churches and charities can't do it all—we must get our government to do its part."[a] The organization lobbies the U.S. government to pass legislation to improve the lives of poor people both at home and abroad; its policy agenda focuses on hunger, health, education, welfare, and development. The work is nonpartisan and inclusive. It is centered on the idea that hunger is very much a solvable problem—albeit a daunting and challenging one.

The statistics on hunger are stark. According to Bread for the World, "More than 850 million people in the world go hungry. In developing countries, 6 million children die each year, mostly from hunger-related causes. In the United States, 12.4 million children live in households where people have to skip meals or eat less to make ends meet. That means one in ten households in the U.S. are living with hunger or are at risk of hunger."[b]

Bread for the World aims to bring people—especially Christians of all kinds—together around anti-hunger and poverty issues. According to David Beckmann, "Within U.S. Christianity, overcoming poverty is the highest-priority policy issue in all families of faith. This is far more than a wish."[c] Bread for the World spearheads campaigns to move its policy agenda forward. For instance, the group was a leading force in the Jubilee 2000 movement, which helped promote a debt-forgiveness agenda at the turn of the millennium.

Bread for the World is about organizing concerned citizens to do the work of the world, and to help alleviate poverty through their own actions. The organization's Website is full of links to other antipoverty organizations, and features myriad opportunities for citizens to become engaged in campaigns, including letter writing; attending interfaith advocacy meetings in their homes, churches, and larger communities; and working on issues ranging from the local and grassroots to the greatest global arenas.

a. See http://www.bread.org/.

b. See http://www.bread.org/learn/hunger-basics/.

c. David Beckmann, April 4, 2007, "Practitioners and Faith-Based Organizations and Global Development Work: A Discussion with David Beckmann, president, Bread for the World," interview by Katherine Marshall for "Faith-Inspired Organizations and Global Development Policy: U.S. and International Perspectives," symposium organized by Georgetown University's Berkley Center for Religion, Peace, and World Affairs. See http://berkleycenter.georgetown.edu/28169.htm.

was founded on ideals of religious freedom, and leaders like Martin Luther King, Jr., have moved people across faith traditions to challenge accepted and entrenched inequality and poverty.

The antipoverty and social service work of U.S. faith institutions has received special focus in recent years with the creation of the White House Office of Faith-Based and Community Initiatives and PEPFAR, which has emphasized faith-based interventions.[1] However, the landscape of faith-based work in the United States extends well beyond any particular administration or initiative.

The terrain of U.S. faith-based development initiatives is wide and varied, with groups of almost every tradition and denomination playing some role. There are activities at all levels, from women's groups and youth groups within congregations, to NGOs, to interfaith movements. Efforts include advocacy and mission work, tithing and sending money abroad, lobbying political candidates and elected officials, protests, media campaigns, petitions, and sustained grassroots work. Some faith-based groups barely scrape by financially, while others have all the funding they could possibly manage and more. The quality of this work varies, as does its motivation and style.

An important feature of this landscape is growing interest in Africa throughout the United States, and grassroots concern and mobilization is an important development. The UN's International Year of Development, the ONE Campaign, which aims to end AIDS and extreme poverty worldwide, and related media attention all have brought Africa into the lives of many Americans, who may not have traveled to the continent but now have many more opportunities to hear and read about it.

African-American faith leaders are increasingly active in directing attention to Africa. Leaders like Bishop Charles Blake in Los Angeles, with his Save Africa's Children organization; T.D. Jakes, the prominent Texas-based evangelical pastor who leads large missionary groups to Africa; Rev. Jeremiah Wright of Trinity United Church of Christ in Chicago, with its explicit focus on the African identity of black Americans; and Rev. Eugene Rivers of Boston, who is outspoken on HIV/AIDS in Africa, are active and passionate advocates for Africa.[2] African-American diaspora groups are helping to make real and close the countries of Africa from which their ancestors originated.

In what some have termed a "conversion," U.S. evangelical Christian groups are also becoming more active in development work. The emergence of evangelical interest in international development has resulted in some unlikely partnerships, with individuals and groups across the political spectrum joining together to tackle conflicts in Sudan and northern Uganda as well as sex trafficking and HIV/AIDS. This work is especially noteworthy given the political roles played by faith groups in the United States, and the fact that they are engaging, rather than simply challenging, secular development agencies (box 13.2).

This chapter explores two important examples of faith-inspired partnerships in the United States that link moral advocacy in combating poverty and HIV/AIDS with a specific commitment to Africa.

BOX 13.2
HEARTLAND TOUR WITH BONO AND THE GATEWAY AMBASSADORS

A remarkable phenomenon in the United States today is the joining together of traditional adversaries in an alliance to combat global poverty. Many of the architects and builders of this new and at times fragile alliance are famous and prosperous. Many are well-known religious leaders. Yao Ewoenam Odamtten, a junior associate at the World Bank, was privileged to contribute to a major milestone in building the alliance when he joined Bono, of the rock band U2, and the Gateway Ambassadors, a remarkable children's singing group from Ghana, for a tour across seven Midwestern states in December 2002. Their goal was to raise awareness of HIV/AIDS, and to marshal the compassionate energies of U.S. citizens behind an effort to increase development assistance for the AIDS emergency in Africa.

The Heartland Tour began on December 1—World AIDS Day— and over 10 days visited the heartland states of Nebraska, Iowa, Illinois, Indiana, Ohio, Kentucky, and Tennessee. A caravan of buses, with accompanying media, met local activists, health practitioners, and students at church halls, university campuses, truck stops, and coffee shops. The caravan started in Lincoln, Nebraska, and included stops

(Box continues on the following page.)

(box continued)

in Omaha, Iowa City, Des Moines, Davenport, Dubuque, Chicago, Wheaton, Indianapolis, Cincinnati, Louisville, and Nashville, with formal and informal stops in smaller communities along the way.

When asked "why the Midwest?" Bono remarked, "We're done grandstanding in London, New York, and Los Angeles. The heartland is the moral compass of America. A certain decency resides here. And what's on the Heart of America soon turns up on the mind of [all of] America."

The tour was organized through DATA, an NGO founded by Bono that aims to raise awareness about the crises swamping Africa: the AIDS crisis, the debt crisis, the trade crisis, and the development assistance crisis. DATA stands for Debt AIDS and Trade in Africa. Because development is a two-way street, Bono is quick to note that DATA also stands for democracy, accountability, and transparency in Africa (this explains DATA's thought-provoking Website address, http://www.datadata.org). DATA works to bring politicians, celebrities, and civic activists together as campaigners, to strengthen U.S. leadership in helping Africans build a better future. DATA's co-founders include U2, the Bill and Melinda Gates Foundation, the Soros Foundations Network, and the Center for Global Development.

Principal tour participants included Bobby Shriver, the tour's executive producer and nephew of former U.S. President John F. Kennedy; actress Ashley Judd; Omaha billionaire Warren Buffet; cycling champion Lance Armstrong; Agnes Nyamayarwo, a Ugandan AIDS activist and volunteer with The AIDS Support Organization; the Gateway Ambassadors; actor/comedian/activist Chris Tucker; Dario Franchitti, Ashley Judd's husband and famed Scottish racecar driver; and country singers Wynonna Judd (Ashley's sister) and Johnny Cash. Other key participants included Dr. Eric Goosby, CEO of Pangaea Global AIDS Foundation; and Dr. Jim Yong Kim and Dr. Joia Stapleton Mukherjee, both of Harvard Medical School and Partners in Health.

The tour featured seven themes: the crucial importance of the HIV/AIDS challenge for Africa, and the imperative for the U.S. to respond more effectively; corruption as an impediment to development in Africa, and what can be done about it; reflection on the prospects for a much more aggressive push to provide HIV-positive Africans with antiretroviral drugs; the need to address stigma and discrimination; the need to involve children and youth in finding solutions; the need for broader partnerships, particularly involving the religious community; and the threat the disease poses to peace, security, and global stability. One religious leader noted that, as Uganda and Thailand have shown, the faith community will be critical in winning the fight against AIDS.

Ashley Judd commented during the tour that "poverty ferments revolution." Noting that the war against terrorism is intertwined with the war against poverty, Bono remarked: "No war is more destructive than the AIDS pandemic." In some parts of Africa, "it's World AIDS Day every day," he said. Deploring the international community's laggard response, he maintained that, "the AIDS emergency is at a level that if we don't get a grip on it, we will be forced to question our civilization and what we're doing."

Note: This box is drawn from a report by Yao Odamtten. Although he was a junior associate in the World Bank's Development Dialogue on Values and Ethics when he participated in the tour, his mission there was to support the children's singing group Gateway Ambassadors.

THE INTERFAITH SUMMIT ON AFRICA

In July 2006, Church World Service, an ecumenical group long active in the cause of international development, working with the All Africa Conference of Churches, convened an Interfaith Summit on Africa: A Dialogue of Religious Leaders from Africa and the United States.[3] It was designed to bring together religious and lay leaders from Christian, Jewish, Hindu, Muslim, Bahá'í, and other faith traditions to come to grips with the challenges before the African continent. The organizers saw it as a chance to exchange lessons learned, explore new ways of influencing and making policy, and "pray together for the intervention of the divine" on critical development issues facing Africa.

The summit drew more than 45 high-level faith leaders from Africa, and they were joined by a range of U.S. faith leaders, representatives from advocacy organizations, think tank analysts, academicians, and congressional policy makers. The conference organizers saw it as their goal to "affect US Government policy and encourage the US Administration to make good on promises made." Topics discussed ranged widely, including small arms trafficking, malaria and HIV/AIDS, durable solutions for the continent's thousands of displaced people, sustainable economic development, interfaith alliances, and the impact of faith voices in policy making.

The summit was structured so that African religious leaders and policy makers from Washington-based institutions and agencies had many opportunities to exchange ideas. Venues included a congressional reception, meetings on Capitol Hill, and many facilitated dialogues and one-on-one discussions. Participants included Agnes Abuom, All Africa Council of Churches; Diana Aubourg, Save Africa's Children; Sheikh Abu Bakarr-Conteh, first vice president, Inter-Religious Council of Sierra Leone; Victor Barnes, director, HIV/AIDS Initiative, Corporate Council on Africa; Rev. David Beckmann, president, Bread for the World; Bishop Charles E. Blake, senior pastor, Western Los Angeles Church of God in Christ; Fr. William Headley, counselor to the president, Catholic Relief Services; Most Reverend Josiah Idowu-Fearon, chair, Programme for Christian-Muslim Relations in Africa, North of Nigeria; Archbishop Winston Njongonkulu Ndungane, archbishop of Cape Town; Curtis Ramsey-Lucas, national coordinator for public and social advocacy, American Baptist Churches, USA; and Rabbi David Saperstein, head of the Religious Action Center of Reform Judaism, and a trustee of the WFDD.

The summit kindled considerable excitement, as it was a rare opportunity for church and development leaders to discuss, together, the challenge of improving assistance to Africa. Ironically, some noted, the meeting actually helped church leaders across Africa in making common cause, as their chances to surmount geographical and language divides are all too rare. The hunger for productive dialogue within Africa itself was clear, and the All Africa Conference of Churches, along with others, called on Church

World Service to support more such exchange. Rev. John L. McCullough, executive director of Church World Service, promised to help do so.

Many and very different U.S.-based organizations played active roles during the summit, bringing clear enthusiasm for Africa and substantial experience across a wide range of issues to the table. The participation of Church World Service, American Baptist Churches, American Jewish World Service, the Evangelical Lutheran Church in America, Bread for the World, Catholic Relief Services, and NETWORK (a lobby of Catholic individuals and organizations) illustrates the range of engagement.

Events like this highlight the challenge of working collaboratively across countries, faith traditions, and perspectives on Africa. Each development topic sparks myriad viewpoints, and each organization prioritizes those challenges differently. At the summit, several sessions challenged participants to outline their major concerns in a given arena, such as HIV/AIDS; everyone then ranked the listed concerns, and the tabulations were very different. As one might suspect, achieving consensus within a diverse group is not a straightforward proposition. Still, much hope emerged that dialogue and interaction in and of itself could bring better understanding and action.

THE 2006 GLOBAL SUMMIT ON AIDS AND THE CHURCH: A RACE AGAINST TIME

Saddleback Church and its dynamic pastor, Rick Warren, are the focus of much attention today. Two major reasons are his remarkable best-selling books, especially *The Purpose-Driven Life*,[4] and, perhaps even more significant in terms of global impact, the fact that his church distributes material for sermons to hundreds of thousands of pastors worldwide every week. Rick Warren has become a leading U.S. voice in the struggle against poverty across the world, and he and his colleagues are deeply involved in many countries, prominent among them Rwanda. It was in part the crisis of HIV/AIDS that inspired Rick Warren to focus on global poverty, and it has become a centerpiece of his work.

Rick Warren is justly classified among America's opinion leaders: he is regularly invited to the White House prayer breakfast and the World

Economic Forum, and many political leaders describe him as their friend. President Kagame has invited him to model his P.E.A.C.E. plan[5] on poverty and HIV/AIDS in Rwanda (see below), and Warren's relationship with Rwanda is growing deeper and wider across a range of issues.[6] Bono has called Rick Warren a "rock star."

Pastor Rick, as he is often called, and his wife Kay Warren, founded Saddleback Church in 1980. The evangelical megachurch has 22,000 regular weekend parishioners, and its reach is far wider. At least 200,000 pastors have been trained worldwide in Saddleback's purpose-driven philosophy, a program that aims to help churches to develop a "balanced growing congregation that seeks to fulfill the God-given purposes of worship, fellowship, discipleship, ministry, and missions."

Only four years ago, Kay Warren came to believe that as a pastor's wife and a pastor's daughter, she had missed a central theme in the Bible: that God was calling Christians to focus on the poor and the sick. She convinced her husband that it was their mission to work on those issues, and today the couple is impassioned and informed on global poverty, and calls powerfully on Christians to feed the hungry, provide treatment to people with AIDS, and eliminate stigma associated with HIV/AIDS.

The Global Summit on AIDS and the Church: Race Against Time, in November 2006 in Lake Forest, California, was the second such summit hosted by Saddleback. More than 2,000 people attended and they included church leaders and people living with HIV/AIDS, government leaders and academics, high-profile and local pastors, and representatives of faith-based development organizations.[7] The event was a call to Christians to learn about HIV/AIDS and determine what roles they can play in working with government, business, and the medical community to respond to the pandemic. Such efforts are part of Rick Warren's larger P.E.A.C.E. Plan, which aims to tackle what he calls the world's five biggest problems—the "global giants": spiritual emptiness, egocentric leadership, extreme poverty, the AIDS pandemic, and illiteracy.

The Global Summit on AIDS and the Church was first and foremost for pastors of local congregations worldwide who wanted practical plans to provide care, treatment, and prevention for HIV/AIDS in their own communities. However, representatives from many secular institutions also came to the summit to learn more about Saddleback's work. The event drew vast media coverage, especially a plenary session featuring U.S. senators (and presidential candidates) Sam Brownback and Barack Obama, who, along with Rick Warren, were tested for HIV on the spot.

The summit's core idea was that Christians represent the single largest network in the world—with 2.3 billion people, it was said—and that the HIV/AIDS pandemic cannot be eradicated without mobilizing and equipping churches. Rick and Kay Warren want nothing less than to "change the Church" (meaning all Christians, in this context), so they seek to inspire and mobilize Christians to respond to HIV/AIDS through congregation-based care, treatment, and prevention. A working assumption seems to be that churches are not prepared on their own to face this pandemic in all its complexity, and that to respond more effectively they need to be engaged and encouraged, and to be given information.

The summit therefore focused on (1) detailing the history and complexities of the HIV/AIDS pandemic, with presentations by government, intergovernmental, and academic leaders; (2) convincing attendees (for example by citing relevant Biblical passages) that it was their Christian duty to become involved; and (3) equipping attendees with a local church-based strategy that enables "ordinary people" to respond.

The summit included technical lectures on various aspects of HIV/AIDS, and 17 workshops a day for two days (participants could only attend two). The event also featured Christian sermons, rock music and ballads, powerful images and videos, and prayers throughout. The summit set out to share basic, scientifically sound information about HIV/AIDS, sketch out an international response, and stir people's emotions and faith, thus moving them to action.

An image repeated again and again at the conference left a striking and lasting impression. A map of part of Rwanda was projected high above the largest church space (which holds 3,000 people) on the Saddleback campus. It first showed the three hospitals in the region, two of them administered by religious groups. The region's 18 clinics—16 of them administered by faith groups—were then superimposed on the map. Finally, the hundreds of local churches were added, at which point it was nearly impossible to see any map details because the church dots obliterated them. The message was that no other network can rival the motivation, reach, human resources, and sheer institutional presence of churches, so they must be mobilized and equipped to respond to HIV/AIDS in their communities.

The conference had a central message: professionals will never be able to end HIV/AIDS and solve other intractable problems on their own. According to Rick Warren, "The greatest need in the 21st century is to release the pent-up, latent power of the average believer in local churches around the world. There aren't enough doctors to solve all the issues in the world; there aren't enough teachers to solve all the issues in the world; and there aren't enough missionaries to solve all the issues in the world. But there are millions of believers sitting in churches waiting to be mobilized."[8]

Rick and Kay Warren have ambitious plans to build on their work around global poverty and HIV/AIDS with seemingly vast human and financial resources. A New Yorker article relays a story that one Sunday Rick Warren asked his congregants to "extend the vision" beyond their normal financial offering: that Sunday yielded US$7 million in cash and US$53 million in commitments.[9]

It is difficult to assess the impact that the Warrens and Saddleback will have on HIV/AIDS and poverty, but it could well be significant. They do not run any institutions—schools, hospitals, or shelters—and have limited experience in the developing world. However, Rick Warren has long trained pastors from many different countries and a vast network of churches looks to him for leadership and guidance. He told of meeting a pastor in rural South Africa who walked hours every week to download Rick Warren's sermons from the Internet. The pastor said that the sermon Website provided the only training he ever had in being a pastor. Experiences like this inspire Rick Warren to believe that he and his wife have a special mission to spread awareness and mobilize Christians around HIV/AIDS, because they can reach pastors and places that no one else can.

Their underlying goal, though, involves bringing God to people whose lives they touch. Their development work is thus hard to disentangle from their evangelizing—and that for many is a sensitive area. Many wonder how they will reconcile faith-based language and style with more secular approaches. Both those who evangelize and those who fear evangelism have some trepidation about working together, and about what might be blurred or lost in pursuit of common ground.

The passionate desire to fight poverty and bring development should echo across points of real difference, and permit room for partnerships. Indeed, the Saddleback bridge and other improbable alliances are allowing many unusual partnerships to take shape today. Evangelical churches and leaders—rarely evident in global interfaith gatherings just a few years ago—are increasingly taking part in them, and joining with those perhaps much more "liberal" on issues from global warming to Sudan, sex trafficking, HIV/AIDS in Africa, and poverty. The new trend is surely an opening for more learning, dialogue, and collaboration.

NOTES

1. For information on the White House Office of Faith-Based and Community Initiatives, see: http://www.whitehouse.gov/government/fbci/. For information on PEPFAR, see http://www.pepfar.gov/.

2. For information on Save Africa's Children, see http://www.westa.org/. For information on T.D. Jakes, see http://www.tdjakes.org/.

3. Church World Service has information on the Interfaith Summit on AIDS at http://www.churchworldservice.org/news/africasummit/index.htm.

4. Rick Warren, 2002, *The Purpose-Driven Life* (Grand Rapids, MI: Zondervan).

5. P.E.A.C.E. stands for: Plant Churches, Equip Leaders, Assist the Poor, Care for the Sick, Educate the Next Generation.

6. See, for example, *Time*, August 15, 2005, "Warren of Rwanda," at http://www.time.com/time/magazine/article/0,9171,1093746,00.html.

7. For the official Website of the 2006 summit on AIDS and the Church Website, see http://www.purposedriven.com/en-US/HIVAIDSCommunity/GlobalConference/2006Conference/Churches_challenged_to_take_lead.htm.

8. This quote is from conference materials.

9. Malcolm Gladwell, September 12, 2005, "The Cellular Church," *New Yorker*, at http://www.gladwell.com/2005/2005_09_12_a_warren.html.

14

Learning from the Extreme Poor

Participatory Approaches to Fostering Child Health in Madagascar

D efinitions of poverty in developing countries used by most devel- opment organizations focus on household income that falls below a given threshold, such as one dollar per capita per day, and on other quantified indicators. While such definitions have the merit of pro- viding a standard by which to measure progress, the very poor use quite different terms and ideas to communicate what extreme poverty means to them.

Extreme poverty results not only from insufficient financial resources but from a lack of basic security in many different areas, including education, employment, housing, and health care, as well as social exclusion. Left to the side in civic, social, and cultural life, and in political

---

This chapter was drafted by Caroline Blanchard, Xavier Godinot, Chantal Laureau, and Quentin Wodon and much is drawn from a book edited by Xavier Godinot and Quentin Wodon in 2006: *Participatory Approaches to Attacking Extreme Poverty: Case Studies Led by the International Movement ATD Fourth World*, World Bank Working Paper No. 77, (Washington, DC: World Bank). The book is available at http://siteresources.worldbank.org/INTRAD/Resources/ParticipatoryApproach- esAttackingPoverty.pdf. The chapter also reflects the engagement in International Movement ATD Fourth World of this book's authors.

decision making, very poor people are often considered ignorant and even incapable of thinking, because they have had no opportunity to gain skill in expression through education. The experience of contempt and exclusion—severely attacking self-confidence—is deep among the poorest, whether they live in rich or poor countries. Very few people listen to them.

"We impose outside interpretations on them that prevent them from reflecting on their own lives," suggests Joseph Wresinski, who founded the International Movement ATD Fourth World,[1] which focuses on the very poor. ATD Fourth World has been persistent over the last 50 years in its effort to engage political leaders the world over, as well as international development institutions (including the World Bank), in the fight against extreme poverty. ATD Fourth World is determined that these institutions should truly recognize the needs of people who are living in situations of desperate poverty, but even more that they should listen directly to their voices. ATD would also like to see its spirit of respect for the poor spread more widely, so that top-down, hasty, and untested approaches and development projects do not further disrupt the fragile and tenuous lives of poor communities. Theirs is a call for an approach that builds on the consent and measured reflection of the people poverty programs purport to target.

ATD FOURTH WORLD'S APPROACH TO LEARNING FROM PEOPLE MIRED IN EXTREME POVERTY

Joseph Wresinski, a Catholic priest, founded ATD Fourth World in France in 1957. A grassroots advocacy organization, ATD Fourth World inspired the UN's annual World Day to Overcome Extreme Poverty (which falls on October 17). The organization runs projects that engage deeply and directly with the very poor in 28 developed and developing countries.

Wresinski and ATD Fourth World's leaders have advocated for investing in the knowledge of the very poor ever since the organization was founded. In a 1980 speech at UNICEF headquarters in Geneva, Wresinski articulated his vision, which still drives ATD Fourth World today. He started by affirming that everyone involved in development projects—including those living in extreme poverty, activists, and researchers—is a thinking human being with goals. He contended that programs will be effective only if they respect the integrity of all three parties: thorough understanding must always precede specific concepts and methods. This fundamental lesson in epistemology, methodology, and ethics has wide applicability for efforts to fight poverty.

Wresinski himself experienced living in extreme poverty, enduring it as a child born in France to migrant parents. He later lived as a priest with the inhabitants of a shantytown close to Paris for 10 years, until all of them were offered new housing. Together with these inhabitants, he founded the International Movement ATD Fourth World, which over time took root in many countries across the world. Together with a Dutch diplomat, he also founded an Office of Social Research, which later became the research and training institute for his movement. This passionate and principled man, trained in the harsh school of destitution and exclusion, became a respected spokesman of the poorest at national and international levels.

HEALTH AND LIVING CONDITIONS IN ANTANANARIVO, MADAGASCAR

A case study helps elucidate ATD Fourth World's approach.[2] The setting is a neighborhood with some 6,000 inhabitants in Antananarivo, Madagascar—precarious and densely populated, with shabby dwellings, a few drinking fountains, no toilets, and flooding during the rainy season that renders hygiene almost nonexistent. Parents have unstable jobs in the informal economy, but nevertheless try to provide their children with an education, using a surprising amount of inventiveness and energy.

In 1991 ATD Fourth World, together with neighborhood parents, launched a two-part program to promote health care (which ended up lasting 10 years) and knowledge sharing (which is ongoing). At first, relations between the inhabitants and health care providers reflected fear and lack of understanding, with inhabitants resorting to ancestral knowledge of traditional medicine, and health care staff reacting mostly in keeping with the norms of Western medicine. However, several years of work that strengthened parents' capabilities allowed new paths to open based on greater understanding and mutual respect.

The case study starts in 1991. At that time, the health situation in the neighborhood, known as Antohomadinika, was worrisome. Infant mortality was very high and life expectancy short. From its first few months in Antananarivo (Madagascar's capital city), the ATD Fourth World team was keenly aware of the fragile health of young children. Over the years, by immersing themselves in the neighborhood, they discovered the chasm separating Antohomadinika's inhabitants from the medical services that were supposed to help.

Malagasy doctors are trained according to Western methods: they search for signs that support a diagnosis of disease in an organ. This approach, which prevails worldwide, rarely considers a patient's background, relationships, or environment, and creates a certain disdain toward traditional healing. The inhabitants of Antohomadinika, on the other hand, have traditional beliefs that give meaning to each event and gesture. These contrasting views of illness, together with a mutual lack of understanding, explained the fear that inhabitants felt when facing the modern medical world, and the sometimes humiliating reactions to their patients of competent doctors.

Although parents were attentive toward their children, this was not immediately apparent to the medical staff. For example, mothers traditionally were afraid that their newborns would suffer if their stomachs were exposed to cold air, and therefore preferred not to undress the baby. This obviously contradicts rules of hygiene that stress the importance of bathing newborns. Such cultural barriers stifled dialogue. People trained in the traditional Malagasy approach simply did not grasp the logic and knowledge that lay behind the technical explanations given by medical staff trained according to Western methods.

In a society where it is essential to be in a group rather than alone during a birth, illness, or death, inhabitants regarded hospitals as cold, fearful places often associated with death and humiliation, and they used them only as a last resort. Doctors did not understand why parents did not follow their advice and why they still preferred to treat their children with the traditional remedies and methods that were meaningful to them. Fed up with being constantly thwarted by people whose illnesses could have been cured if they had sought help earlier, the medical staff became aggressive and judgmental toward parents they considered irresponsible. The staff concluded that parents did not love their children because they did not administer prescribed treatments, or because they waited until a child was in agony before bringing him or her to the hospital. The total lack of mutual understanding was illustrated by the attitude of one mother who refused to come to the Mother and Child Protection Clinic and traveled instead for miles to take her poorly nourished child to a healer.

Traditional Malagasy medicine has enormous potential in many situations; it alleviates certain illnesses very well. For example, *tambavy*— plant infusions—can be highly effective, but also very dangerous if they are used incorrectly. Matrons, who live in the same neighborhood and often in the same conditions as very poor people, hold a privileged position in administering this medicine. They are the close and preferred contact who accompanies a woman before birth. They recommend prenatal visits held in their own homes. They give massages that are often effective: when necessary, they can change a baby's position inside the womb. They also play an important role during the birth and in the first few months of a baby's life.

In the neighborhood, the sick willingly use traditional remedies, which they know and understand, and which respect their beliefs. In fact, most Malagasys use tambavy; only those who suffer from negative side effects are hospitalized. Because doctors see only these people, and therefore only the downside of these remedies, they advise people not to use them at all. Those who are hospitalized do not dare say that they have used tambavy. Mutual distrust is hence built on a combination of misunderstandings and ignorance.

For Antohomadinika inhabitants, hospitals are places where they are stigmatized and seen as poor and different. They often have no time to change or wash their clothes before coming, especially in an emergency, and are quickly labeled and criticized by the medical staff because of their appearance. Hospital fees and incidental costs, which can be substantial, present an additional barrier for those who have little to no money. Patients must also bring their own sheet or blanket. What should they do when there is only one blanket for the whole family? Because of unfamiliarity, lack of understanding, and humiliation, inhabitants were very fearful of the hospital. Yet there were openings for change. Even though most medical personnel in Madagascar work in very difficult conditions and are poorly paid, many are open-minded and some even used their own resources or special initiatives to set aside medicine for poor families.

To address this situation, ATD Fourth World started a knowledge-and-health program in cooperation with the Missionaries of Charity Brothers. Dr. Chantal Laureau, a member of ATD Fourth World's team, complemented medical visits to the Brothers' facility with nutritional follow-ups, starting in January 1991. Mothers who arrived for a checkup were invited, when necessary, to a second, longer checkup, to organize a nutritional follow-up to talk about the food they were feeding their children. The ATD Fourth World team suggested to mothers whose children had symptoms of malnutrition that they learn how to make a simple and cheap dish that provides all the needed nutrients, and a monthly "dish demonstration" complemented the nutritional followup.

Children who came to a checkup received home visits—especially very poorly nourished children, who are fragile and fall sick easily. The mothers talked about how much these visits meant to them: "Nobody had ever come to our home except for you." These visits fostered trust and created a certain dynamic: inhabitants awaited ATD Fourth World team members and cleaned their homes to welcome them. During these visits, team members often suggested development activities for very young children. The visits then became a time for the family to enjoy itself around books. The young children were the center of attention, and the other family members played an active part.

The program developed by trial and error through discussions with the mothers and efforts to meet their aspirations in various ways. For a long time the ATD Fourth World team members did not understand why the children were so poorly nourished. When trust started to blossom, the parents expressed themselves more fully and shed light on this question. For example, they were convinced of the fundamental importance of rice, a staple food in Malagasy cooking. Their proverbs state that children are well if they eat rice. Conversely, if they do not eat rice, even if they eat enough overall, parents worry. Such information became apparent only with time. To take advantage of volunteers' growing understanding of such views, ATD Fourth World posted volunteers to other locations. For example, Chantal Laureau accompanied a doctor visiting a pediatrics clinic, another permanent volunteer worked in a nursery school, and a third worked in a home for children run by Madagascar's justice ministry.

In 1992 ATD Fourth World began to hold informal meetings in Antohomadinika to give neighborhood women the chance to ask questions about their health and that of their children, and to allow volunteers to present fundamental facts on malnutrition. These meetings made clear the volunteers' growing appreciation of parents' contributions to their children's development. Indeed, parents proved highly inventive considering the lack of means at their disposal. For example, one mother recounted how she cut out pictures from magazines and covered the walls of her home with them to teach her daughter the names of objects.

These meetings also encouraged women to talk to each other—to exchange experiences and advice, thereby strengthening their solidarity. The team had noticed a certain distrust within the neighborhood, heightened by a fear of poisoning, which people spoke about a great deal. At first the neighborhood meetings occurred once a month, hesitantly, with light attendance, and always in the same place. By the end of 1993, meetings with the mothers were held weekly in different places, complemented by activities for their children. Relations in the neighborhood improved as a result. One mother said, "We are happy: we have hope for our children's future. If we are sick, there is someone to cure us." Another positive sign was the continued presence of the mothers at the nutritional checkups arranged for their children.

In 1995, the ATD Fourth World team began to incorporate health into all its cultural activities. This stepped-up work included larger meetings in two small courtyards. Volunteers would start these meetings by inviting all participants to wash their hands, giving them a chance to exchange news and perhaps invite the volunteers to visit sick people at their homes. A coordinator would then tell a story. After the story, volunteers presented simple educational and development games to the mothers, and invited them to play with their last-born child for the rest of the session. This made the mothers their children's first teacher, and they were more at ease in asking questions when they saw themselves in this role. The informal discussions also allowed the women to learn gradually more about their bodies, the nutritional value of food, and family planning. A street library and a health program, as well as home visits, complemented these moments of leisure between mothers and their young children.

The ATD Fourth World team noticed the overwhelming appeal of books among the children and their parents. One day in October 1997, some mothers asked the coordinators of the street library if they could borrow books to read to their children at home. Nine parents soon started to borrow books, and four years later some 340 youngsters and adults had registered for this service, and the coordination team could no longer meet the demand. In 2003, 10 adults from the neighborhood hired for this task built a library on donated land.

To complement the activities in the small courtyards, the ATD Fourth World team organized a systematic followup of children born in 1995 and early 1996. Mothers began to create a development book for their children, recording key moments at the start of life as well as their progress. Some mothers also recorded their hopes for each child: "I would like you to learn to read and write, and to talk about how we should talk." Others explained their view of education: "The aim of parents is to see their children succeed in life." "We encourage you so that you learn manners and know how to write." "When he does something naughty, we give him a good telling off." In 1997, 26 women completed a development book for a child.

These books helped deepen discussions between team members and the mothers on cultural practices. In the life of the least-favored families, health is often secondary to family unity. For example, a mother cannot be hospitalized without risking the death of a breastfeeding child, who could not be cared for if the two were separated harshly. The ATD Fourth World team observed, "parents often prefer keeping the family together to healing a child. In any case, the child may not be cured, and if he is it won't last if the family goes through particularly hard times." "Health is the balance between a person, his environment, and the community in which he lives. Illness upsets this balance." Health also depends on community solidarity: adults can be hospitalized only if neighbors agree to look after their children, and to offer financial support. Improving hygiene in a neighborhood therefore requires a change in attitude on everyone's part.

Lack of understanding between medical staff and neighborhood parents as well as fear had prompted parents to put off a hospital visit as long as possible. As trust became firmly established and parents grew accustomed to speaking about health and cultural practices, the ATD Fourth World team invited mothers to visit health care centers around Antohomadinika, to meet the staff and learn about the care they offered. The mothers thus discovered facilities they had not known existed, like the Isotry dispensary, Tsaralalana children's hospital, and the Marie Stopes international dispensary.

ATD Fourth World also invited health professionals, mostly from Befelatanana Hospital, to meet with neighborhood mothers to learn about their living conditions. These professionals came to realize how expensive a hospital stay can be for poor people, beyond formal fees, as people need to spend time traveling to the facility and the time they spend there is time they when they cannot work. Precarious living conditions also present a barrier for specific treatments. During these meetings, the mothers dared to talk unashamedly about resorting to traditional methods—something they would never have done inside a hospital—while the professionals saw women who appeared frightened and ashamed in a hospital in a different light.

Few books have been written in Malagasy, and practically none on early childhood. The idea therefore arose to produce a book that would help answer the questions parents ask most often. The book could also illustrate the inventiveness of parents who confront multiple challenges in educating their children, and help smooth discussions with health care professionals. The book was published in May 2000 under the title *Sarobidy Ny Silaky Ny Aina*, which means *Our Children Are a Treasure*. At first seen as a simple collection of parents' insights, the book eventually came to include information from the child development books that mothers had prepared. Health care professionals helped correct information they considered wrong, and highlighted ideas they considered important to the development and health of young Malagasys. This work helped create a common language between the two very different worlds.

Inhabitants are very proud of the book, and it has served as a starting point for conversations between the neighborhood and institutions. "This book aims to be an invitation for health care professionals to dare meet very poor families.... The book says that such a meeting is possible and that everyone comes out on top if we heed the concerns of others: if both professionals and parents look for a better future for their children together, parents could learn from the professionals and the professionals, having learned why the parents are afraid, could cure their children better." Funding provided by the World Bank through Madagascar's Health Ministry financed the printing of 200 copies of the book in 2002. By showing how much parents love their children, think about their education, and expend energy on their behalf, the book helped change the reputation of a neighborhood that was all too often regarded in negative terms.

LESSONS FOR OTHER PROGRAMS

A seminar on extreme poverty at the World Bank on October 19, 2005, highlighted lessons from the Madagascar experience as well as other case studies. A key conclusion was that development projects should not only take people mired in extreme poverty into account but make them the highest priority, because they are least able to improve their daily lives without the help of others. However, numerous obstacles prevent them from participating in projects and services designed for their benefit. Daily survival requires all their energy and attention, and, perhaps even more significant, they often find it too shameful, painful, and terrifying to take advantage of services—especially those that address only their deprivations rather than their aspirations. Indeed, the projects that are the most successful in reaching the poorest tend to tap the aspirations they carry deep inside but often have difficulty expressing.

Many activities designed to reduce poverty fail to reach the most disadvantaged people, who are often so excluded that they seem beyond reach. This exclusion also means that outsiders have difficulty understanding their situation and efforts to emerge from poverty. To acquire in-depth knowledge of their aspirations and build projects with them, outsiders need tools, commitment, and proximity. At the same time, people in situations of chronic poverty need to be able to appreciate the intentions of those who want to help them.

The Madagascar case and other case studies have implications for grassroots organizations, governments, and international financial organizations working to eradicate extreme poverty:

Working with people trapped in extreme poverty requires a long-term process, not a one-shot intervention. Reaching them requires a significant human investment, not only by outsiders but also by themselves. Institutions must make it clear from the beginning that partnering with them does not mean entering into a short-term agreement. Community mobilization often begins with finding the local groups that may exist out of sight and focal places such as community centers and schools. From then on the building process can continue.

Programs that attack extreme poverty should build a new social contract that allows those who endure financial deprivation (and other excluded people) to take an active role in revamping the institutions that redistribute assets and control decision making. Programs and projects will not work if people trapped in chronic poverty do not participate. Just as outsiders require training, so do they, so they can build their own expertise and share it with others. This requires building their capacity to transform their existing knowledge into a powerful creative force that will break down their dependence and allow them to construct new social relations among themselves and with others.

This approach requires a new relationship between people trapped in extreme poverty and external agents, including government officials and civil society volunteers. This new relationship should derive from a process where each agent strives to share their own knowledge and to learn from others. These agents must generate knowledge that will help individuals, communities, and institutions transform the reality in which they live. Yet these agents occupy very unequal positions in society. Making discussion and sharing possible among them thus depends on creating balanced conditions where everybody's voice is listened to.[3] This implies humility from the better-off, courage from the worst-off, and a constant monitoring by the mediators who bring them together. At the project level, agents need to develop indicators of transformation of those social relationships that hinder the capacity of the most disadvantaged to move out of poverty. One approach is to require projects to meet preestablished benchmarks before moving to the next level of investment.

Overall, people mired in extreme poverty must not only be reached but also met as equals in dignity, deserving the respect and the human rights they are lacking and longing for. Ensuring them this respect and these rights is an undertaking that can transform both the excluders and the excluded, empowering the latter. Projects aiming to fight extreme poverty might be evaluated based on a very simple question: Has this project allowed those who endure it to advance toward greater freedom, pride and responsibility rather than remaining in a cycle of deprivation and dependence?

NOTES

1. ATD Fourth World Movement's Website is http://www.atd-fourthworld.org/en.html; it describes their history, current programs, and philosophy.

2. Chantal Laureau, Caroline Blanchard, and Xavier Godinot, 2006, "Making Health Services Work for Poor People: Ten Years of Work in Tananarive, Madagascar," chapter 4 in *Participatory Approaches to Attacking Extreme Poverty: Case Studies Led by the International Movement ATD Fourth World*, World Bank Working Paper No. 77, (Washington, DC: World Bank).

3. These conditions are described in International Movement ATD Fourth World, November 2006, *Guidelines for the Crossroads of Knowledge and Practices and How to Apply Them to People Living in Situations of Poverty and Social Exclusion* (Paris: Research and Training Institute, International Movement ATD Fourth World).

PART III

Extending
the Reach

Global Dialogue,
Partnerships, and
Movements

Introduction

The work of faith communities crosses many boundaries. Faith can be an intimate and personal aspect of an individual's life, but faith has also long been a banner, rallying cry, and the principle inspiration for many social movements. Today faith communities are supported by the Internet, which has made rapid communication possible across land and sea, country and continent. The possibilities for connection, collaboration, and information sharing have never been greater. Thus faith communities are increasingly joining with others of the same faith and in interfaith settings, and with secular partners, to address myriad concerns.

The globalization facilitated by Internet technology and less expensive and faster transport has brought home the idea that we live on one shared planet: the challenges of global migration and trafficking, global warming, global money-laundering, and terrorist networks have all underscored connections across time and place. Many hopeful signs abound, with people across the world joining together in movements: movements for peace, movements against genocide in Darfur, movements for debt relief and better prospects for poor countries, movements to protect and save the environment—all aiming for deeper cultural understanding and transcontinental collaboration to address seemingly intractable challenges. There is a coming together today that is unprecedented.

This section brings together stories of dialogue and joint response that cross traditional boundaries of difference in the interest of making a better and more just world. Chapter 15 examines a monumental challenge facing the world: some 12 million orphans on the African continent, many deprived of their parents by HIV/AIDS. The work of responding to the needs of these orphans is being taken up by grandmothers and other family members, and also by faith communities joining together locally and globally both to support orphans directly and to call attention to a virtually unimaginable situation in which so many children are growing up without parents. Where will these children go, what will they become, and how will they engage the world?

Chapter 16 tells of an unprecedented process of dialogue among the World Bank, the International Monetary Fund, and the World Council of Churches—an ecumenical Christian organization that encompasses some 340 churches, denominations, and church fellowships representing as many as 550 million people in more than 100 countries. All three global institutions have much to learn from each other, and while the dialogue process proved challenging, it bore much fruit in terms of better relationships among the institutions and recognition of common ground, as well as of important and continuing differences.

One key arena where faith work is gathering momentum is the world of finance. Chapter 17 introduces this engagement and explores the efforts by faith communities to provide investment opportunities and financial services that are socially and environmentally conscientious, and also to hold companies to higher standards.

Chapter 18 looks at the Fès Forum, which for six years promoted a dialogue integrated deeply into the vision and experience of a sacred music festival celebrating the diverse religious cultures of the world. This dialogue brought together representatives from governments, environmental movements, and businesses, women's cooperatives and global media, advocacy groups and international organizations, to debate the thorny challenges inherent in globalization.

Chapter 19 examines the roles that faith leaders and communities are playing in tackling corruption and identifies the challenges ahead. The premise is that faith communities should be and can be more involved in global alliances that are working to end this debilitating scourge.

Chapter 20 provides an overview of important work by the World Faiths Development Dialogue to review a cross-section of faith-inspired institutions and programs, large and small, that work to empower and engage citizens to build sustainable societies based on spiritual values.

Finally, four boxes explore, with short vignettes, very different examples of innovative, boundary-crossing work by faith communities.

Box 17.1 illustrates the expanding excitement of faith institutions about the potential of microcredit, focusing on a small specific organization, Five Talents, which brings microfinance services and entrepreneurial skills to poor communities, at the same time seeking to build on their rich wisdom and potential. Box 20.1 shows how the Pastoral Social of the Diocese of San Marcos, in the mountains of western Guatemala, is wrestling with integrating ancient cultures and beliefs with the challenges that come with fast-paced modernization. Box 20.2 describes a promising international community initiative to address the problems of Senegal's street children, while Box 20.3 also treats street children, but in a very different part of the world; a leading Jewish charity is working in a Muslim country to develop effective programs that can respond to the urgent needs of children living on the streets.

CHAPTER **15**

Responding to the
Orphan Crisis in Africa

Adevastating consequence of the HIV/AIDS pandemic, felt most
acutely in Africa, is the growing number of orphans left behind
when parents die in the prime of their lives. The figures are staggering.
Africa is home to at least 12 million orphans today, with rapid increases
projected into the foreseeable future. A far larger group of children are
affected by HIV-related illness among their parents, siblings, and community. As many as 2 million African children are themselves HIV positive or suffer from AIDS.

This tragic situation is eroding recent gains in child survival in the
African countries hardest hit by the HIV/AIDS pandemic, and stymies
every facet of efforts to advance social and economic development
through education and health. Children affected by HIV/AIDS represent a
humanitarian, development, and human rights crisis of unprecedented
proportions. Every organization engaged in fighting the pandemic needs
new strategies to combat both its scale and duration.

Given the pervasive presence of religious bodies of virtually all faiths
throughout Africa, and their social justice missions, it should come as no
surprise that they are at the forefront of efforts to respond to the needs of

---

This chapter is largely based on the WCRP/UNICEF report of May 2004, *Documentation Study of the Response of Faith-based Organizations to Orphans and Vulnerable Children*, but also draws on other research on orphans in Africa. Geoffrey Foster was the report's principle author; James Cairns of WCRP oversaw the report,
and provided valuable comments on this chapter.

177

vulnerable children, especially orphans. Faith-based organizations (FBOs) are developing rich experience across virtually all dimensions of the HIV/AIDS pandemic, but place special emphasis on children. However, their activities are generally small in scale and difficult to measure. This helps explain why the cumulative impact of faith-led activities is often underestimated compared with the more visible responses of development agencies. Two important results are generally poor coordination, networking, and sharing of experience; and relatively low levels of financial and technical support from the major international and also national HIV/AIDS programs.

To help address significant information gaps regarding these efforts, WCRP, together with UNICEF, in 2002–03 surveyed the activities of religious groups working to meet the needs of orphans and vulnerable children in six countries in eastern and southern Africa. Of the 85.2 million total population in these countries—Kenya, Malawi, Mozambique, Namibia, Swaziland, and Uganda—orphans number some 5.8 million, with nearly half resulting from HIV/AIDS. The report projected an increase in this figure to 6.9 million by 2010; numbers are likely to grow until at least 2020 before leveling off.

The carefully designed survey engaged some 690 Christian, Muslim, Bahá'í, Hindu, traditional, and Jewish FBOs, including 410 congregations and 167 religious coordinating bodies, as well as faith-based community organizations and faith-based NGOs. Personal interviews or focus groups involved more than 500 children and 200 key informants.

The report portrays an extraordinary range of efforts to support children and families. For example, an estimated 9,000 volunteers in the surveyed groups provide spiritual, material, educational, and psychosocial support to more than 156,000 children, mostly through community-based initiatives. Many activities involve material support—food, basic health care, and help with schooling—for orphans and vulnerable children.

Faith-inspired programs for children present challenges also. Among them are their generally ad hoc nature, the absence both of strategic approaches and coordination habits and systems to link them with other efforts. They can do great good but barely scratch the surface of the need. Yet the potential is enormous. And the role of regional, national, and global organizations with broader mandates—both faith-specific and interfaith—is growing. Faith groups—widely present in communities and able to mobilize volunteers and resources—should be central partners in efforts to support children affected by the HIV/AIDS pandemic. The key question is how to do so most effectively. The report's findings help answer that critical question.

THE IMPACT OF HIV/AIDS ON AFRICAN CHILDREN AND COMMUNITIES

African tradition maintains that there is no such thing as an orphan. Children who lose their parents are normally incorporated into a relative's family, commonly treated as that relative's own children. The sharing of children's care among members of the clan is evident in high rates of child fostering: the proportion of children 5 to 14 years old fostered by relatives was 35 percent in Namibia, 24 percent in Uganda, 19 percent in Malawi, and 14 percent in Kenya.[1]

Communities go to great lengths to keep orphans in school, for example borrowing money through informal networks and even selling their own assets. But the HIV/AIDS pandemic has led to such rapid increases in orphan number that it has strained families and communities to the limit.

Because of its sheer scale, Africa's HIV/AIDS epidemic has repercussions that are qualitatively different from other regions. Teachers, health workers, and civil servants as well as parents are dying of AIDS. Orphan numbers grow at the same time that caregivers become fewer and fewer. Families are weakened. The result is increasing numbers of children living on the streets, in child-headed households, or engaged in harmful child labor (though the latter is fairly limited considering the pressures).

The children suffer from malnutrition, migration, homelessness, and poor access to education and health care. Psychological effects include depression, guilt, and fear, and potentially long-term mental health problems. The HIV/AIDS epidemic also increases children's vulnerability to many other consequences, including HIV infection, illiteracy, poverty, and economic and sexual exploitation. Girls who are orphaned face particularly acute challenges and demands.

HIV/AIDS has a devastating impact on caregivers, with women bearing the brunt of those burdens. Women's low legal, social, and political status leaves them more vulnerable to HIV infection. More than 50 percent of the 28.5 million people already infected with HIV in sub-Saharan Africa are female. As the key providers of food, clothing, and household support, women's early deaths from AIDS have profound social and economic consequences. A woman's health and life situation—including the time and energy she can devote to her children, conditions in the home, her material resources, skills, and knowledge—are critical to the health and life chances of her children.

Families and local communities demonstrate remarkable resilience and creativity as they try to address these myriad challenges. Substantial evidence suggests that the traditional African social system of fostering could continue to meet most children's basic needs—but only with support, both financial and social. Communities do need help if they are to respond. Proven interventions need to be expanded through all levels of society to address the multiple dimensions of needed care. And long-term commitments are necessary, for it is the duration as well as the scale of the pandemic that presents its unique challenge.

WHAT DRAWS RELIGIOUS ORGANIZATIONS TO OFFER PROGRAMS FOR CHILDREN?

Deeply rooted and deeply held traditions of care for orphans are embedded in virtually all religious traditions and explain both why faith organizations are so deeply engaged and special dimensions of their approach.

The Bible, Qur'an, and Veda instruct believers to protect and care for orphans. Giving alms to the needy, including orphans and widows, is an ancient feature of both Christian and Muslim congregations; it is enshrined as one of the five pillars of Islam. Judeo-Christian traditions refer frequently to care of widows and orphans:

> *Religion that God our Father accepts as pure and faultless is this: to visit and look after orphans and widows in their distress.*   (James 1:27)

> *God defends the cause of the fatherless and the widow, and loves the alien, giving him food and clothing.*   (Deuteronomy 10: 17–18)

The Qur'an similarly includes a body of teaching about orphans:

> *Give orphans the property that belongs to them. Do not exchange their valuables for worthless things or cheat them of their possessions, for this would be a grievous sin…. Those who unjustly eat up the property of orphans eat up a fire into their own bodies; they will soon be enduring a blazing fire!* (Sura 4:1, 10)

> *They ask you, Muhammad, what they should spend in charity. Say: whatever wealth you spend, that is good, for the parents and children and orphans and those in want and for wayfarers. And whatever you do, that is good—Allah knows it well.* (Sura 2:215)[2]

The Hindu scriptures teach that believers should be nonjudgmental and demonstrate a selfless spirit toward the disadvantaged:

> *He is liberal who gives to anyone who asks for alms, to the homeless, distressed man who seeks food…. He is no friend who does not give to a friend, to a comrade who comes imploring for food; let him leave such a man—his is not a home—and rather seek a stranger who brings him comfort…. For wealth revolves like the wheels of a chariot, coming now to one, now to another.* (Rig Veda 10.117.1–6)

> *O Lord of the home, best furnisher of resources for orphans and vulnerable children are you. Grant us the strength from you for a healthy domestic life.* (Hindu prayer)

Traditional African religious beliefs and practices buttress the extended family and community safety nets. They specifically reinforce the notion of providing care and support to orphans and neighbors, as illustrated by a proverb from the Shona of Zimbabwe and Mozambique:

> *What has befallen me today will befall you tomorrow.*

A saying, which resembles the African proverb "it takes the village to raise a child," reminds community members that everyone is responsible for raising children, not just the birth parents:

> *The child of the mother is the one in the womb but once born everybody plays with it.*

HOW HAVE FAITH ORGANIZATIONS RESPONDED?

Much evidence, including surveys, testimony of activists, and observation, attests to the proliferation of faith-based activities that respond to the HIV/AIDS orphan crisis. A 2001 study, for example, analyzed the establishment, development, and capacity needs of church initiatives to respond to orphans in Zimbabwe.[3] It reported that pastors initiated these programs after seeing orphans going hungry, kept from school, and lacking clothes and spiritual guidance. Services to these and other vulnerable children focused on providing food, clothing, and school fees, and relied on volunteers affiliated with local churches for regular visits, to help establish income-generating projects, and to provide psychosocial support. While the creators of most such initiatives wished to expand, they faced severe organizational capacity and financial resource constraints.

Six founding partners established the Hope for African Children Initiative in 2000, to scale up the response to the orphan crisis. The WCRP was one of these six partners (with Plan International, Save the Children Fund, Care International, World Vision International, and the Society for Women and AIDS in Africa), reflecting its focus on the actual and potential role of faith organizations in combating the crisis.[4] The Hope for African Children Initiative provides important support for programs focused on children in several African countries.

The WCRP/UNICEF study highlighted the extraordinary diversity of religions in the six countries it examined. Christianity claims the largest number of adherents, accounting for some 75 percent of the population in these countries. About 10 percent of the people are Muslim, with a similar percentage following traditional African religions. Followers of the Bahá'í, Hindu, Sikh, and Jain religions are also significant minorities (see figure 15.1).

The six countries report more than 150,000 Christian congregations. Densities range from one congregation per 880 adherents in Uganda to one congregation per 140 adherents in Swaziland, which has many small independent African congregations.

Five types of religious organizations address the needs of children affected by HIV/AIDS. *Congregations* are local groups of believers who meet on a regular (usually weekly) basis. They include local Christian churches, Islamic mosques, Hindu temples, Jewish synagogues, and Bahá'í

Figure 15.1 Faith Adherents in Six African Countries (Kenya, Malawi, Mozambique, Namibia, Swaziland, and Uganda)

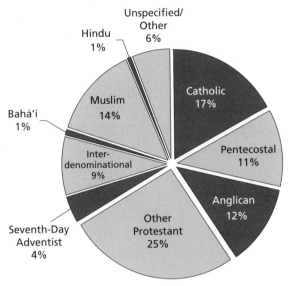

Source: WCRP/UNICEF survey, 2002–2003.

assemblies. Many initiatives serving orphans and vulnerable children (OVCs) receive material or financial support from a congregation, and are supervised by one or more religious leaders. These initiatives may be jointly administered by several congregations from the same area, and draw participants from other congregations and the community. Some congregations employ staff to operate orphanages and shelters.

Most congregations belong to a coordinating or governing organization. The WCRP/UNICEF report coined the term *religious coordinating bodies*, or RCBs, to describe this broad category. Within it, larger faith communities provide indirect supervision and support to congregations through lower-level bodies. For example, the Muslim Supreme Council in Kenya supervises 72 district councils. These bodies are known by various names, depending on the faith community and whether they are national, subnational, district, or subdistrict. RCBs function mainly through the religious and pastoral ministries of participating congregations.

Some RCBs appoint coordinators to oversee their own OVC projects or administer those run by their daughter congregations. Interfaith RCBs are growing in importance in serving children. They include national religious councils like the National Council of Churches of Kenya (NCCK), with 26 denominational members; and the Inter-Religious Council of Uganda, which coordinates bodies representing different faiths, including Catholic, Protestant, Muslim, and Bahá'í.

Nongovernmental organizations usually are registered welfare groups, depend on external donor support, have constitutions and bylaws, and employ staff. Most are guided by established policies, plans, and monitoring systems, including audited accounts. International NGOs work in multiple countries and are governed or advised by international boards; local NGOs are overseen by local boards.

Some established NGOs have added HIV/AIDS or OVC programs to existing activities, while other have responded with new initiatives. Two approaches predominate. Many local—also called implementing—NGOs deliver services directly, often relying on volunteers supervised by staff. Other NGOs work with or through community-based organizations that deliver services. NGOs that facilitate service delivery by others are also known as intermediaries.[5] NGO initiatives include church or mission hospitals and clinics, religious schools, orphanages, shelter and outreach initiatives, including to street children, vocational skills training and business development centers, scholarship-granting organizations, and community mobilization.

Community-based organizations (CBOs) differ from NGOs in their greater reliance on volunteers rather than employed staff. CBOs may provide direct services or cooperate with NGOs. Volunteers sometimes receive allowances or stipends, and CBOs occasionally grow into NGOs with paid staff, project proposals, and external donor funding.[6] Faith-based CBOs differ from congregations in their governance structures: most CBOs function under an appointed board, while congregations are accountable to congregation leaders or an RCB.

CBOs have characteristics in common with NGOs. They are governed by members according to a constitution, and may be registered welfare organizations. Many raise donations in cash or in kind from outside the community; a limited number receive substantial funding from outside the country. Most CBOs have an office and a bank account and produce annual accounts, although they tend not to be externally audited.

Missionary organizations and religious orders mobilize and support religious missionaries. They may be based within or outside Africa.

Most of these groups receive little or no external technical or financial support for their OVC initiatives, relying heavily on volunteers. The 231 FBOs surveyed reported a total of 9,236 volunteers, averaging one for every 10 children they served. The average number of volunteers per initiative was highest for RCBs (107 per initiative) and NGOs (101), and lowest for congregations (21) and CBOs (30). Most volunteers are women between the ages of 30 and 50 who are members of a congregation, while a majority of volunteers involved in HIV/AIDS prevention activities are youth. The RCBs reach the largest number of children, followed by congregations (see figure 15.2).

Volunteers are motivated by goodwill, compassion, the plight of vulnerable children, a desire to help the needy, and a calling to serve God. Other incentives include certificates of appreciation, attendance at workshops, and exchange visits with other OVC initiatives. A few volunteers receive material support, transport, and meal allowances from a community or congregation.

Figure 15.2 Number of Vulnerable Children Supported by Different Types of FBOs

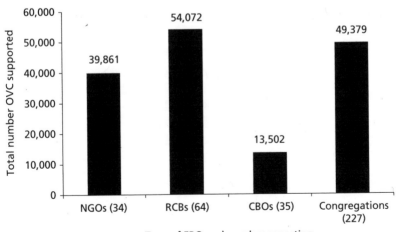

Source: WCRP/UNICEF survey, 2002–2003.

Volunteers face many challenges, including creating time for OVC activities, overwork because the numbers of needy children are so large, and inadequate training. Indeed, lack of training is the norm. Some volunteers gain knowledge by attending workshops, seminars, talks, and exchange visits. RCBs and NGOs facilitate training in some congregations on program management, child development, home-based care, counseling, and the impacts of HIV/AIDS.

WHAT DO FAITH-BASED CHILDREN'S PROGRAMS DO?

Faith-based organizations provide a broad range of services to support vulnerable children, with many offering more than one type of service (see figure 15.3):

Material support: Clothing and food, sometimes in the form of prepared meals, often constitute the backbone of community response to orphans and vulnerable children. Such support is more prevalent in poorer countries like Malawi, and most often provided by congregations.

Figure 15.3 Main Activities of FBOs to Address the Needs of Orphans and Vulnerable Children

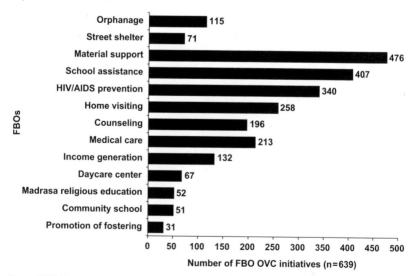

Source: WCRP/UNICEF survey, 2002–2003.

School assistance: Many FBOs pay fees so that children can attend primary and sometimes secondary, vocational, and tertiary school. Some FBOs also provide uniforms, equipment, books, and boarding fees.

HIV prevention: About half the organizations surveyed are involved in raising awareness of HIV among vulnerable children, and providing moral guidance. Few FBOs, however, focus on sexual and reproductive health skills, for example by providing information on condoms and promoting HIV testing as a preventive measure. And few provide treatment for sexually transmitted infections.

Visiting and home-based care: Volunteers often visit the most vulnerable households in their communities, including child-headed families, several days a month or even daily, acting as surrogate parents. They provide advice and household supervision, prepare meals, eat with the children, help maintain dwellings, and assist with household agriculture and income-generating activities. Some such programs have evolved from home-care programs for the terminally ill.

Counseling and recreational activities: Many FBO initiatives provide counseling and other support to address children's psychosocial needs, as well as recreational opportunities. Examples of the latter include sports and cultural activities such as choirs and plays, which can bring vulnerable children and other members of the community together.

Medical care: Some faith-based initiatives provide medical fees or medicines to vulnerable children.

Income generation and vocational training: Some community-level FBOs raise money to support vulnerable children while also giving them experience in managing projects and training in specific vocational skills. Projects include nutrition gardens, husbandry projects, manufacturing cooperatives, and buying-and-selling initiatives.

Daycare centers: These provide care and food for preschool children during the day, often while caregivers are working.

Community schools and child development centers: Some faith-based groups have set up facilities to provide primary education to vulnerable children who would otherwise be out of school.

Other areas: Some FBOs promote foster care, train staff and volunteers, provide financial support to other organizations, foster community development, build houses, and provide transportation for volunteers.

Most organizations provide more than one service. Congregations are more likely than other FBOs to provide material support, home visits, and daycare centers, and less likely to promote fostering, offer HIV/AIDS prevention, medical care, income generation/vocational training, community schools, and religious education. Regional and NGO programs tend to provide school fees more often than do CBOs and congregations, possibly because such sponsorships require sizable sums of money (see table 15.1).

Longstanding Christian and Muslim traditions have spurred adherents to establish residential institutions for vulnerable children (orphanages). However, many congregations are moving from institutionalizing children to supporting them while they live with guardians. This approach is seen as less costly and more sustainable, and children can remain with their siblings and other relatives, grow up within their communities, retain their identity, and safeguard their inheritance. Institutionalization, in contrast, assists individual children but not families, creating dependency.

Some institutions have established residential units catering to small groups of children and ensure frequent visits among children and relatives on weekends and holidays; others have removed the uniforms worn by staff. The WCRP/UNICEF report proposed a set of principles to help assess whether the larger facilities that remain are "child friendly" (see table 15.2).

Most faith-based programs offer care and support to vulnerable children irrespective of their faith. Some care for young children under five years of age, including HIV-positive babies and children, and run rehabilitation centers for street children. Some daycare centers double as feeding and education centers.

Table 15.1 Sample of Large-Scale Faith-Based Initiatives Serving Orphaned and Vulnerable Children

Country	Name of FBO	Brief description of OVC activities	No. of OVC (date est.)
RCB			
Namibia	Catholic AIDS Action (CAA)	Coordinates 105 groups with 1,516 active volunteers reaching, some 3,000 homes directly. CAA also offers training to other churches and organizations.	14,500 (1998)
Malawi	Livingstonia Synod AIDS Control Programme. (Presbyterian)	Established committees & volunteers, including people of different denominations working with traditional, political, and religious leaders, to support OVC in five districts. Volunteers are trained in orphan care, counseling, and AIDS awareness. Support includes school fees, vocational training, spiritual support, clothes, and groceries.	12,056 (1989)
Kenya	Africa Inland Church	Africa Inland Church runs 18 children's homes around the country, managed from church headquarters in Nairobi. The church is experimenting with enabling children to remain in their communities rather than moving them to group homes. The homes provide children with education, food, shelter, clothing, counseling, medical care, and spiritual support.	2,000 (1993)
NGO			
Uganda	Africa Evangelistic Enterprise (AEE)	AEE oversees 30 projects in 21 districts of Uganda, working through Anglican and some Catholic congregations. AEE works with government officials to identify needy orphans, and committee members drawn from the community vet these beneficiaries, selecting some 200 children in each locality to receive school fees. AEE provides grants to groups for income-generating projects, and supports child-headed households.	5,000 (1971)
Namibia	Tate Kalungu Mweneka Omukithi wo "AIDS" Moshilongo Shetu (TKMOAMS)	Translation: Our Mighty Father Protect Our Nation from the Deadly Disease "AIDS" This organization coordinates home care for 32 community groups supporting 900 volunteers. These groups operate from schools and churches and work with local headmen.	3,000 (1996)
Kenya	Mandera Education Development Society	This NGO supports orphans and vulnerable children within the Mandera district, running an orphanage while also assisting other children. Committees oversee the program, while community volunteers help implement the activities. The children receive food, clothing, education, and shelter.	4,034 (1989)

(Table continues on the following page.)

(table continued)

Country	Name of FBO	Brief description of OVC activities	No. of OVC (date est.)
		Congregation	
Uganda	Kampala Pentecostal Church: Watoto Child Care Ministries	This initiative built 50 family dwellings, each with eight orphans and a housemother, throughout the community. The children receive shelter, food, medical care, education, family life, and training in values. Female church members visit the homes weekly to deliver food, encourage the mothers, and provide attention to the children. Regular visits by men enable the children to relate to a father figure. Men also arrange sporting activities and special outings for the children. The project sponsors the children's primary and secondary education.	1,200 (1992)
Malawi	Naotcha Mosque Area, Blantyre	Some 22 volunteers who serve as committee members provide material support to children, as well as HIV/AIDS prevention and counseling activities.	2,000 (2001)
Kenya	Al-Kahf Islamic Orphanage and Dev. Centre	This NGO provides food, clothing, and madrasa lessons to children in a rural community.	2,000 (2000)
	African Children in Need	This NGO offers community-based care and support to OVC in a rural area. Some 80 volunteers provide education, food, clothes, medical care, counseling, and visits.	2,414 (2001)
	Omongina Self-Help Group	"Mothers" visit children in their homes regularly to discuss problems and pray and eat together. The group runs a pharmacy, income-generating activities, loan schemes, and orphans and widows clubs, and provides advocacy and spiritual care.	1,842 (2000)

Source: WCRP/UNICEF survey, 2002–2003.

Table 15.2 Best Practices for Child-Friendly Institutions Caring for HIV/AIDS Orphans

Child-friendly principle	Goal for institutions	Examples of best practice
Integration of children into families	To integrate children with relatives or long-term foster families	• Children requiring placement should live in orphanages close to their community of origin. • Orphanages should try to trace relatives and maintain contact with extended families. • The standard of living, culture, diet, and clothing of children should be similar to those of the families of origin. • Institutions should try to integrate children with relatives or long-term foster families.
Parenting within small family units	To meet children's need for consistent parenting within stable family units	• Children in institutions should be cared for within small family units. • Caregivers should be married couples living with children on a semi-permanent basis and committed to providing long-term parenting. • Caregivers should not wear uniforms. • Caregivers should not be young unmarried employees working shifts to provide housekeeping chores with additional child-minding responsibilities. • Children and caregivers should live, eat, and share ablution facilities in their own family units. • Family units should be semi-permanent—children should not move from one family unit to another.
Psychosocial and cultural development	To establish activities that increase children's psychosocial development and maintain their cultural identity	• Caregivers should be trained in child development and psychosocial support. • Visits by outsiders should be minimized. • Attempts should be made to connect children to the culture and religion of their community of origin.
Community involvement by institutions	To move beyond the provision of quality care to a small number of vulnerable children by developing community involvement and support programs	• Those setting up institutions should do so in partnership with communities. • Community members should have advisory or decision-making roles in the institutions. • Resident children should have opportunities to interact with nonresident children. • Funding or in-kind contributions should be raised from surrounding communities. • Institutions should minimize discrimination against resident children by those living nearby. • Institutions should provide community-based support to nonresident vulnerable children.

Source: WCRP/UNICEF survey, 2002–2003.

CHALLENGES IN SCALING UP

Questions often arise about the capacity of faith-inspired organizations to implement and manage larger initiatives, which often take them into new fields of activity. However, the WCRP/UNICEF study concluded that the governance and financial accountability of local FBOs that address the needs of orphans and vulnerable children often compared favorably to those of larger NGOs.

Over 80 percent of 192 congregations assessed had strong governance structures. Most have an approved constitution guiding their programs and committees responsible for supervising OVC support activities. Most committees meet regularly, and have six or more members appointed by their congregations and headed by religious leaders. These committees sometimes incorporate people from outside the congregation. In congregations without committees, religious leaders managed OVC activities with the help of a few volunteers. Programs are usually ad hoc, and provide quite modest support to children. Most congregations have bank accounts, effective financial systems, and treasurers who present monthly or quarterly accounts, although some smaller initiatives with limited funds do not feel the need to appoint a treasurer. Still, because their capacity is weaker than that of larger FBOs providing OCV services, less than a third of congregations have outside financing.

In sum, the report cites lack of funds as the major limitation that FBOs face in providing direct assistance in the form of school uniforms and food, and in providing incentives to volunteers and covering their transportation costs (see table 15.3). Some FBOs need funds to cover operating costs such as salaries for personnel and office equipment, and few FBOs have the resources to address the burgeoning numbers of orphans and vulnerable children in their communities.

While they are eager to respond to the needs of vulnerable children, congregations often lack confidence about what are best practices and strategies for doing so. The WCRP/UNICEF report underlined weak communication and partnerships among local FBOs, with most groups unaware of initiatives by other FBOs. Most also lack policies or guidelines for OVC programs and HIV/AIDS interventions, and few rely much on government policies. Stronger links within the religious community could

Table 15.3 Priority Needs of FBOs Serving Orphans and Vulnerable Children (Percent)

Requirements	Congregations (n = 54)	RCBs (n = 16)	CBOs and NGOs (n = 25)
More funds	53	62	44
Training	20	37	20
Other materials (mainly information)	19	24	16
Food	14	12	12
A facility (center/building)	14	12	8
Human resources (more skilled people)	12	37	12
More community support/involvement	10	31	16
Better adherence to religious teachings	8	12	0
Planning skills	8	12	0
Clothes	6	6	4

Source: WCRP/UNICEF survey, 2002–2003.
Note: Information shown here is based on results from Namibia.

allow FBOs to exchange information, share experiences, and learn from one another.

Interviews with HIV/AIDS personnel at the national level echo some of these weaknesses. Respondents see congregations as well placed to spearhead community responses to OVC, but recognize that they need more tools and stronger structures to manage and sustain projects, including better-trained personnel, better program monitoring, and greater accountability.

BUILDING LOCAL CAPACITY

Although too little is known about community initiatives that support orphans and vulnerable children in countries with severe HIV/AIDS epidemics, FBO responses clearly have been proliferating quietly over the last few years. Many religious individuals, officials, and institutions have become deeply involved in caring for children affected by HIV/AIDS out of moral concern and sheer necessity. Congregations and other community-based organizations have assisted thousands of destitute children in the absence of significant support from public authorities or external agencies.

External organizations, especially those lacking local knowledge of communities, have tended to view these efforts as weak and failing. That view is incorrect: FBO responses are innovative and robust. Still, the full potential of FBOs for supporting orphans and vulnerable children affected by the HIV/AIDS epidemic has not been realized.

Communities put much trust in religious organizations. To sustain and expand their efforts to support children, FBOs need additional resources and assistance. "Water, water everywhere, and not a drop to drink" is the cry of many groups desperately looking for small injections of capital to expand their initiatives. The need for new mechanisms to channel outside funds, advice, training, and capacity-building efforts is urgent. The emerging network of religious coordinating bodies can offer an important vehicle for fulfilling such a "wholesale" role.

NOTES

1. M. Ayad, B. Barrere, and J. Otto, 1997, "Demographic and Socioeconomic Characteristics of Households," DHS Comparative Studies No. 26 (Calverton, Maryland: Macro International). Cited in S. Hunter, 2000, *Reshaping Societies: HIV/AIDS and Social Change* (New York: Hudson Run).

2. Other Sura references from the Qur'an: 2: 83, 22; 17.7; 4: 2–3, 36; 59: 7; 89:15–20; 90: 4–17; 107:1–7.

3. G. Foster, J. Webster, and P. Stephenson P, 2002, "Supporting Community Initiatives Is Crucial to Scaling Up Orphan Support Activities in Africa," Abstract MoPeF4099, XIV International Conference on AIDS, Barcelona,

4. See http://www.hopeforafricanchildren.org/.

5. Intermediary organizations have been defined as those with the skills to mediate between grassroots groups and funding organizations. Intermediaries may provide training, build capacity, channel resources, perform advocacy, share information, and facilitate networks between communities.

6. The distinction between NGOs and CBOs is not always clear. For example, some organizations (sometimes termed *emerging NGOs*) straddle the divide by changing from volunteers to paid staff to administer their activities.

16

A Pathfinding Dialogue among the World Council of Churches, the IMF, and the World Bank

T he World Council of Churches (WCC), the International Monetary Fund (IMF), and the World Bank engaged in a pioneering dialogue process over a two-year period, culminating in a meeting of the organizations' leaders in Geneva in October 2004. The dialogue addressed far-ranging topics, including the roles and histories of the three institutions, but above all focused on their common work in fighting poverty. The dialogue was unique, in that it was without precedent between international financial institutions and institutions of faith; intentional, in that it was thoughtfully and deliberately entered into; and challenging, in that it engaged participants in exchanges on mutual interests and common concerns, as well as differences in philosophy, perception, and activities. As of mid-2007, the formal dialogue process had concluded, and possible next steps were under discussion. Overall, the experience offers lessons

Richard Newfarmer (World Bank) and Graham Hacche (IMF) provided valuable comments on this chapter.

about what such a dialogue entails, and the benefits it can offer in fostering greater understanding of real-world challenges as well as key institutions involved in fighting poverty.

ORIGINS OF THE PROCESS

In late 2000, the IMF proposed a meeting—a straightforward discussion in the usual style of such encounters—involving the World Bank, the IMF, and the WCC. This overture came in response to a blistering critique from the WCC in June 2000 of a joint report from the United Nations, the World Bank, and the IMF, entitled *A Better World for All*.[1] The WCC's critique (which caught the World Bank and IMF quite by surprise) decried above all the process that had produced the report, which the WCC described as reflecting the domination of Northern countries, and as undercutting parallel processes of reflection and negotiation already under way. The WCC, self-described as a fellowship, and representing a significant part of the Christian world, has an active and engaged interest in social justice issues.[2] On this occasion, WCC presented its views on behalf of a larger group of faith and secular organizations and movements.

After initial contact and discussion, there was a protracted period of silence between the WCC, the IMF, and the World Bank. During this period, the WCC engaged in intensive reflection with its membership as to whether, in what form, and on what conditions it was prepared to engage with the international financial institutions. A remarkable document resulted from this process, entitled *Lead Us Not into Temptation*, which outlined the WCC's analysis of its far-ranging reservations about the motivations, governance structures, policies, and programs of the Bretton Woods institutions (BWIs).[3] As the title implies, this document also reflected concern about how the WCC could engage in dialogue with the BWIs without compromising its principles. In early 2002, following these internal consultations, Konrad Raiser, then the WCC's general secretary, formally invited the heads of the World Bank and IMF to participate in a high-level meeting in May 2002. His letter made clear that the WCC vision of the meeting went well beyond a routine exchange of views, and was aimed at a comprehensive review of institutional mandates and approach.

This letter, in turn, spurred a process of reflection within the IMF and the World Bank, and some informal discussions with WCC staff. The elapsed time since the IMF's initial approach to the WCC, and the unprecedented nature of the proposal for a dialogue, generated considerable discussion. Staff members within the BWIs raised questions about resources and priorities, and about engaging so intensively with a Christian organization (what should be the response if, for example, a Buddhist federation made a similar proposal?). These concerns were met with a recognition of the large membership of the WCC, and an understanding that such proposals for in-depth discussion (from faith institutions) were rare and could be addressed as they came.

In September 2002 a letter jointly signed by James D. Wolfensohn (then president of the World Bank) and Horst Koehler (then managing director of the IMF) proposed that, *instead* of a single meeting, the institutions should engage in a dialogue process that would allow them to explore differences and common ground. The process was to lead, notionally in late 2003, to a meeting of the leaders of the three institutions:

> We agree that the process should proceed along these lines, with a combination of seminars on fundamental issues of principle complemented by engagements, which will allow our two institutions to benefit from the rich experience of your membership. At the culmination of this process, we look forward to a meeting in which, hopefully, the three of us could participate, where we could benefit from the results of the dialogue and look with vision and hope to the path ahead. We particularly hope that you will contact us, or our teams, about any issues of special concern. These might include specifically sharing with us the experience of your churches in participating in the Poverty Reduction Strategy Paper Process, given its vital importance as a new instrument for addressing the challenge of putting poverty reduction at the center of the international agenda and any ideas that you might offer on how best to advance towards achievement of the Millennium Development Goals (MDGs).[4]

The general secretary of the WCC responded with a statement about what he saw as the issues at stake in such a dialogue:

> We believe that only by addressing the root-causes of the present injustices can the programs and instruments that are set in place be effective. Therefore, our main concern will continue to be focused on critical analysis and the ethical implications of neo-liberal economic policies in the world today so as to discern whether they address current global economic inequity and related violence. We believe that there are alternatives to the current unjust economic system and hope that the upcoming seminars as planned by our teams will provide us with an opportunity to articulate new ways of promoting equitable human development so that all people can live in dignity and in harmony with our earth. We stay committed to this process of preparation which I hope will culminate in a global summit which will include not only the three of us but also participants from our governing bodies and members from the civil society.[5]

The differences in approach reflected in the two letters are telling. The IMF and the World Bank focused on the poverty objectives of their institutions, and the assumed common concern with implementing the MDGs. They saw a practical benefit in learning from the field experience of WCC member congregations. The WCC, in contrast, made it clear that it was concerned with fundamental ethical issues, and the very nature of the financial institutions. Nonetheless, the letters attest to the parties' joint commitment to exploring key issues.

THE DIALOGUE PROCESS

The two-year dialogue process began shortly after the exchange of letters. It involved a series of structured and formal meetings, the first in Geneva (February 2003) and the second in Washington (October 2003). The dialogue also proceeded via a series of planning meetings (in May 2002 and May 2004), and IMF and Bank staff participated in an internal WCC meeting in September 2003. The culmination of the formal process was a leadership meeting, called "a high-level encounter," in Geneva in October 2004.

The dialogue process took place largely at the staff/secretariat level, but had the support of the leaders of all three institutions. Each meeting involved parallel delegations and considerable advance discussion of the agenda and participation. The WCC tended to rely on formal presentations by academics associated with it, while the IMF and World Bank generally relied on operational staff—that is, practitioners of their work with client countries.

The agenda setting was far from easy or straightforward, perhaps not surprisingly, given the rather different objectives of the institutions from the outset. The WCC particularly wanted to discuss the economic ideologies and models that, in its view, guided the policies and approaches of the World Bank and the IMF. The WCC also wished to discuss institutional governance, which it saw as a fundamental flaw of both the IMF and the World Bank. The latter, in contrast, were more concerned about establishing the strong common interest of the three institutions in fighting poverty, and moving from there to practical efforts to discern lessons and address bottlenecks. The BWI teams saw little merit in addressing the governance structures of the institutions, as staff members have virtually no influence on them. Each meeting agenda thus represented an elaborate compromise.

Vocabulary and assumptions were often a central focus of the meetings themselves. To move forward, participants had to refocus frequently on efforts to establish that there was indeed considerable common ground and common purpose. One of the more interesting sessions involved presentations on the parallel histories of the three institutions, as all developed after World War II and were much shaped by the events of the period. However, these parallel narratives also revealed how much the histories of the institutions differed, in substance but above all in how they were narrated.

The dialogue process was also hindered by strongly held and generally negative WCC perceptions that IMF and Bank policies, operations, and governance are firmly set within the neoliberal ideological framework of "the Washington Consensus."[6] The WCC team also seemingly felt it necessary to defend, within its own network, its decision to engage in dialogue with the BWIs. The WCC's documents tellingly characterize its role as a "spirituality of resistance" aimed at reforming the BWIs, or stopping the ethically abominable results of their policies.

The IMF and the World Bank teams, in contrast, sought to establish the pragmatic bent of their institutions, and the complex realities of widely different economic programs in member countries. The BWI participants brought layer upon layer of arguments and examples to persuade the WCC that its portrayal of the neoliberal model poorly reflected the ideas guiding the BWIs. While they were comfortable offering their own critiques of IMF and World Bank programs, BWI participants plainly had fundamental disagreements with the far-ranging WCC images of their institutions.

Discussions about the WCC, its constituent churches, and their role were far more muted, as the IMF and World Bank did not view it as their right or purpose to contest in any form the WCC's governance structure, purpose, or theology (which makes sense, given that—unlike the BWIs— the WCC is not supported by public funds). Still, the BWIs delicately suggested at various stages (and some WCC delegates agreed) that self-reflection and criticism within the churches was necessary and salutary.

On balance, these mutual perceptions shifted only at the margins, although progress in understanding occurred on both sides. The differences between the institutions—their constituencies, systems of accountability, and styles and approaches—also resulted in a somewhat imbalanced discussion at times. Still, the IMF and the World Bank saw benefit in learning about a complex and unique institution and the Christian churches that were behind it, and the exercise yielded insights into how perceptions of the BWIs form in quite different parts of the world.

Information on the dialogue process was widely diffused from start to finish, especially within the WCC family worldwide. The IMF also published articles about the dialogue in the *IMF Surveys*.[7] WCC published virtually all the papers prepared for the dialogue in several volumes. *Wealth Creation and Justice* includes papers from the first encounter in February 2003, while *Passion for Another World* covers the second encounter in September 2003. These compilations reveal the complex underpinnings of the dialogue, and progress, albeit partial and slow, in highlighting clear commonalities in stating economic and social problems, and real differences in understanding causality and appropriate ways to address them. Papers from the October 2003 meeting in Washington were published under the telling title *Common Goals, Different Journeys,* reflecting the shared missions of the WCC, World Bank, and IMF, as well as their contrasting ideas and tools for achieving them.[8]

Two enduring images emerged from the successive discussions. The first was that the institutions were like "ships passing in the night," seeing each other, dipping their lights, but making no meaningful contact. The second was the notion of a "fellowship of the road," an ideal that emerged toward the end of the two-year process. The fellowship drew on the medieval practice for travelers navigating dangerous roads to converge at recognized spots to make the journey together. This practice offered protection and the chance to share difficulties and benefits, but the travelers were free to resume their separate paths when the danger zone had passed. The metaphor suggested agreement that the fight against poverty was a difficult and dangerous road, and the BWIs and the churches would do well to travel it together.

The WCC/World Bank/IMF dialogue helped foster mutual knowledge and better understanding, and areas of common ground. Still, significant divides between the BWIs and the WCC remain. The WCC, in particular, seemed to have more ambivalent goals, with some participants accepting the spirit of learning and others approaching the encounters as an exercise in converting the Bank and the IMF to greater consciousness, and perhaps even repentance for sins. However, throughout, the parties consistently tried to focus the content and tone of the dialogue on encouraging mutual understanding and closer alliance in the global fight against poverty.

THE FINALE: A HIGH-LEVEL ENCOUNTER IN GENEVA

As originally planned (though with some delay), the culmination of the formal dialogue process occurred with a meeting of the leaders of the three institutions at WCC headquarters in Geneva. James D. Wolfensohn, as president of the World Bank, Agustín Carstens, deputy managing director of the IMF, and Rev. Sam Kobia, the then new general secretary of the WCC, took part, with Cornelio Somarruga of the Caux Initiatives for Change, an independent foundation, acting as moderator. Rodrigo de Rato, the IMF's managing director, was present for part of the event, and

Dr. Agnes Abuom participated on behalf of the WCC's Governing Council. Other participants included members of WCC's Governing Council and staff, a range of invited representatives from institutions that WCC considered part of its network, press representatives, and staff from the World Bank and the IMF. (See box 16.1 for the formal statement issued after the meeting.)

BOX 16.1

JOINT STATEMENT BY THE GENERAL SECRETARY OF THE WORLD COUNCIL OF CHURCHES, PRESIDENT OF THE WORLD BANK, AND DEPUTY MANAGING DIRECTOR OF THE INTERNATIONAL MONETARY FUND, GENEVA, OCTOBER 22, 2004

1. This afternoon, Rev. Dr. Samuel Kobia, General Secretary of the World Council of Churches (WCC), Mr. James Wolfensohn, President of The World Bank Group, and Mr. Agustín Carstens, Deputy Managing Director of the International Monetary Fund (IMF), met together at the headquarters of the World Council of Churches in Geneva, Switzerland, to discuss matters of common interest, particularly development and related economic policy issues. Mr. Rodrigo de Rato, Managing Director of the IMF, was unable to participate in the meeting because of an official commitment, but met with Rev. Kobia earlier in the day. These meetings of the heads of the three organizations, in which a number of other representatives of the WCC and staff of the World Bank and IMF participated, followed several preparatory meetings held since May 2002. The series of meetings were initiated by correspondence expressing the wish of the managements of the two Bretton Woods Institutions (BWIs) to engage in dialogue with the WCC to improve mutual understanding of the organizations' work in development. Reviewing the discussions held since February 2002, including today's meetings, and looking forward, the leaders of the three organizations issue the following statement.

2. These discussions have been significant and useful. The WCC and BWIs have improved their mutual understanding of their positions on

development and related issues. Areas of common ground but also differences of view have been identified. (See paper on "Common Ground and Differences of View between the Bretton Woods Institutions (IMF and World Bank) and the World Council of Churches," prepared by the staff involved in the discussions and available from the organizations). Central to the common ground is the fight against global poverty—particularly the extreme poverty that remains all too prevalent in much of the world. We all agree that poverty reduction at the pace that is needed requires policies to improve both economic growth and equity. We all emphasize the importance of keeping the focus of the global agenda, national leaders, and international organizations on the objective of poverty reduction.

3. In particular, at the present time, we all agree on the importance of the UN Millennium Development Goals (MDGs), which focus on eradicating extreme poverty and hunger; achieving universal primary education; promoting gender equality and empowering women; reducing child mortality; improving maternal health; combating HIV/AIDS, malaria and other diseases; ensuring environmental sustainability; and developing a global partnership for development.

4. While each of our organizations can best serve the MDGs and the objective of poverty reduction that they represent by working in the respective areas of our mandates, responsibilities, and expertise, we believe that more can be achieved in making progress to our shared goals by improved communication and cooperation between the BWIs and the WCC, including through policy dialogue, case studies and advocacy, which can help increase the effectiveness of the international fight against poverty.

5. We agree on the need for sharing experience further on a range of policy issues of common concern, on some of which the BWIs and WCC have differences of view, including development issues such as approaches to development, financial markets, and the impact of

(Box continues on the following page.)

(box continued)

globalization, along with economic policy issues such as those relating to macroeconomic stabilization, government budgets, and international trade.

6. The three organizations are committed to a continuing dialogue to increase further their understanding of their respective experience and learning, as well as to build stronger alliances where appropriate. A key instrument for the continuing dialogue will be a series of country and sector case studies.

The October meeting was designed to summarize the dialogue process and focus participants on future directions. A carefully negotiated joint concept paper defined the meeting's aims as: (a) exploring common and differing perceptions of the three organizations regarding the roles of economic growth, distribution and redistribution of resources, and ideas of equality and participation in poverty eradication; and (b) working towards a statement stressing the common commitment of the three organizations to fighting poverty and working for social justice, and outlining the areas of disagreement and possible plans for future collaboration amongst the three organizations. The intent was also to discuss present and future WCC roles in achieving the MDGs and engaging with the Poverty Reduction Strategy Paper (PRSP) process; to address how the three institutions were integrating into their work concerns about human rights and social justice; and the "democracy deficit"—that is, the perception and concern that the BWIs are undemocratic. WCC hoped to gain greater appreciation for its objective of winning a stronger voice and more decision-making power for the BWI's poorer client countries.

The meeting, in content and in tone, was focused on the commitment of all three institutions to poverty, reflecting the lengthy and labored efforts over the two-year period to establish that they had indeed created significant areas of common ground. Nonetheless, the reality of wide differences in diagnosis, method of approach, and even objectives was apparent. The meeting ended on a positive note of rededication to the common priority of addressing global poverty, and willingness to explore continuing differences in approach and views on central issues. Several themes were woven through the discussions:

Poverty eradication: The status of global partnerships to fight poverty and how the three organizations perceived them were discussed, with emphasis on critical barriers and how economic growth, distribution and redistribution of resources, and equality were related. WCC speakers, notably, stressed their hope that the BWIs would do more to promote poverty eradication by addressing inequality and promoting "growth with distribution" that also safeguards the environment. The BWIs hoped to see greater WCC mobilization behind the MDGs.

Human rights and social justice: Discussions explored the complex and sometimes contentious issue of how the three organizations approached and integrated human rights and social justice objectives, above all, in daily practice. The question was posed as to how these ideas might contribute more directly and effectively to each institution's work. Would such integration indeed change operational norms, and how might the three institutions assist each other on the path ahead?

Voice and vote in the World Bank and IMF: Different views of the impact and above all the path forward on what WCC termed the "democracy deficit" were discussed, as were broader governance objectives, including how all three institutions might work toward greater transparency, accountability, and open debate.

Putting partnership to work: Pursuing the promising dialogue was a central theme, as the three institutions agreed on the merits of the engagement and the long road ahead.

The meeting's central conclusion was that, indeed, given significant areas of common ground, the three institutions should find more effective ways to work together. They agreed that the dialogue process should continue, and that it would focus on specific topics lending themselves to common action. Mr. Wolfensohn proposed five such areas: (a) continued advocacy and action in implementing the MDGs, with particular emphasis on education; (b) work to address the needs of indigenous peoples; (c) better governance, including but by no means limited to fighting corruption; (d) the PRSP process, with a focus on key countries; and (e) HIV/AIDS.

As was the case throughout the dialogue process, the tone of the meeting was both frank and positive, not masking the wide differences in approach and views but underscoring the good intentions on all sides and strong common ground. The meeting took the form of formal statements followed by discussion. Rev. Kobia reviewed the history of the dialogue and its high points. He stressed the issue of voice: the WCC has, he said, represented the voiceless throughout its history. Values and ethics, he said, are not abstract concepts but the essence of the task before us all. The objective is a world economy that is truly people centered. Growth is not enough; we must deal also with inequality. He also highlighted two large challenges: the environment and democratization of the BWIs. "We have come a long way," he concluded.

Dr. Abuom spoke largely through stories: the first, a parable about the sun, most appreciated when it is absent, highlighted the complexity of differing objectives and perceptions; the second, a grandmother reflecting about the tensions between tradition and modernity. She characterized the visible gaps between the wealthy and the poor ("the champagne glass economy") as risking turning the wealthy into tourists gazing at animals in a zoo. WCC's concerns, she stressed, centered on unregulated forms of markets, not markets themselves. The world's problems cannot be resolved by the tools of economists: ethics are essential, and solutions belong in the realm of "agape"—love. She urged the BWIs to view their work constantly and directly in a human rights framework. The dialogue must continue, she urged.

Mr. Wolfensohn reflected first on why he had come to the meeting, and his concerns as he prepared for it. As to why he had come, he reiterated his deep conviction (against many doubts within his organization and its board) about the critical role of religions in development. He had spent eight years, he said, trying to build bridges with faith institutions. More broadly, his deepest concerns on the development agenda were the role of youth, gaps between rich and poor, and the overemphasis on short-term security versus long-term global imbalances. We face a serious crisis of inaction on poverty, he noted, even in the face of so many promises and commitments. As to his concerns, he was deeply troubled by the WCC's *Lead Us Not into Temptation*, which presented such an untrue picture of the World Bank's mission, work, and staff. He discussed how the Bank approaches human rights: largely through its actions. He noted that concerns about governance of the BWIs were issues for their shareholders, not for management. He called, in concluding, for a two-year amnesty on harsh public criticism, and a determination to work together against poverty.

Mr. Carstens reviewed highpoints of the IMF's evolving role, focusing on its responsibility for surveillance of economic performance, in part with a view to anticipating and avoiding crises, and in handling crises when they occurred. The IMF is charged with helping governments make difficult decisions in difficult times. He noted the grave misconceptions about the IMF's role and work. He offered many details on the PRSP process and its origins, and also emphasized the progress made through the dialogue process as a result of the hard work of the staffs of the three institutions. He saw much to be hopeful about in common ground.

A brief discussion included frank exchanges on governance of the BWIs, the "disciplinary role" of the IMF, the role of the Bank and IMF in dealing with indigenous peoples, and the potential for innovative sources of financing for development (for example, the Landau proposals[9]). In concluding, the participants focused on their common commitment to greater equity and the importance of using the MDG framework as a vehicle for mobilization and action. Sam Kobia and Agnes Abuom highlighted how important they considered the path the three institutions had traveled together, and the common cause that linked the three institutions.

NEXT STEPS?

The agreed two-year dialogue process formally ended with the high-level encounter. Contact among the three institutions has continued since then, albeit in a far less structured and formal way; at the time of writing specific next steps on the continuing dialogue were still under discussion. Meanwhile, WCC invited the World Bank to be an observer at their 9th global Assembly in Brazil, and staff members of the three institutions maintain their connections.[10] The dialogue process built a foundation for better communication and more collaboration than before, when the BWIs and the WCC were largely unknown to each other—in many ways working in parallel, perhaps somewhat at odds, certainly with different styles and languages, but to great extent with similar motivations and priorities.

NOTES

1. For the WCC general secretary's letter to the UN secretary general, see http://www.wcc-coe.org/wcc/news/press/00/22pu.html.

2. For the World Council of Churches Website, see http://www.wcc-coe.org/wcc/english.html.

3. World Council of Churches, October 2001, *Lead Us Not into Temptation: Churches' Response to the Policies of International Financial Institutions: A Background Document* (Geneva: World Council of Churches).

4. Letter from James D. Wolfensohn, president, The World Bank Group, and Horst Köhler, managing director, International Monetary Fund, to Rev. Dr. Konrad Raiser, general secretary, World Council of Churches, September 17, 2002.

5. Letter from Konrad Raiser, WCC general secretary, responding to the World Bank and the IMF, October 1, 2002.

6. John Williamson, Senior Fellow, Institute for International Economics, introduced the term "Washington Consensus" in the 1980s to refer to a set of economic policy prescriptions of the World Bank, the IMF, and the U.S. Treasury.

7. For example, see http://www.imf.org/external/pubs/ft/survey/2003/031703.pdf; and http://www.imf.org/external/pubs/ft/survey/2003/120103.pdf.

8. The books are available from WCC, edited by Rogate Mshana, at http://publications.oikoumene.org/index.php?id=2069.

9. These proposals by the French government were presented shortly before the meeting. For details, see http://www.conservationfinance.org/Documents/CF_related_papers/Landau_commission_article2.pdf.

10. For information on the WCC's 9th Assembly, see http://www.wcc-assembly.info/.

CHAPTER 17

Faith and Finance
Unlikely Partners

Management of assets has never been an entirely alien topic to leaders and institutions of faith. Indeed, many concepts of finance and economics themselves, as schools of thought and disciplines, trace their roots to religious teachings and practices, both in ancient times and throughout history. Nonetheless, in financial circles today, a common assumption is that faith bodies operate in a somewhat different realm from business, and that they are not prominent participants in corporate boardrooms or on the trading floor.

However, the reality is that many assets are in fact held by faith organizations of many kinds. Precise estimates are hard to come by; one study by a Citibank team for the Alliance of Religions and Conservation (ARC) suggested that faith groups hold as much as 10 percent of the world's liquid financial assets, and probably more than 15 percent of its land resources, with influence in both areas extending considerably beyond. Overall, the role of faith players in financial realms is on the rise. Ethical and religious concerns also motivate the financial practices of many citizens, at least in part. Thus the world of finance offers an important and little-traveled bridge linking different worlds that are concerned about global poverty.

A recent marked increase in discussion and action on socially responsible investing can be traced at least in part to activism by faith organiza-

This chapter draws on the author's engagement with 3iG. Michiel Hardon and Seamus Finn, 3iG directors, provided helpful comments

tions over the past few decades. Likewise, a sharper spotlight is trained on links between investment and issues of poverty, whether they touch on the labor practices of multinational companies or the potential of microcredit to serve the "unbanked." This arena engages many faith communities (see box 17.1 for one example).

BOX 17.1
FAITH-BASED MICROCREDIT: FIVE TALENTS

Faith communities, inspired by their confidence in poor people's ingenuity and determined to offer them paths out of poverty, are prominent among those working with the myriad small-scale financial programs in poor communities the world over—programs that fall under the heading of microfinance. Nearly 3 billion poor people lack access to the most basic financial services. The Consultative Group to Assist the Poor (CGAP)—housed at the World Bank Group—was founded to address this gap. Today this consortium of 33 public and private development agencies works to expand access to financial services for the poor in developing countries.[a]

Microfinance is one of the most dynamic sectors in the development world today, with a plethora of new institutions committed to filling gaps in providing financial resources and services to the poor. The UN's naming of 2005 as the Year of Microcredit, and the awarding of the 2006 Nobel Peace Prize to Mohammed Yunus and the Grameen Bank he founded in Bangladesh, are major markers of progress.[b] But even before Yunus won the Nobel Prize, the Grameen model had spread and evolved the world over, with many thousands of groups interpreting the microcredit model as their own.

Faith-based organizations are among these creators of innovative microcredit models. Opportunity International is one of the best-known Christian microfinance organizations, founded in 1971 and recognized and supported by the Bill and Melinda Gates Foundation.[c] Opportunity operates in 28 countries worldwide and provided nearly 1.5 million loans in 2006—85 percent of them to women. Other Christian organizations involved in microfinance include Food for the Hungry International, Adventist Development and Relief Agencies, Mennonite Economic

Development Associates, World Vision, and Christian Children's Fund. Dozens of NGOs offer Shari'a-compliant microfinance services in Muslim countries from Indonesia to Morocco.

Five Talents is an interesting example of a small faith-inspired microfinance institution. Founded in 1999, Five Talents works from its faith principles to fight poverty, create jobs, and transform lives by empowering the poor in developing countries through innovative savings and microcredit programs, business training, and spiritual development.[d]

Five Talents was launched at the 1998 Lambeth Conference of Anglican bishops, in Canterbury, United Kingdom. The aim was a long-term response to debilitating poverty—"not only to assist but also to guard the dignity of the poor," many of whom survive only on a dollar per day. Diane Knippers, one of Five Talents' founders, wrote in the *Wall Street Journal*, that it was conceived to "link two strengths of the Anglican Communion: the wealth of its North American and British adherents and the outreach of their African sister churches."[e]

The organization's name was inspired by the book of Matthew from the Bible. "Master," he said, "You have entrusted me with five talents. See, I have gained five more." His master replied, "Well done, good and faithful servant! You have been faithful in a few things; I will put you in charge of many things; enter into the joy of your master" (Matthew 25:14–30). The parable highlights that every human being has dignity and has been granted God-given abilities. Access to loan capital and business training can empower the poor to recognize and develop their talents.

Five Talents has its headquarters in the United States in Vienna, Virginia, with offices in London and Kampala, Uganda; an office in the southeast United States coordinates the organization's Latin American program and curriculum development. Hundreds of volunteers across the United States and United Kingdom support Five Talents, and it has financed thousands of US$50 to US$300 loans to poor entrepreneurs in nine countries: Bolivia, Honduras, India, Indonesia, Kenya, Nigeria, Peru, the Philippines, and Uganda. In countries, Five Talents works through partnerships with local entities, whether Christian microfinance institutions affiliated with local Anglican churches or international institutions like the Geneva-based Ecumenical Church Loan Fund.[f] Five Talents is also part of numerous international microfinance networks.

(Box continues on the following page.)

(box concluded)

Five Talents aims to give people the opportunity to lift themselves out of poverty by providing access to basic savings and microcredit services built on trusted community traditions. Five Talents also provides business training, grounded in biblical teachings, to help poor people start small businesses and begin to build their future. Five Talents also supports local institutions working in microenterprise development. The organization's primary programs include consulting services, training and education for savings and microcredit programs, materials that promote ethical business principles, and loan capital for the poor.

One aspect of Five Talents that sets it apart from other microcredit enterprises is its effort to provide business training and one-on-one business counseling to loan recipients, thereby enabling them to pursue new and creative ways to use their skills and talents. Management professionals—who are generally Anglican or Episcopal—travel on short trips to train entrepreneurs in the countries where Five Talents operates.

The goal is a transformative experience for all involved. Toward that end, the biblically based curriculum covers the basics of entrepreneurship, business planning, marketing, and record keeping, thus equipping loan recipients to run and expand their businesses, at the same time that it emphasizes dignity and values and provides spiritual support.

Note: This box is drawn from an interview with Craig Cole, executive director of Five Talents, and from the Five Talents Website: http://www.fivetalents.org/. Elizabeth Littlefield, Director CGAP, provided useful comments and amplifications.

a. For information on the Consultative Group to Assist the Poor, see http://www.cgap.org/.

b. See http://www.grameen-info.org/.

c. See http://www.opportunity.org/.

d. Another international faith-based microcredit model is Oikocredit. See http://www.oikocredit.org/.

e. See http://www.fivetalents.org/content.asp?contentid=503.

f. See http://www.eclof.org/.

Active faith communities often raise concerns about the environmental and social impacts and practices of investment managers. This work includes critiques of the World Bank, with faith leaders and communities among those that have questioned specific policies and programs most actively. These critiques range from fundamental and broad challenges, such as the Jubilee 2000 campaign against poor country debt,[1] to ethical concerns about specific projects in specific countries, expressed, for example, through letters from religious orders about water projects in Bolivia and factory conditions in Cambodia seen as harming the poor. More positively, dialogue with critics, including those within faith communities, is on the rise and there is increasing consciousness of important common ground, including in areas involving investment and finance.

While different faith traditions approach business very differently, those involved in the socially consistent investing arena work with a conviction that sound investment with good returns can and should be quite consistent with keen attention to social and environmental dimensions. At one recent meeting, a faith leader who oversees investments called on his colleagues to be "as shrewd as the sons of this world" in using finance to achieve socially responsible ends.[2]

Religious institutions are thus part of the trend toward the "triple bottom line," where investment is guided by constant attention, in equal measure, to financial, social, and environmental impact. A strong common interest in making transparency a reality—in the sense of being publicly clear about the criteria and risks of investment decisions—offers real potential for involving faith institutions in partnerships that advance sound, sensible approaches and effective tools. The potential for synergy is substantial. This path requires carefully crafted processes for dialogue that addresses topics such as approaches to privatization and regulatory frameworks, and parallel work on practical options for collaboration, such as in diagnosing obstacles to growth in a given country, advocating specific policy changes, and building a microfinance institution or program.

LEADING UP TO THE PRESENT

Organized efforts to bring together the voices and resources of faith communities to influence broader investment policies have been particularly developed in the United States. A pioneering institution providing leadership to faith institutions in investment policy is the Interfaith Center on Corporate Responsibility (ICCR).[3] Originally a Christian group founded in 1971, today it includes Jewish and other socially responsible investors, and is reaching out to other faith communities in the United States. ICCR's 275 faith-based institutional investors include national denominations, religious communities, mutual funds, public and private pension funds, foundations, hospital corporations, economic development funds, asset management companies, colleges, and unions. The organization both provides concrete advice and works on specific topics, such as in its engagement with Wal-Mart, Disney, McDonalds, Pfizer, and Citigroup. The combined portfolios of ICCR members are estimated at about US$100 billion.

Besides investing for solid financial returns, ICCR members examine the social and environmental performance of the companies in their portfolios. Rather than simply selling stock when these policies and practices are seen as harmful to people or the environment, ICCR members press corporations to change. Thus a key element of ICCR's approach is sponsoring, each year, more than 200 shareholder resolutions on major social and environmental issues. Overall, ICCR members rely on their investments and other resources to change unjust or harmful corporate policies, in the process working for peace, economic justice, and stewardship of the Earth.

Members use their investments to open doors at companies and attempt to raise concerns at the highest levels of corporate decision making. They use the power of persuasion backed by economic pressure from consumers and investors to hold corporations accountable. They sponsor shareholder resolutions, meet with management, screen investments, divest stock, conduct public hearings and investigations, publish special reports, and sponsor actions such as prayer vigils, letter-writing campaigns, and consumer boycotts. ICCR members also make investments to promote economic development in low-income and minority communities.

A listing of the priorities of ICCR members illustrates this approach:

- eliminating sweatshops and corporate involvement in human rights abuses

- reversing global warming
- halting the proliferation of genetically modified foods until safety is proven
- guaranteeing equal employment opportunity for all
- working to make retailers of violent video games more accountable
- making pharmaceuticals and health care safe, available, and affordable to all
- ending tobacco product advertising
- seeking more accountable corporate governance structures
- ending foreign military sales
- achieving international debt forgiveness for the world's poorest countries

THE INTERNATIONAL INTERFAITH INVESTMENT GROUP

Inspired in good measure by the ICCR experience, a new institution is working to build an even broader interfaith network that provides similar services at the global level. The International Interfaith Investment Group (3iG) was formally launched in April 2005, and its first secretary general, Joost Douma, took up his position in early 2006.[4]

The coalition has several origins. The initial idea and work was the inspiration of Martin Palmer of ARC, which also shepherded the nascent institution in its formative stages. It was during ARC meetings of faith leaders on environmental issues that the proposals were first mooted. The motivation was a common wish among an extraordinarily diverse set of individuals from public and private institutions to challenge faith investors around the world to align their financial investments with their religious and ethical beliefs.

In developing 3iG, organizers put great emphasis on a religious-secular partnership. A broadly interfaith group, including Buddhist, Christian, Hindu, Islamic, Jain, Jewish, Muslim, Sikh, and Zoroastrian members, served as an interim steering committee. Over several years, these members sought to encourage each denomination to assess its portfolios with "due regard to the faith's beliefs, values, the environment and human rights so that all life on Earth can benefit."[5] The group also coined the term "faith-consistent investment" as a form of socially responsible investment. The group benefited from the advice of secular investors, including philanthropists, who found their values and ethics aligned with those of the 3iG charter. The group invited a number of actors to assist the different faith communities in developing 3iG, including major foundations and banks such as Citigroup, Rabobank from the Netherlands, and the World Bank; organizations such as Innovest and World Wildlife Fund International; and economic think-tanks such as Medley Global Advisors.

Today 3iG's mission is to promote investments that are consistent with the common core beliefs of the members coming from different faith traditions that combine the potential for good returns with beneficial social and environmental consequences. The interaction that 3iG fosters between religious worlds and the world of finance, including secular value systems and networks, offers an exciting new model of collaboration. As a resource center for faith-consistent investing, proactive brokerage, and a marketplace for people, projects, and ideas, 3iG stands alone in bringing together people of faith to invest in a better world. Box 17.2 summarizes one example of an investment scheme, which serves as something of a harbinger of 3iG investments, involving a partnership bridging Scandinavian churches and communities across southern Africa.

BOX 17.2
FAITH-CONSISTENT INVESTING IN DEVELOPMENT:
RESPONSIBLE FORESTRY

The Global Solidarity Forest Fund (GSFF) has a total value of about US$100 million. Founded by the Diocese of Västerås, the Lutheran Church of Sweden, and the Norwegian Lutheran Church Endowment, it offers a fascinating example of a growing trend for practical, finance-based involvement of faith organizations in the development process. It aims both to produce solid financial returns and to benefit communities in forested regions across Southern Africa through solid, ethical, and sustainable investments. The investments help the communities involved directly through revenues generated by forestry investments, but the hope is also that successful projects will encourage other investors to engage in Africa. This innovative scheme is illustrative of the path being traced by institutions like the International Interfaith Investment Group (3iG), which aim to bring together financial resources, commitment to engaging and supporting local communities, and ethical investment principles of faith communities to serve the cause of development.

GSFF's history traces back almost a millennium, as Christianity developed in Scandinavia. As communities were Christianized during the 12th century, villages had to build a church and donate sufficient forest and farmland to allow the priest to support himself. These gifts form the foundation of the churches' present forest and farmland assets; today this ancient legacy translates into nearly 100,000 hectares of managed forests that produce steady revenues. As the churches engaged in dialogue with Mozambican communities about their problems and needs, a plan emerged to extend this special Scandinavian church experience to Mozambique, through a scheme that combined sound investment and forestry principles and mechanisms to benefit people living there directly.

GSFF runs several distinct investment projects. The Chikweti Forest investment in Niassa Province (northern Mozambique) focuses on reforestation; commercial forest plantations are coupled with programs for natural ecosystem management. Land is leased from the government on a 50-plus-50-year lease agreement. The investments are long term (felling at age 18 to 30, depending on species) and export focused, but short-term benefits come from products sold on the local market and the creation of jobs. (Chikweti employs 400 full time and 150 seasonal workers, about 20 percent of them women, and the number will double at full capacity.) The project involves capital investment of US$60 million during the first 10 years, with US$30 million invested by GSFF and the rest by a U.S.–based institutional investor. Returns are currently projected at 13 percent a year.

The Responsible Wood Angola investment is focused on a 100,000 hectare concession of natural forest in northern Angola. Here, management of existing forest resources, with extensive consultation with the communities in the area, is at the core of the program.

(Box continues on the following page.)

(box concluded)

All GSFF investments are subjected to strict certification. The Forest Stewardship Council, a third-party, accredited verification organization, confirms that forest management plans are economically viable, socially beneficial, and environmentally appropriate. GSFF also works with local partners to ensure that communities are deeply engaged from start to finish. GSFF's local partner in Mozambique is the Anglican Diocese of Niassa; in Angola, it is the Anglican Diocese of Angola. These partners have a 10 percent ownership in the individual investments, building a long-term financial base for church social development activities.

The "five F" project (forests, finance, food, fuel, and future) runs in parallel, involving the Anglican Diocese of Niassa, GSFF, and the U.S. Forest Service International Program, so that community development, training, and concerted efforts at environmental protection bolster the financial benefits accruing from forest investments.

Source: Margaret Rainey, Vice President, Global Solidarity Forest Fund, provided background information and useful comments.

As it looks to the future, 3iG plans to make an impact by helping more faith investors to integrate their core beliefs into their investment policies and decisions, to allow those who are already committed to this work to invest their assets even more effectively in ways that are consistent with their traditions, to do so in collaboration with other faith traditions, and also to do so in ways that bring fiscally responsible returns. The group is thus building on and expanding the experience and determination of faith organizations to advance a more just and environmentally friendly society that takes seriously the contribution of the faiths and respects the rich reservoir of cultures and traditions. It also aims to provide access to a wide range of solid research on the gifts which faith traditions can bring to this field, including the education and formation opportunities for advisory and investment services that are willing to serve the needs of faith investors and institutions from every corner of the world.

NOTES

1. See Katherine Marshall and Lucy Keough, 2004, "Learning with Jubilee: World Bank Engagement with the Jubilee 2000 Debt Campaign," chapter 3, in *Mind, Heart, and Soul in the Fight against Poverty*, Katherine Marshall and Lucy Keough (Washington, DC: World Bank).

2. Meeting of Oikocredit, a financier of microcredit, on faith-consistent investing, Amersfoort, Netherlands, December 2006.

3. See http://www.iccr.org/.

4. See http://www.3ignet.org/about/.

5. See http://www.3ignet.org/about/history/.

18

Paths to Hope through Music and Culture
Dialogue at Fès

Dialogue can evoke a deep and meaningful exercise when it is inspired and facilitated by spiritual leaders. Processes of dialogue are common within and among faith traditions. These processes can be elaborately structured and conducted with careful rituals designed to ensure balance and mutual respect. They can transpire over decades and even centuries. The term "dialogue" tends to suggest something different to most development practitioners—at best an effort to exchange views at a deeper level than the normal conversation around operational work or academic interchange, and at worst just more words instead of action.

In Fès, Morocco, a different venture in dialogue tried to bring together the best elements of intercultural learning and exchange in an effort to address knotty global problems and areas of great tension.[1] The dialogue that formed part of the Fès Forum was deeply integrated into the vision of a sacred music festival whose objective is to celebrate and appreciate the diverse religious cultures of the world. Thus this dialogue brought the world of art and culture together with a range of pragmatic topics around globalization. The core philosophy is that diversity is the essence of what is best in human life and culture. The Fès dialogue's aim has been to reach new understandings and styles of exchange around a very worldly issue: globalization. Still more fundamentally, it aimed to help bridge the divides that provoke conflict among peoples, by fostering a deeper understanding of the rich tapestry of the world's cultures, and by demonstrating concretely how this diversity can enrich life at every level.

THE IDEA

A group of strangers assembled in a rather gray hotel conference room in Fès, in June 2001, for the first venture in dialogue. They were curious, if tentative, about a social and cultural experiment in which they had been invited to take part. The renowned Fès Festival of World Sacred Music, and the mystique of the ancient and magical city of Fès, attracted and intrigued them, but the invitation to participate spoke to a much broader challenge. This was to face directly the controversies, divisions, and passions that the topic of globalization evoked in different parts of the world.

The challenge set forth for this colloquium in Fès was to work toward a different kind of dialogue that would focus on listening and transformation. It would build on the inspiration of the multicultural music festival, and the city's celebrated history of a lived pluralistic society where people of different faiths take pride in long centuries of living together in harmony. Could adversaries from government ministries, environmental movements, and large companies, from women's cooperatives and global media, from advocacy groups and international organizations, find a spirit of communication that would allow them to learn and reshape their visions for future action?

Over the next five years, participants in this Fès dialogue came to form a network and committed themselves to a process. The group was no longer made up of strangers; some participants returned year after year while others came only once or twice, but the sense of a community existed nonetheless. The setting of the meeting changed from a conventional hotel conference space to the open air of the Baatha Museum, beneath the vast canopy of a Barbary oak, which inspired countless analogies in presentations and conversations over the years (the link between roots and branches, for example, and the harmony of the different birdsongs).

The participants were skeptical at first as to whether such a different dialogue—one that eschewed the formalities of seminars and international meetings—was possible. These doubts were dispelled as the years went by. The spirit of Fès succeeded in remarkable fashion in sparking a rich dialogue in a very unusual form. The style resembled a "jazz" approach to dialogue: unscripted, not composed, and allowed to roam and take its inspiration from the spirit and vision of the moment. This very different quality of dialogue owed much to an insistence on personal engagement, encouraged by a well-established tradition of using symbols and words, which was cherished by the core group of Fès participants.

The underlying goals of the Fès Forum were to engage in continuing reflection about the direction and efforts of globalization, with a specific agenda that evolved and developed over time. The spirit of Fès also had a less visible but equally important side: it transformed the people who engaged in the discourse. Thus the colloquium, now renamed a forum, moved from a brave, lonely venture with visionary patrons to a partnership that engaged public, private, Moroccan, and international partners. Besides its Moroccan patrons, the forum benefited from the active support of the European Commission, the Aga Khan Foundation, and the World Bank.

Beyond Fès, debates about globalization changed over the years, and perhaps the spirit of Fès played its small part. The cymbals of globalization disputes are less noisy and more nuanced today than they were six years ago, and the sounds of debates mingle with tensions of war and peace and the intertwined issues of poverty, culture, and social justice. The forum has witnessed a remarkable set of challenges: to revitalize the fight against poverty; to bring peace; to elucidate debates about identity, respect, and tolerance; and to address the clashes among nations and institutions. The Fès forum has been a rare place where opposing or blindly unseeing perspectives meet and truly engage. Its organizers and supporters see this as a precious opportunity for hope.

RUMI'S ELEPHANT

An ancient story tells much about the vision for the Fès forum. Many cultures and faiths tell the story of how blind men—that is, people without light—explore an elephant and speculate on what nature of creature it is. Participants in the forum represent, in many respects, the blind eagerly exploring the very large elephant of globalization, each bringing different perceptions and experiences to bear. All have different but very real visions of what they see, and still more, what they hope to bring to these powerful global forces. They seek to direct light to what they, as individuals, can glean from their differing experiences.

One verison of the tale of the blind men and the elephant suggests an important difference. The seekers are not blind but in the dark, in need of traces of light. As the great poet Rumi told it many eons ago:[2]

An elephant was in a dark building. Some people from India had brought it for exhibition.

Many people kept going into that dark (place) in order to see it. Each one was stroking it with his hands in the dark, since seeing it with the eyes was not possible.

In the case of one person, whose hand landed on the trunk, he said, "This being is like a drain pipe." For another one, whose hand reached its ear, to him it seemed like a kind of fan. As for another person, whose hand was upon its leg, he said, "I perceived the shape of the elephant to be like a pillar."

And in the case of another one, who placed his hand upon its back, he said, "Indeed, this elephant was like a throne."

In the same way as this, any one who reached a part of the elephant used his understanding in regard to any particular place he perceived by touch.

Their words were different and opposing because of the different viewing places. One person gave it the nickname of the bent letter "dâl;" this other one, of the straight letter "alif."

If there had been a candle in the hand of each person, the disagreement would have gone out (completely) from their speech.

The eye of physical sense is like the palm of the hand, nothing more. And the palm of the hand has no access to the whole of the elephant.

The eye of the Ocean is one thing and the foam is something else. Abandon the foam and look out of the Ocean's eye.

The movement of the surface foam continues night and day from the Ocean. You keep seeing the foam, but not the Ocean. How amazing!

We are colliding against one other like boats. We are darkened of eyes—and yet we are in the clear and brightly lit water. The physical water has a universal water as its source which drives it forth. Likewise the spirit has a universal spirit calling it.

We live in a world today where we grapple with issues of power and violence, of breathtaking beauty and hideous conflict, of enormous possibilities and of pain. We see the contrasts and seek paths to bring the differences into focus—to turn the kaleidoscope of diversity into rich and positive harmony.

PATHS TO HOPE?

The Fès Festival and Forum are grounded in an ambitious vision: to explore and contribute to world peace and social justice by celebrating cultural diversity and by building on a profound respect for the interconnectedness of world cultures. The music festival's expressions in music, film, and other arts are woven together with the forum's explorations of religion, culture, politics, and economic and social systems—particularly insofar as all are affected and shaped by globalization and dynamic changes in the modern world. The Fès Festival provides a treasured opportunity to explore the complex interplay of spiritual and secular, religious and social, and political and economic facets of contemporary challenges.

The forum's agenda has built year by year on central themes, such as identity, wealth and poverty, tolerance and respect, the roles of religion and spirituality, and the resolution of conflict. At the 2006 forum, Faouzi Skali, festival and forum director, proposed a new credo: "committed to enhancing the conscience of the world"—an echo of the World Economic Forum's motto "committed to improving the state of the world." The Fès Forum set as its central aim to strengthen bridges among widely differing perspectives—whether those of leaders and champions of world business, radical critics of contemporary economic life, political leaders, or civil society activists—and to trace paths to greater understanding and partnership among different cultures and disciplines.

Although the spirit of dialogue at Fès is grounded on ideas and exchange, never far away is a will to action. Practical ideas include the restoration and revival of the city of Fès, and extending the Fès network beyond Morocco—for example, through similar models of dialogue across Spanish, Italian, and French cities. In 2004 and 2006, music groups which had performed at the Festival toured the United States under the banner of "the Spirit of Fès," with a primary goal of increasing understanding. The creation of an Institute for Cultural Diplomacy and Mediation for the Muslim world at Al Akhawayn University in Ifrane is directly linked to Fès discussions. Media and communications are central to this vision, as is the transmission of culture through education in its broadest sense.

The annual five-day dialogue has addressed many very different topics over the years. Some have recurred with some regularity—notably identity, human rights, and democracy. In 2004, the forum turned to an issue that was always present but little discussed in earlier years: challenges in the Middle East, and the nagging drama of the conflict between Israel and Palestine. The theme of memory was a recurring topic in 2004, with painful recollections evoked of lost heritage, lost homes, and loss of cherished images and memories. The following year the central theme was healing, highlighting the essential work of linking memory and forgiveness, memory and understanding, and memory and hope. In 2006, the environment and the responsibilities of all for its care emerged as a central theme.

Peace, hope, equity, and development are threads woven through the life of the forum. It has explored how these themes and challenges are shaped by the very evident interconnections of lives exemplified by music and the interconnected futures of different societies and cultures that grow ever more apparent. How can we, together, build a better future upon the foundation of rich identities, profound appreciation of rights, heartfelt admiration for cultural heritage in all its domains, and respect for memory of both joy and pain?

THE 2006 FORUM

The Fès Forum builds on the music festival's founding and binding vision, reflected in its enduring title—Giving Soul to Globalization—but each annual festival also has its own theme. In 2006 it was harmonies. This theme linked the intricate harmonies and rhythms expressed in music—including Syrian sufi chants, the ancient music of Andalusia, English gospel, and Japanese drummers—to the challenge of perceiving and amplifying the subtle harmonies found among the world's diverse societies and cultures. This challenge is far from an abstraction: it presents urgent and real demands for enlightened understanding and action. In today's global community, identity, relationships, and survival of different cultures, religions, and communities are widely seen as under threat from the juggernaut of globalization. The issues at stake are life and death matters for many communities, reflecting visions of "clash" and "conflict" versus calls for "dialogue" and "alliance" of civilizations.

During its sixth year, the Fès Forum remained faithful to the customs and style that marked the dialogue process and reflected the core of its ethos. Each discussion was introduced with music, which had the effect of sparking inspiration. Participants presented symbols and metaphors that reflected their personal engagement. The ambiance of the forum—set beneath the great Fès Barbary oak—fostered creative expression of personal views, and encouraged participants to venture into areas rarely explored in typical seminars.

The forum is open to the public, and media from many countries follow its course (it was Webcast live in 2006). The gathering had built a remarkably loyal fellowship of people who returned year after year, and who followed the forum start to finish—notwithstanding the festival's competing artistic performances, late-night offerings of sufi music and dance, and the heat of Fès at noontime as each day's discussions reached their conclusion.

Participants in forum panels are truly citizens of the world, coming from all continents and most professions; some return year after year, while new fellows join each year. Films and art exhibitions are integral parts of both festival and forum. Highlights in 2006 included presentations by Wim Wenders, filmmaker and advocate, who discussed the implications his film *Land of Plenty* for global responsibilities for wealth and poverty.

The forum, president Mohammed Kabbaj has stressed, is not a festival of words but a festival of action. Its aim is transformation, grounded in probing exploration of leading challenges on the global agenda. The annual dialogue in Fès is thus the lodestar of an intricate series of events—guided by its director and partners—that includes music festivals and associated dialogue on several continents, development projects in Morocco and Fès, the movement towards an "interdependence day," and the Al Akhawayn University's Institute of Cultural Diplomacy, which aspires to develop leadership for peace, especially in the Islamic world. Each venture of ideas is matched by calls for immediate and specific action; the calls in 2006 ranged from an exhortation to fight sex trafficking in Germany during the World Soccer Cup, to appeals to share the sacred heritage of Jerusalem, to workable ways to sustain a focus on children, to ideas for guiding development in the city of Fès along a path of spiritual tourism. Migration also was an insistent theme, as was the need to address global warming.

The forum constantly looked for ways to distill ideas and link them to action. Each day began with a summary and reflection on the previous day's work. These summaries (available in English, French, and Arabic on the Websites of the Fès Festival and the World Bank's development dialogue team)[3] are designed to bind discussions day by day, and year after year. Also worthy of mention are four books emerging from the forum, with the latest, *Les Chemins de l'Espoir*, edited by Nathalie Calmé.[4]

The 2006 agenda illustrated the reach of the dialogue, as it focused on five quite distinct daily themes—each echoing earlier discussions in Fès, but also profoundly shaped by the contemporary global agenda. The first day's discourse, on economy and spirituality, was generally somber in tone, with many participants expressing concerns about inequity and the "spiritual poverty" of lives dominated by cultures of consumption and assumptions that put "homo economicus" at the center. Yet talk of ecological destruction, conflict, and the injustice of inequality contrasted with real hope for new "knowledge" economies and exciting progress in many domains. The discussion took as a starting point the dilemmas that confront the private sector today, especially multinational enterprises. The discussion, however, was dominated by links to economic and political behavior—throughout history, and in the world today.

The second day brought a complex and challenging discussion of wealth and poverty, led off by Wim Wenders. His questioning of crude assumptions—that wealth is good, poverty bad—set the tone. The reflections on poverty highlighted a highly nuanced understanding of the interrelationships between wealth and poverty, rich and poor, and their implications for many dimensions of policy and advocacy

Islam and globalization was the challenging topic for the third day. Participants explored the realities and difficulties of "lived Islam," and the tensions between moderate Islam and tendencies to hijack it through fundamentalism, across many dimensions and places. The humane and deeply rooted voices of a tolerant, diverse, and very moderate Islam echoed through the day.

The fourth day, on the topic of forgiveness, began with the painful witness of two women working for peace in Israel and Palestine, in the shadow of their personal loss of family to violence. The theme was how to help resolve conflict through efforts ranging from individual, personal work to civil society action to political "space." The forum explored the roots of wisdom and practice involving peace keeping that link the three Abrahamic faiths: Judaism, Christianity, and Islam.

The fifth and final day, on ecology and spirituality, featured an urgent and far-ranging exploration of challenges to the global environment. Among the many ideas and proposals was a multifaceted call to appreciate far more deeply the world's extraordinary array of spiritual traditions that touch on humankind and nature, and to work with more energy and creativity to engage both these traditions and the institutions of faith in preserving our "beautiful and fragile blue planet."

SUSTAINING THE FORUM

The Fès Forum has been a widely acclaimed and remarkably integral part of the Fès Sacred Music Festival. Today it stands at a crossroads and different paths lie ahead. The five-year partnership with the World Bank has concluded. Several possible paths—not mutually exclusive—lie ahead. The forum could pursue its original focus on bridging the divergent worlds of the World Economic Forum at Davos (in Switzerland) and the parallel World Social Forum at Porto Alegre (in Brazil), thus above all working to bridge tensions around the processes of globalization. It could also take inspiration from the sacred music to refocus dialogue on the significance of spirituality and religion. Another possible route is to take advantage of Morocco's special strategic and cultural position to focus more explicitly on the Middle East, with the aspiration of contributing more directly to peace. The forum could also focus more sharply on Morocco and Fès itself. It could, in contrast, address more rigorously the enduring challenges the forum has considered over the years, including ecology, values in education, the responsibility of the private sector, the roles of women, and the urgent need to resolve conflicts throughout the world.

NOTES

1. See, for example, "Fès Forum 2006: Giving Soul to Globalization," World Bank Development Dialogue on Values and Ethics, at http://www.worldbank.org/developmentdialogue.

2. Drawn from Rumi, Mathnawi III 1259-1274; found at http://www.dar-al-masnavi.org/n.a-III-1259.html.

3. See http://www.fesfestival.com; and http://www.worldbank.org/development dialogue.

4. The four books published specifically about the Fes Forum are: Edgar Morin et al, 2003, *Donner une ame a la mondialisation: Une anthologie des Recontres de Fès publier sous la direction de Patrice van Eersel* (Gordes, France: Albin Michel); Helmy Abouleish and Nathalie Calmé, 2004, *L'esprit de Fès*, (Paris: Rocher; Patrice van Eersel, 2005, *Tisseurs de Paix* (Gordes, France: Les Editions du Relie); and S.A.R. le Prince Charles presente *Les Chemins de l'Espoir: Une ame pour la mondialisation, Actes du Forum de Fes 2005*, Collectif sous la direction de Nathalie Calmé (France: Editions de Rocher, 2006).

19

New Alliances for Integrity, Against Corruption

Because they have special "expertise" in values and integrity, and because of their extensive presence and reach, faith institutions, leaders, and networks offer a powerful potential force in raising governance standards in the work of development. Throughout history, faith leaders have raised some of the most courageous and effective voices in efforts to combat corruption and promote good governance. Today, however, with growing attention to ensuring high standards of governance everywhere, there is a broader and more public expectation that faith leaders and institutions should go beyond their traditional focus on personal and community values to play even more active roles in alliances against corrupt behavior—whether at the community, national, or global level.

The religious world claims a classic prophetic role of "speaking truth to power," thus helping to set and preserve social standards (even when faith communities themselves are not without fault). Personal values and ethics, and religious beliefs and teaching, are tied together in many ways. Faith teachings help people define and monitor standards of behavior in many contexts. And private morality and values—whether or not derived from religious principles—link to public morality. There is a common expectation that religious teaching and preaching will instill solid values, remind and admonish people to follow them, and raise voices in denunciation when and where standards are breached and public integrity fails.

The morality of pulpit and temple are widely expected and understood, even if many would suggest that the lessons heard there too seldom travel far beyond the church or temple door. Parables and teachings of different faiths are common points of reference in debates about public ethics across the globe.

The developing world offers many contemporary examples of faith leaders working within a variety of partnerships to fight corruption. In 2003, the International Anti-Corruption Conference (IACC) in Seoul—in alliance with Transparency International, the global coalition and movement against corruption—included an unprecedented effort (within that movement) to involve both religious leaders and approaches explicitly in the dialogue.[1] Cardinal Oscar Rodriguez Maridiaga of Honduras offers an example of a widely respected leader within the Catholic Church who is well known and appreciated for his active role in working for higher standards of governance. He sits on many international bodies and speaks out frequently to this end.[2]

Nonetheless, the general observation is that global movements and discussions on integrity and governance have involved faith leaders less than might be expected.

The spotlight now shining on the damage that corrupt practices inflict on development work has more direct implications for faith institutions when they themselves are engaged in designing and running development programs. The question arises whether faith institutions are sufficiently sensitive to the potentially corrosive effects of "leakage" of funds and conflicts of interest, and whether they are well equipped to combat those problems. As faith organizations become more involved in relief operations, HIV/AIDS programs, and other development work, through both congregations and development institutions, new demands for accountability arise.

Should religious leaders and institutions be more directly engaged in both national and global efforts to define and raise standards of public governance? To what extent are they already doing so? Can they participate effectively, and if so, how? What is needed to reinforce and expand alliances between faith and development institutions, and to reinforce a culture and practice of integrity, both so essential to fighting poverty? These questions are of immediate significance in intense public debates about how to fight corruption in development work, and about the relationships between religious and secular, church and state.

This chapter explores six broad and public policy challenges that relate to the actual and potential roles of faith leaders and institutions in fighting against corruption and for higher standards of public integrity. These challenges include: building on common religious teachings to enhance public integrity; pursuing purposeful dialogue on areas of difference and disagreement; exploring the potential for mobilizing faith organizations to combat corruption; concentrating on religious education and teaching to encourage integrity and public ethics; strengthening fiscal management and accountability within faith communities and programs; and monitoring poverty levels and public sector expenditures.

COMMON RELIGIOUS ETHICAL TEACHINGS AND PUBLIC INTEGRITY

Religious leaders are often not at the center of secular discussions about public integrity and ethics because many "integrity alliances" hold that the values underlying good governance are common to all faith and secular traditions—that it is possible (and desirable) to define a global ethic. The effort to focus on universal standards and principles is often seen as countering arguments of particularity of cultures and religion.

Some also fear that invoking the moral teachings of individual faith traditions could be divisive in plural societies. And some proponents of global ethics are frankly skeptical about whether all faith leaders and institutions truly live up to their own preaching and teaching on morality.

Thus most efforts to define common ethical values that underlie good governance have focused on those that cut across different social and legal traditions, and that encompass threads of many religious traditions. As an example, the final declaration of the 2006 IACC meeting, entitled "Common Values, Different Cultures," highlighted strong common values around integrity: "Convinced that corruption should be condemned and eradicated for the sake of the universally held value of integrity, participants declare that cultural and historical particularity should not be used as a pretext for justifying corruption, or conversely, for labeling certain societies as corrupt. At the same time, anticorruption measures tailored to the specific circumstances of a particular society should be devised in order effectively to deliver practical solutions."[3]

A good case can indeed be made that many of the basic values underlying principles of civic integrity stem from deep common culture roots and a common consensus. However, some of these values, though not all, can be linked to the teachings of various religions, and that is useful to underscore. As an example, a directive along the lines of "thou shalt not steal" appears in some form in most faith traditions, as do admonitions to be honest and, more broadly, to serve the common good.

The most extensive work to define and document the roots of a global ethic has been led by Hans Kung, the renowned Swiss Catholic theologian. Kung and his colleagues have traced a well-articulated set of principles to core teachings of the world's major religions. The basic message is that there is indeed a powerful common core of shared principles, which these proponents set out as a Global Ethic. This Global Ethic has among other things been the focus of the 1993 World Parliament of Religions meeting in Chicago and its successor parliaments, and of successive discussions by the InterAction Council, an assembly of former heads of state.[4] Innumerable conferences and discussions, including those of the International Monetary Fund and the World Economic Forum, have also considered the concepts and specifics. And the Global Ethic features prominently in university ethics curricula.

Framing a persuasive case that common ethical norms bind cultures together and offer a basis for universal standards can serve as a powerful counter to cynics and doubters who argue that corruption is embedded in specific cultures. The Global Ethic can also be an effective instrument for finding common ground and promoting public education. It thus offers a potentially powerful tool for dialogue and teaching in a wide range of settings, and a positive mechanism for highlighting the importance and strength of shared values and norms against a perception of diversity and difference among individuals and communities.

EXPLORING DIFFERENCES

Questions of ethical values are, however, not always as straightforward and simple as the Global Ethic would suggest. Public debate often emphasizes cultural differences that impede institutional arrangements to ensure integrity. And different faith traditions as well as cultures do bring shades of difference to interpretations of public morality and integrity.

Yet fairly simplistic assumptions sometimes underlie supposed differences in policy approaches, and holding these assumptions up to the light can be beneficial. As an illustration, thoughtful analysts, including World Bank economists, at one stage suggested that Confucian family values militated against effective public norms of accountability and objectivity, for example with their perceived emphasis on hierarchies in society which might militate against entrepreneurial behavior. These analysts were pessimistic about the development prospects of Asian societies as a result. Of course, history has prompted a sharp reassessment of these contentions. Similar arguments have been advanced relative to traditional African religions with the high value they accord to traditional hierarchies and obligations to the community.

Similarly, some see honesty as a culturally varying virtue. However, when experience is examined and people are actually asked about their values, such differences often fade or decline in importance.

Nonetheless, differences—and above all perceptions of difference—are worth examining. Significant benefit might be drawn from deeper exploration of traditions, teachings, parables, and practice among different faith traditions related to ethics, accountability, and integrity.

At least two dimensions bear scrutiny. First, a comparative exploration, drawing on theology, of how different faith traditions approach corruption could yield useful insights. The objective would be to define not only areas of common ground but also significant differences, and matters that deserve closer examination. For example, there could be merit in exploring faith teachings about conflicts of interest and hierarchies of values in personal and professional relationships.

Second, there has been little systematic exploration of how religious traditions, leaders, and institutions have confronted governance issues in development programs, particularly with a comparative focus. Examining how Christian, Buddhist, Muslim, and Hindu leaders have diagnosed problems of corruption in a range of countries and communities could prove instructive.

Thoughtful faith leaders from different traditions could usefully reflect on norms of public behavior and their links to faith traditions. Such exercises have yielded important insights on poverty, labor standards, and health care.[5] A similar set of consultations on public integrity and account-ability could produce significant insights and guidelines for setting standards and guiding public officials. Differences among traditions—both obvious and blunt, and deep and subtle—can also suggest solutions well-honed and adapted to local settings, as well as avenues for construc-tive dialogue.

MOBILIZING THE ORGANIZATIONS OF THE WORLD'S FAITHS

Faith organizations have vast networks and infrastructure at their disposal, including communications channels that are often sophisticated. While these institutions have sometimes actively mobilized to address corruption and public integrity, as was the case in Malawi and Kenya, their potential has not yet been fully tapped. It would be useful to explore why faith leaders and networks have been somewhat reticent to highlight these problems, and what kinds of training might help mobilize them against corruption.

The June 2006 conference on corruption organized by the Vatican's Pontifical Council on Justice and Peace underscored the potential for organizing the vast network of the Roman Catholic Church. Such efforts might find echoes in other faith organizations. Other avenues to pursue include finding ways to encourage a more effective prophetic voice by spiritual leaders and their vast communications networks. Ensuring more explicit dialogue and focus by faith-based NGOs, churches, and spiritual movements might also spur them to engage more actively in "integrity alliances."

The major global interfaith organizations—including the World Conference of Religions for Peace, the Parliament of the World Religions, the United Religions Initiative, and the WFDD—could offer important vehicles for addressing public integrity and accountability, if they chose to make those challenges a priority. Each organization is increasingly engaging in practical and prophetic work on social justice, so public integrity and good governance would seem to offer a logical extension of this work.

EDUCATION AND RELIGIOUS TEACHING

Faith institutions play significant roles in many dimensions of education. Churches and mosques run extensive school networks directly, they offer

Sunday or Friday religious education classes to both children and adults, and they influence public school curricula in important ways.

An important question is how faiths can build on these efforts to advance the cause of integrity and good governance. Model programs, case studies, and best practices in effective teaching of ethics in educational systems at all levels—especially those that illuminate the roles that faith institutions can and do play—could provide the answer. Potential arenas for such activities include teaching through preaching, programs in faith-run schools, direct and indirect contributions to teaching values in public school systems, the curricula of theological training institutions, and communication through faith-led media at local, national, and international levels.

If faith leaders and institutions are to fight corruption effectively by both influencing public policy and engaging in activities such as monitoring development programs, those involved need good information. This includes information on what works in fighting corruption, and access to information on effective monitoring efforts. Workshops on governance would equip faith leaders and communities with better tools and foster more active engagement.

INTEGRITY WITHIN FAITH COMMUNITIES AND PROGRAMS

To preach and teach about corruption, one's own house must be in order, and that applies equally to faith leaders and communities. A practical, straightforward avenue for action to assure such integrity is more transparent record keeping and clearer mechanisms for accountability within religious communities themselves. Exemplary cases of clear public accountability and monitoring of community resources within faith communities do exist. However, their accounts, audits, and reports are often fairly rudimentary, and demands by development agencies for adherence to strict procurement, monitoring, and reporting practices can generate resistance.

Faith communities often maintain that such processes are too cumbersome and intrusive, and that they constitute a breach of the trust that binds their communities. However, demands for greater accountability are becoming more important as faith communities become more active in programs to combat HIV/AIDS and malaria, and receive external funds on a significant scale.

Focusing on "corruption-proofing" faith-run programs also offers the potential for teasing out some reticence among religious leaders to address corruption. While some religious leaders in Africa are unambiguous about the evils of corruption, others tend to see the problem in more nuanced ways—holding that both "briber" and "bribee" share responsibility. The concern of these religious leaders is that critics of corruption have focused unduly on those who accept bribes, who normally reside in poor countries, and too little on the patterns and mechanisms that allow those in rich countries to bribe with impunity.

FAITH ENGAGEMENT IN MONITORING POVERTY AND PUBLIC SECTOR EXPENDITURES

Faith institutions have actively participated in the poverty reduction strategy process supported by the World Bank and the International Monetary Fund in a range of countries, sometimes as a direct outcome of prior activism on debt relief (for example, in Zambia). Such engagement involves faith leaders in key policy decisions on poverty and social spending, and opens pragmatic avenues for monitoring public programs.

This engagement is an essential part of the widely acclaimed participatory approach to creating the antipoverty strategies. However, much remains to be done to make this engagement truly effective, including both an opening to effective participation by faith leaders and enabling faith actors to gain the knowledge and confidence that they need to be well positioned to discuss issues in terms of economics and finance, where they might lack training and experience.

Several prominent African religious leaders are taking active roles in public alliances to fight corruption and raise standards of integrity. At the national level, examples include Malawi and Kenya, where such leaders include Rev. Mulava of the Kenya Council of Churches. At the regional and continent level, the nascent Africa Monitor, inspired in large measure by Archbishop Njongonkulu Ndungane of Cape Town, offers significant promise (see Chapter 2). Africa Monitor aims to tap clear local roots and the respect accorded to the Anglican Church to develop effective mechanisms for monitoring public services and expenditures.

INTEGRITY, ETHICS, AND ACCOUNTABILITY: HIV/AIDS AND GENDER-LINKED VIOLENCE

In institutional settings, "ethics" commonly focuses on rules governing spending, procurement, and conflicts of interest. This is particularly the case today, in light of the intense spotlight on lapses in public honesty. Discussions with leaders and thinkers from different faith traditions underscore, however, to what extent some communities find the rule-grounded framing and definition of ethics and integrity wanting. For example, a discussion of flawed procurement turns imperceptibly toward questions of equity, and touches raw nerves that turn on fairness. Are the rules of the game truly open to all or are they stacked against local and small participants? Norms, standards, and rules are vitally important, as are honest and forthright efforts to address the broader ethical issues embedded in contemporary debates about globalization.

A broader framing of ethics, accountability, and integrity can link pragmatic concern about the management of public finances to the drive for equity and social justice, including, for example, wider access to health care. A broader framing can also encourage a willingness to confront, boldly, long-hidden problems such as domestic violence, and discriminatory treatment of women within households and communities.

Too often lacking in all these debates is a desire to promote greater understanding, respect, and curiosity—to seek out common concerns and values, and to explore areas of significant difference. Given the present-day urgency of fighting global poverty, which is so closely linked to international peace and security, we can no longer afford such divides. All must come to the table to devise and agree on ethical standards, and to build better mechanisms for enforcement and accountability.

NOTES

1. For more on the 11th International Anti-Corruption Conference in Seoul in May 2003, see http://unpan1.un.org/intradoc/groups/public/documents/APCITY/UNPAN019160.pdf.

2. See, for example, the cardinal's statement at a meeting of the International Development Bank, at http://www.iadb.org/news/articledetail.cfm?artID=1930&language=EN&arttype=WS.

3. See http://www.stt.lt/lt/files/global_forum3_on_fighting_corupption.pdf.

4. For the text of the Global Ethic, see http://astro.temple.edu/~dialogue/Center/
kung.htm. See also Hans Kung, ed., 1996, *Yes to a Global Ethic* (New York: Continuum); and Hans Kung, 1993, *Global Responsibility: In Search of a New World
Ethic* (New York: Continuum). See also *Report on the Conclusions and Recommendations by a High Level Expert Group on In Search of Global Ethical Standards*,
chaired by Helmut Schmidt, March 22–24, 1996, at http://www.interaction
council.org.

5. The WFDD organized consultations on approaches to poverty in 1999–2000;
see http://www.WFDD.org.uk. The International Labor Organization and the
WCC organized consultations on decent work; see Dominique Peccoud, 2004,
Philosophical and Spiritual Perspectives on Decent Work (Geneva: ILO).

20

From Community Initiatives to Movements
Faith-Inspired Work for Social Transformation

I believe Gandhi's answer would have been a concern for the poorest of the poor; in moving towards a simpler life style, a life style which ultimately can be shared with everyone; an emphasis on truth and non-violence; and a fearlessness to fight for issues of ecological security and sustainability. —Kamla Chowdhry

The cases presented in this book (and its predecessor volume, *Mind, Heart, and Soul in the Fight against Poverty*) were chosen because they reflect partnerships that engage both secular development and faith-inspired actors and institutions. Thus each example represents a bridge linking the strengths and resources of different partners, even as it reveals the challenges involved in joining actors from often quite different worlds.

In parallel with efforts to assemble these stories, two leaders of the WFDD, Wendy Tyndale and Kamla Chowdhry, were also exploring case studies of faith involvement in development work—but selected based on different criteria. Their cases focus on faith-inspired movements and organizations that are working from the inspiration of their beliefs, without necessarily engaging in partnerships with development institutions. These organizations are very different, one from another, but all seek to change the economic and social life of communities along idealistic and spiritual lines. The objective of the work led by Wendy Tyndale and Kamla Chowdhry was both to understand and document such work better and, specifically, to explore common themes in faith-inspired approaches to the challenges of poverty and development.

Several of the movements and organizations studied are well known because of their large size and impact, while others are less visible. However, knowledge about the actual work of these entities and its effects on economic and social change—like information on the efforts of faith-inspired organizations that focus more specifically on development—is limited. A fundamental and only partially answered question is how and how far these movements and organizations differ materially from secular international development agencies and national governments and the better known faith-based organizations (like Catholic Relief Services or Islamic Relief) that work on development. The premise of this book and of the work of Wendy Tyndale and Kamla Chowdhry is that we can learn much from these unique entities—many of them remarkably successful, even transformational. This chapter provides a brief overview of their work and highlights the major conclusions suggested by their experience.

TWO SETS OF CASE STUDIES

The case studies fall into two main groups, one led by Wendy Tyndale, the other by Kamla Chowdhry,[1] although there is some overlap. The two women worked closely together over many years as colleagues and friends (Kamla Chowdhry died in December 2005), but their professional paths and thus approaches to the case study work was somewhat different in focus and style. However, they worked together on many of the case studies, with teams drawn from different parts of the world and, by design, different faith traditions. The teams met several times as small groups to review findings.

In February 2004, many in the case study group joined a workshop in Dehli—jointly organized by WFDD and the Vikram Sarabhai Foundation (which Kamla Chowdhry founded and led) and supported by the Ford Foundation—which examined the full range of case studies.[2] The workshop focused on the underlying question: what motivated the different faith-led movements and programs? The aim was to discern common elements and differences—and, above all, the visions of development that motivated and propelled the organizations and their leaders. Relationships with governments and secular development organizations were also a common theme of the discussions.[3]

The analysis led by Wendy Tyndale is reflected in *Visions of Development: Faith-Based Initiatives.*[4] This collection, a compilation of case studies from a variety of authors, examines the work of 13 faith and faith-inspired movements in different regions of the world and draws on the work of many who undertook individual case studies. The work of Kamla Chowdhry, which was based in Delhi and supported in part by the Ford Foundation, is brought together in a book edited by Makarand Paranjape entitled *Dharma and Development: The Future of Survival,*[5] which again reflects a distillation of the case study work. The book *Dharma and Development* is broader in its discussion of faith dimensions of poverty work, with several general discussions, though most of the chapters focus on what it terms a "sacred India" and the subcontinent, whereas *Visions of Development* is centered on case studies and its coverage is worldwide. However, at the heart of both works is a focus on looking at different, faith-inspired approaches to development and an effort to shed light on remarkable work by a set of extraordinary organizations, ranging from the Swaminarayan experience in Gujarat, to the Brahma Kumaris, to small projects in Cameroon, and human rights work in South America.

All these case studies fall somewhere between storytelling and analysis: they reflect an intense effort to listen and learn, and far less to judge. The documentation is done with great care, as well as great respect. These are not quantitative evaluations, but rather mark an effort to see through the eyes of participants and organizations how they define their objectives and path in their own terms. These books make clear that the faith-inspired organizations studied differ markedly from secular development organizations in how they regard development itself, as well as the processes that lead to change. A thread that runs through them all is the inspiration of Mahatma Gandhi's work, which the editors and the faith leaders in the case studies mention often.

TYNDALE'S *VISIONS OF DEVELOPMENT*

The case studies in Wendy Tyndale's edited volume cover a wide range of organizations, but all have a deep spiritual motivation, and all work in very poor communities.[6] The main criterion for selection was not that these organizations performed spiritual or religious work per se, but that they were changing people's lives for the better, or had the potential to do so.

The organizations tend to describe their work in language that differs significantly from that of development organizations—notably in their focus on life purpose. However, their work overlaps with development institutions in many arenas, from ensuring adequate water supplies to women's empowerment and rights. The central theme that runs through each and every case study resonates with contemporary secular ideas on development: the importance of empowering communities and basing development plans on their cultures and preferences.

The 13 organizations fall into five groups. The first includes two examples of very large grassroots movements, one Hindu in origin, the other Buddhist: the Swadhaya movement in India, and the Sarvodaya Sharmadana movement in Sri Lanka (see Chapter 10). Spirituality has given each a particular vision of development. Swadhyaya is often described as a movement of social regeneration (*swadhaya* is a Sanskrit word meaning "self-study," which implies self-empowerment and a life-changing experience). Both movements focus more on culture and meaning than on equity, but they do not distance themselves from what can be described as "impersonal"—or material—wealth. Both work through thousands of volunteers, and represent a new kind of nonsectarian and creative social movement. While their core motivation is spiritual, these organizations have come to focus on many development tasks in practice, particularly the challenge of providing livelihoods for some of their regions' most impoverished people.

The second group includes three small grassroots organizations working in Brazil, Cameroon, and Guatemala, all led by courageous women who are inspired and empowered at least in part by ancient spiritual traditions. These organizations struggle to improve the lives of very poor people who have been abandoned by virtually all other segments of society. Spirituality is a common source of strength and guidance, though different values do lead to different development priorities among the three.

Zarkan Zoumountsi is a Muslim organization in Cameroon driven by the goal of environmental conservation. Born in 1995 in Yaoundé, its name means "chain of solidarity." The organization's wide-ranging activities include resolving disputes among Muslims and between Christians and Muslims, as well as stopping the spread of HIV/AIDS.

Terreiro Ile Axe Omin Funko is a Candomblé—or spirit worship—organization working in the city of Salvador, Brazil, with a focus on water. Its name focuses on traditions around the importance of water in the African Yoruba culture that Brazil inherited. The organization has also come to fight for people's rights to education and other services. The third organization is Awakatan, a women's group with a Christian and Mayan focus that works in the mountains of Guatemala. Education is its principal focus, but it is also engaged in women's health. (See box 20.1, which highlights another Christian/Mayan partnership.)

BOX 20.1
MAYAN SPIRITUALITY MEETS CATHOLIC TEACHING
IN SAN MARCOS, GUATEMALA

The Pastoral Social of the Diocese of San Marcos, in the mountains of western Guatemala, is a Catholic organization wrestling with how to integrate ancient cultures and beliefs with the fast-paced forces of modernization. Most Mayans are Catholics, yet they also hold dear their traditional culture, including its practices and rituals. The practical question today is whether and how a partnership between what were long seen as cultures and religions in contradiction can produce an authentic, locally grounded development path that promises a better way of life.

The backdrop is a region that is desperately poor. San Marcos has been left behind in many respects: at least a third of adults are illiterate. Visible and dramatic challenges to the environment are apparent in erosion and disappearing forests. Social problems are never far

(Box continues on the following page.)

(box continued)

away, as the region works to reconcile tensions that are a legacy of long years of armed conflict. The pull of modern life—in the capital city and the United States—is strong, as are pressures to adopt what is seen as a monolithic cultural model alien to the values and traditions of ancient Mayan culture.

In the face of these pressures, the Catholic bishop of San Marcos, Alvarro Ramazzini, and Mayan leaders are deeply supportive of a new approach to development that binds the best of Catholic teaching with genuine respect for Mayan traditions and values. Wendy Tyndale, who works with the Pastoral, highlights the powerful synergy that can result from a creative and compassionate joining of Catholic and Mayan traditions. The commandment of Christ to love our neighbor, she says, is mirrored in the Mayan concept that "my face is your face. When I look at you I see myself."

A dynamic and respected leader, Alvarro Ramazzini not only consciously navigates Catholic teaching and traditional beliefs, but he is ready to mobilize the Church's resources to support the new vision. Thus the Pastoral has galvanized people to contest the allocation of new mining licenses, and to frame their objections in persuasive terms that document the damage to people and land that will result. He also supports residents in arguing in local and municipal councils for more development funding for their region. This work has helped frame an alternative vision that promotes security of land tenure in a region where land titles are obscure, and where poor people rarely have formal rights to the land they farm.

The Pastoral also supports a solidarity fund that is locally based, but that echoes successful microcredit programs. This fund stresses savings, clear criteria for providing loans that emphasize hard work and respect within the community, and both solidarity and compassion in addressing problem cases. Meanwhile, new women's councils are building on ancient Mayan traditions that emphasize learning from each other by offering training in reading, writing, accounting, and tailoring.

San Marcos faces difficult challenges of history, geography, the ever-present pull of migration, and a "system" that seems always stacked against those without power, wealth, and influence. What the work of the Pastoral and local Mayan leaders brings is above all hope that a better future can be built on a foundation of respect for the people, including their complex identities and authentic culture.

Note: This box is drawn from exchanges with Wendy Tyndale, former director of the World Faiths Development Dialogue, and from her November 2006 article "Mayan and Catholic Spiritual Traditions: A Foundation for Development in the Mountains of Guatemala," *Mountain Research and Development* 26 (4): 315–318.

The third group of cases includes two integrated development programs that work with tribal mountain people in India and Cameroon. Both have strong ties to the religious traditions of their founders, who came from outside the regions, but both have also developed an ethos and approach deeply grounded in local traditions. They are examples of religion "brought down to earth."

Vivekananda Girijana Kalyana Kendra is a private voluntary organization working among the Soliga tribes in Karnataka in southern India. It was founded by a Hindu doctor who arrived with his own ideas but learned to adapt them to what the people wanted. Tokombere in Cameroon was founded as a Christian missionary venture but similarly transformed itself to address the complex needs of the community. Both organizations focus on health and education. The leaders hold that there can be "no development without faith," which means "not a step forward without knowing where we come from and what we walk towards."[7] If the project is a tree, the roots are local tradition, the Gospel is the sap, the health project is the trunk, and the different branches are structures created over time.

The fourth group comprises three women's organizations with a similar ethos but very different faith origins—Muslim in Ethiopia and Indonesia, and Bahá'í in India. Their vision of development links a faith-inspired concept of justice with a passion for getting rid of poverty and injustice in all aspects of society, including the family.

The Addis Ababa Muslim Women's Council began with a focus on women's rights and a determination to stand up for those rights. The council cites a major lesson: that women can be empowered only if they believe in their own strength. Thus a consciousness-raising process is essential. Convincing men to participate in the program is also essential, so they become aware of their own responsibility.

Nahdlatul Ulama (NU) in Indonesia—the world's largest Muslim association—includes two women's associations, Muslimat NU and Fatayat NU. NU initially opposed Indonesia's birth control programs, especially when agencies seemed to be pursuing a coercive approach. Faced with opposition, the government took steps to involve the two women's groups, and this eventually led to a transformation of the governmental program itself into a broader family-planning effort. According to Christopher Candland and Siti Nurjanah, the story of NU's involvement in national family planning "shows ... how Islam can be a powerful resource for women's empowerment.... Islamic associations helped Indonesians to achieve one of the highest mother and infant survival rates among lower-income developing countries."[8] The program builds on respect for families and values—often attributed to its tie to the NU women's organizations.

The third program is a Bahá'í women's program in Barli, India, with a focus on education. The group has created a training institute that sets out to transform the lives of young women—and succeeds in doing so.

In all three cases, women were motivated to take action when they observed the suffering of women around them, and concluded that oppression and disempowerment of women were contrary to the principles of their religious traditions. All focus on the balance between rights and responsibilities and seek to include men in their programs. All struggle to balance the interests of the community and the individual, all work with technology as one element of transformation, and all focus on human welfare and the care of nature.

The fifth group includes three organizations from very different parts of the world—Chile, India, and Thailand—that are deliberately political and that focus on action on behalf of persecuted, marginalized, and outcast people. Their faith inspirations are Buddhist and Christian, but all three organizations have created their own path within their tradition. The thread running through them is spiritually inspired solidarity as a way of life, and freedom as a deeply held underlying value. All three movements were founded by people who allowed themselves to become fully aware of uncomfortable truths. For them, compassion for others transforms a sense of solidarity from a rhetorical slogan into a truly uniting force.

The engaged Buddhist movement reflects the inspiration of Sulak Sivaraksa, who with firm determination has worked against what he regards as the perils of modernization. His gentle nonviolent anarchism bypasses state power and works to create self-reliant communities.[9] He pursue his work at many levels, from modeling a simpler way of life to countering the pressures of modernity, from protesting dam construction to offering a Buddhist perspective in international settings.

The National Fishworkers Forum is a spiritually inspired movement in the Indian state of Kerala. Its origins are Christian: the Latin Catholic Bishop of Trivandrum originally founded a village for fisher families that grew as an independent cooperative, accompanied by committed priests and nuns. The forum has emerged as both an example and an advocate, serving as a catalyst for a movement of fish workers who aim to improve their communities. Over time the group has broadened its faith focus, and today it is molded by Tagorean religiosity (Tagore is a Hindu mystic poet) as well as more mainstream Hinduism. The forum thus offers an example of an all-embracing spirituality.

The Sebastian Acevedo Movement in Chile emerged from a Catholic community whose members determined to stand up against torture, although the Catholic archbishop was not initially convinced that this was wise or right. The group took its name from a man who set himself alight in November 1983 to protest torture.

Arvind Sharma's introduction to *Visions of Development* calls the potential of the case studies revolutionary, because they focus on non-economic factors in development.[10] Their premise is that spiritual and moral development can lead to material development, and, more broadly, that a spiritual vision of the world is essential to understand completely the aspirations and motivations that drive many communities. Sharma concludes with a piece of advice attributed to the Hindu mystic Ramakrishna (1836–1886): "Religion is like a cow. It kicks, but it also gives milk." Sharma suggests that the cases show how religious movements do give milk, but they also have a utopian vision that might "make the land flow with milk and honey."[11]

The 13 case studies all illustrate the regenerative power of religion when it is brought down to earth and made real, so that people's beliefs are intertwined with practical matters. Religion is not primarily about an abstraction or transcendence. Rather, it involves a host of activities that are part of the daily life of communities and people, practiced through rituals, symbols, and customs that are usually forms of communication with the divine (thanksgiving, petition, penitence), as well as more contemplative, meditative processes that are a means of heightening one's awareness of the presence of God.

Both Tyndale and Sharma address the question of what these movements and leaders can tell us about religious fundamentalism, as the views of some of those studied might be so described. The cases do illustrate how fundamentalism can be a reaction against secularization and economic, political, and cultural globalization.[12] Sharma suggests that the work highlights a conundrum: that some fundamentalist movements which might be seen as authoritarian or hierarchical may succeed in empowering their followers more than their secular counterparts (because of their powerful human pull). More broadly, however, the cases highlight the diversity and dynamism of all the faiths. They show that no single group can monopolize a religion, nor can repressive laws, dogmas, and practices control the essence of a spiritual or faith experience.

A central call arising from the work is to secular aid agencies, to understand the nature of religion if they want to work with faith-based organizations. They cannot do so through intellectual study of sociological dimensions alone. Religion is intertwined with all dimensions of life, and its emotional and cultural as well as very practical aspects need to be lived and appreciated. The spiritual orientations of the groups are similar in many respects, but some aspects are also very different, and understanding those differences yields insights.

An example is the basic distinction between cyclical and linear understandings of the process of life. The cyclical view of Hinduism and Buddhism is very different from the linear view of the Abrahamic religions, for example: Buddhists tend to see all things as a flow reflecting causes and conditions. All religions are inherently syncretic: they entail an amalgamation of their own received wisdom and beliefs with those of indigenous cultures and other religions. The movements cannot be understood or appreciated outside their social, political, and historical context.

The core messages from the case studies are twofold: that a deep understanding of poverty requires understanding its religious context, and that the values underlying each faith-based program need to be explored. The case studies speak to different levels of perception, and different ways of understanding. They also highlight how adherents of faiths view secular approaches to development. Tyndale often heard adherents express bewilderment about the motivations and seemingly quasi-religious mission of secular development agencies. Most significant, the models that drive secular development efforts are generally assumed and rarely justified.[13] This argues for greater self-awareness, and consciousness of impact and preconceptions, among secular development specialists.

DHARMA AND DEVELOPMENT

The case studies that Kamla Chowdhry inspired focus on large movements that mobilize millions of people in India and Sri Lanka. Although based in specific countries, these movements have often inspired global activities and followings, in some instances on a very large scale. While *Dharma and Development* highlights a few such movements, and stresses how little is known about them, the editor suggests that there are at least a hundred stories of successful and large organizations like them. The book's hypothesis is that spiritual organizations are often unaware that what they are doing is development, but that they often exert a more positive and lasting impact than government and secular development organizations.

These movements often differ markedly in approach, style, and philosophy, but they also share concerns and orientations. They work with the poor, and often use a different language to talk about poverty. They are concerned in the first instance with inner change, and the underlying philosophy of what it is to be human, and they believe that to serve other human beings is to serve God. Most maintain a high degree of integrity and enthusiasm, and many are also managed remarkably efficiently.

The case studies ask a basic question: "What makes these guys tick?" and focus especially on what motivates and inspires the founders and leaders. The movements all exhibit charismatic leadership, and that helps explain their extremely dedicated cadres of workers. More broadly, they have developed remarkable organizational strategies, mobilize huge funds, and communicate in an exemplary yet often unique manner—often through very modern methods.

The Swaminarayan movement, founded in Gujarat by Sri Swami Narayan, is now a remarkable global movement that mobilizes millions. The case study focuses on the remarkable juxtaposition in its messages and work between traditional spiritual Hinduism and engagement with the secular and modern. The case emphasizes the movement's noteworthy work on water: the "miracle" of producing water supplies for poor communities. In essence, for the Swaminarayan movement, spirituality and social service are inseparable. There are many seeming contradictions. At one level, with its enormous temples, monks who entirely avoid women, focus on spiritual trance, and acceptance to a degree of caste distinctions, the movement appears to be a rather conservative branch of modern Hinduism. Yet viewed in a different light it is a force for social transformation, taking an active part in relief activities and urging followers to work hard at their daily pursuits.

The movement works through the Bochasanwasi Shri Akshar Purushottam Swaminarayan Sanstha (BAPS), based in Ahmedabad. BAPS administers a huge organization that includes temples, youth centers, hospitals, educational institutions, tree-planting programs, well and dam construction, and far more. The movement claims to have helped 251,000 people quit addictions. It is well financed, in part through contributions (normally 10 percent of income) from its members. Five charitable trusts support close to 500 centers worldwide, visited by some 150,000 pilgrims each day. Thus the movement is both spiritual and social. It is also bewildering in its complexity, with subsects that are constantly reshaping.[14]

The case study of the Ramakrishna Mission focuses on its sanitation work in the Medinipur district of West Bengal. Founded in 1897 by Swami Vivekananda, the movement is a fellowship concerned with both the material and spiritual welfare of the masses. Its headquarters near Calcutta include a hospital, dispensary, college, primary and secondary schools, an academy for the blind, and an agriculture and animal husbandry training center. The mission works all over the world in a wide variety of efforts, including many with the character of relief and development.

The Brahma Kumaris describe themselves as catalysts of socio-spiritual change. The movement has grown at an extraordinary pace, from a small community of 350 women in provincial Sindh 50 years ago to at least 700,000 followers in 80 countries today. And it continues to grow fast. Founded by Lekhraj Kriplani, a Sindhi jeweler, it is a rare organization that is led and managed by women. It believes deeply in empowering people and promoting values. While much of its work focuses on a clearly spiritual practice, its social work with prisoners and its medical practice and research are also remarkable, seen from a secular development perspective. As in the other cases, the movement is well funded and displays a remarkable power to organize people. Still, its leaders assess their effectiveness and efficiency based on their impact on people's lives, not on numbers.

The Chinmaya Mission pursues activism based on the Hindu Vedanta philosophy. Its founder, Swami Chinmayanda, looked to the wisdom of the Vedanta as a practical means for spiritual growth. Today the mission is clearly also a development organization, with 280 centers all over the world, 30,000 paid staff members, and far more volunteers. It has a loose federal structure, with the Central Chinmaya Mission Trust headquartered in Mumbai. The mission describes its calling as working to reawaken Hinduism by providing values-based spiritual education, and contends that by changing themselves, people can change the lives of others. The mission touches vast numbers of people through its projects and services.

Mother Teresa's story and example are well known and widely honored, notably through the 1979 Nobel Peace Prize and her beatification by Pope John Paul II in 2003. Not without criticism, Mother Teresa's legacy lives on in the work of the Missionaries of Charity. The extraordinary reach of this movement is less well known than its founding Mother, but it has grown from a small leprosy center to a network of several hundred homes caring for those in great need, in 123 countries.

Svadhyaya is a mass movement inspired by the teachings of Pandurang Sastri Athavle. Its former leader, Svadhyaya afer Dada, was an extraordinary force and took the organization in many new directions. The movement focuses on translating theory into practice, with devotion expressed through action. It has concentrated on empowering dalits (untouchables) and working for women's equality, with its philosophy emphasizing the value of cooperation. Its highly practical work includes mounting cleanup campaigns, improving public health, and planting trees; its school near Ahmedabad trains farmer philosophers to be agents of change in rural areas. The movement's schemes are designed to bring people together and foster community, and it works to create *apaurushiya Lakshmi,* or impersonal wealth (wealth created by diligence and hard work but involving the community not the individual).

The case study of the Sarvodaya Sharmadana movement in Sri Lanka overlaps with Tyndale's description and the partnership approach highlighted in this book (see Chapter 10). The movement's inspirational leadership, its meshing of spiritual and practical, and its organizational genius have much in common with the characteristics of other movements. The description of the National Forum of Fishworkers in *Dharma and Development* similarly overlaps with Tyndale's summary in *Visions of Development.*

Sri Sathya Sai Baba leads a movement that focuses on service and spirituality and has attracted a following of millions across the world. Born of the Hindu tradition, its broad spirituality today has universal appeal, stressing love and service. The leader became known for miracles that changed people's lives, but the movement now looks to "modern miracles," such as ensuring drinking water supplies. The vast spiritual organization operates some 8,000 Sai Seva Centers, with at least one in almost every district of India and almost every country. The movement focuses on both spiritual development and education, and it runs colleges, schools, cultural programs, and rural development schemes. As with the other cases, this movement resists the pull of quantification: "I value quality, not quantity," Sai Baba says.[15]

The final case study explores the Integral Education movement in Orissa, India. This movement arose in response to widespread perceptions that the public education system is failing, and that the explosion of private education often does not meet the needs of the poor—and to combat apathy in facing those problems. The movement follows principles enunciated by Sri Aurobindo, who founded the first Integral Education center in 1970. Today the movement's New Life Education Trust runs more than 261 schools and promotes a new kind of pedagogy that counsels loving and caring relationships between teacher and taught, and involves parents, students, and communities.

A HOLISTIC VIEW OF DEVELOPMENT

The diverse experiences highlighted in these case studies defy simplistic conclusions, but they do cry out for further study and exploration. All the movements promote the idealistic notion that a change of consciousness will enable people to build more just and harmonious societies that, in the words of the engaged Buddhists, are no longer "open to greed, hatred, and delusion." The groups focus on the unacceptability of material destitution but see development as a holistic process that must embrace all elements of human existence. Material development is seen as an essential counterpart to spiritual development because, as the Buddha put it, "if stomachs are empty, there is no ear for preaching."

The practical work performed by these spiritually inspired groups embraces a wide range of activities, including building houses, roads, and fishponds; planting trees; setting up small businesses; promoting local crafts; and providing services such as education and health care. These movements contend that such development activities cannot occur at the expense of either spiritual or traditional cultural values. Economic development programs will be sustainable only if they address the cultural, spiritual, political, social, and environmental dimensions of life.

These movements highlight education again and again as the key to development, but this does not imply merely attending school. Education must enable people not only to get jobs and earn money but also to open their minds and "understand the world." In this context, development must promote positive change while opposing obstacles to it, such as corruption and exploitation.

BOX 20.2
A PARTNERSHIP TO ADDRESS SENEGAL'S NUMBER-ONE SOCIAL ISSUE: GETTING CHILDREN OFF THE STREETS

As many as 30,000 children live on the streets of Senegalese cities—a substantial number in a country with a mostly rural population of some 12 million. Many factors drive these children—mostly boys—to the streets, with poverty foremost among them. Madani Tall, the World Bank's country director for Senegal, calls street children "the number-one social issue in Senegal." A particular aspect of this phenomenon—young boys who beg for food each day as part of their education through Koranic schools—has galvanized a new partnership in support of change.

Senegal's Koranic schools, known as Daaras, trace their history to the earliest days of Islam in the country, when Islamic schools were an essential part of each community's social fabric. Parents sent their children to work in the fields of the Koranic teacher, or *marabout*, in return for a religious education and preparation for adult life.

When a succession of droughts in the 1970s and 1980s led to economic and social upheaval, many marabouts and their pupils, or *talibés*, moved from their villages to large cities. There many students began to beg to provide a source of revenue for their marabouts. The practice is dangerous, and the children suffer many health risks from malnutrition and unhygienic living conditions, not to mention psychological scarring.

Some marabouts say they do not have the financial means to take care of the boys, and justify their exploitation by saying that begging teaches humility. However, many talibés are abused, and few who beg complete their childhood equipped with a good formal education and reasonable prospects for a better life. Thus the system often leads to what are essentially child exploitation networks reminiscent of Dickens' portrayal of Oliver Twist's London. Senegal's religious leaders have denounced the practice, lamenting that the country's noble tradition of teaching young boys the Koran has been distorted and exploited.

Despite considerable advocacy on behalf of street children, various concerned groups have so far not ended the phenomenon. Government laws designed to protect families and children are too sporadically enforced. The public has become complacent at the sight of boys as young as four begging on city streets, and many unwittingly encourage the situation through their own charity, compassion, or whatever motivates them to give the children money, food, or other small gifts.

New Hope

A promising new partnership to support the street children and return them to school has brought together a wide array of organizations—both Senegalese and international. Launched in late 2006, the Street Children's Campaign Partnership has won active support from the Senegalese government, UNICEF, the African Development Bank, the French Cooperation, the International Labor Organization, national and international celebrities, religious leaders and other members of civil society, NGOs, the media, and the private sector.

The World Bank's Senegal office has been active in the partnership. As a first step, a steering committee led by the country office studied the problem and sought to raise awareness of it. Staff members stress that the problem has many different facets, and can be solved only by collective effort. Such an effort must include the government, focusing on policy, leadership, and law enforcement; religious leaders, highlighting the vital importance of education, and helping address underlying the problems that cause parents to avoid public schools; and the private sector, focusing on the transition from school to good jobs.

Senegal's president, Abdoulaye Wade, has lent his personal support to the campaign. It will start with a pilot project in Kolda, Tamba, and Matam—the three main cities where the majority of street children live. The pilot program will transport some 500 of these children back home, or place those who cannot return home in a dozen rehabilitated residential centers.

(Box continues on the following page.)

(box continued)

A major communications campaign is planned to raise public awareness by working with children to produce songs, poems, and artwork for public service announcements, and the use of recreational activities to draw vulnerable children into the pilot program. Women will be mobilized to act as godmothers of the street children, giving them occasional food, clothing, and a wash, and, where possible, initiating dialogue with mothers of talibés to facilitate their reintegration into the family.

This campaign illustrates the complexity of a single development issue, and the diversity of partners with contributions to make in solving it—from mothers and teachers to the worlds of government, business, and faith.

Note: This discussion draws on materials of UNICEF and the World Bank Senegal office, and benefited from comments by Madani Tall and Maurizia Tovo.

BOX 20.3
TURKEY'S STREET CHILDREN

The number of children living or working on the streets of Turkish cities has visibly grown in recent years. Children as young as five years of age work as peddlers, garbage collectors, flower sellers, shoe-shiners, car parkers, and porters, often to supplement household income. Some come from abusive families and seek refuge on the streets. Unable to attend school, many of these children grow up with little hope of gaining certification or training for a skilled job. While on the streets, many children are also subject to maltreatment, physical and sexual abuse, disease, malnutrition, and substance abuse.

A successful project in several Turkish cities, including Diyarbakir, Adiyaman, Sanliurfa, Istanbul, and Izmir, has developed centers that provide these children with health care, nutritious meals, basic education, skills, recreation, and psychosocial support. Social workers conduct outreach and facilitate family sessions. The centers provide the children with textbooks and other materials for school, and offer after-school courses and access to a library and computer lab. The centers also offer sports and arts activities and arrange cultural events, such as visits to museums and theaters and attendance at concerts. Above all, these centers offer the children opportunities for education and job training.

A primary example is the center in Istanbul. It serves 80 boys who live on the premises, as well as other children who live at home, for a total of about 130 children. The residents—street children who live at the center for a transitional period that may last several years—are educated at nearby schools or in special courses at the center, and have access to a computer lab and an outdoor sports space. The center employs a director, two deputy directors, teachers, and social workers. Volunteers conduct workshops for the children on a regular basis

Partnership is an important program element, and the centers aim to establish good working relationships with local businesses, street merchants, and the police through outreach campaigns and seminars that encourage identification of working children and their referral to the centers. The International Labor Organization is a key partner overall as well as in each city. The centers are part of a network throughout Turkey that shares experiences. The program aims to increase awareness among local authorities of the needs of children, and to empower children and youth so that they can better chart and navigate their own future.

The American Joint Jewish Distribution Committee supports the project to improve the quality of life for working children and their families. The committee and Jewish individuals provide funds and gifts in kind, and send professionals to provide occasional training and seminars. Local partners, most of whom are Muslim, have primary responsibility for the project. Charity is a shared motivation, as are the obvious dangers to global society posed by children so visibly and tragically without hope.

Note: This box is based on information from William Recant of the American Joint Jewish Distribution Committee.

NOTES

1. Kamla Chowdhry, 2005, "The View from Gandhi's Window," in *Dharma and Development: The Future of Survival*, Makarand Paranjape, ed. (New Delhi, India: Samvad India Foundation), p. 101.

2. Wendy Tyndale worked with the WFDD from 1999 to 2005, and before that was with Christian Aid and worked as a journalist. Kamla Chowdhry had many roles in her long life, including working with the Ford Foundation in India, helping to found the Management Institute at Ahmedabad, and serving as a member of many international bodies, including the Earth Charter. She was a WFDD trustee.

3. Notes on the February 2004 workshop in Delhi are available at http://wfdd.org.uk/programmes/case_thematic.doc.

4. The questions that guided the case study work were as follows:
   • What does "development" mean to those who run and participate in the programs studied?
   • How important is the way in which the work is carried out?
   • How does the spirituality of these faith-based groups and movements influence their vision of development and ways of working?
   • Do these spiritually inspired groups and movements differ from official development agencies and secular NGOs in their vision of development and the way they work?
   • What is the relationship between these movements and their religious sponsors?
   • How do these faith-based organizations relate to their governments?

5. Wendy R. Tyndale, ed., 2006, *Visions of Development: Faith-Based Initiatives* (Aldershot, Hampshire, U.K.: Ashgate).

6. Makarand Paranjape, ed., 2005, *Dharma and Development: The Future of Survival* (New Delhi, India: Samvad India Foundation).

7. The following section includes summaries of case studies in *Visions of Development*.

8. *Visions of Development*, p. 76.

9. Christopher Candland and Siti Nurjanah, 2006 (February 2004), "Women's Empowerment through Islamic Organizations: The Role of Nahdlatul Ulama in Transforming the Government's Birth Control Programme into a Family Welfare Programme, in *Visions of Development*.

10. Many books have been written by and about Sulak Sivaraksa. An example is Sulak Sivaraksa, 1992, *Seeds of Peace: A Buddhist Vision for Renewing Society* (Berkeley, CA: Parallax), which includes a foreword by the Dalai Lama and a preface by Thich Nhat Hanh.

11. Sharma is professor of comparative religion at McGill University in Toronto.

12. *Visions of Development,* p. xiv.
13. *Visions of Development,* p. 154.
14. *Visions of Development,* p. 156.
15. See http://www.swaminarayan.org/introduction/.
16. *Dharma and Development,* p. 256.

PART **IV**

Conflict, Rebuilding, and Reconciliation

Introduction

In contemporary discussions of the role of religion in international affairs, peace and war are the most prominent topics. The core question has two faces: What roles do religious ideas and organizations play in conflicts? And what can be done to reinforce, expand, and deepen their historic roles in making and building peace? Catholic theologian Hans Kung has often reiterated a message summarized in four propositions: no peace among the nations without peace among the religions; no peace among the religions without dialogue among the religions; no dialogue among the religions without common ethical standards; and finally, no peace without a global ethic.[1] This understanding of the links among dialogue and understanding and peace and welfare explains the focus of the major world interfaith organizations and interfaith gatherings on peace among religions, and the growing body of research and advocacy on the resources faiths can devote—both individually and together—to peace.

This book does not purport to offer an academic introduction to the subject of peace building. However, two books on the topic stand out among the many dozens published in recent years. The first is a classic, produced under the direction of former diplomat and advocate Douglas Johnston, with a self-explanatory title: *Religion: The Missing Dimension of Statecraft.*[2] The second is from the Tanenbaum Center for Interreligious Understanding, *Peacemakers in Action: Profiles of Religion in Conflict Resolution.*[3] The structure and purpose of the latter are not dissimilar from those of this book, in its focus on pragmatic case studies; it highlights a wide range of creative and determined efforts of 16 religious actors working for peace in countries from Sudan to West Papua, Ethiopia to Afghanistan,

Northern Ireland to Bosnia. Among the key lessons that the book draws is the important role that women play in peace making in widely different situations.

The chapters and boxes in this section present cases of partnerships that involve numerous organizations and efforts within the common theme of active engagement in promoting reconciliation in conflict-torn areas and rebuilding peaceful societies. The challenges facing northern Uganda are monumental, and at the time of writing peace negotiations—with faith-linked participants playing central roles—were still under way. Chapter 21 focuses on the importance of religious faith and religious institutions in this deeply scarred region, and thus on their potential contributions in the vast task ahead to foster reconciliation among warring parties and rebuilding on firmer ground.

Chapter 22 presents a brief overview of the challenges of reconciliation, which are closely tied to success in post-conflict rebuilding. It highlights discussions at the 2006 Fès Forum, which looked at forgiveness and reconciliation with the dual lens of current realities in the Middle East and religious teachings of the three Abrahamic faiths, and a remarkable body of research by journalist/scholar Helena Cobban comparing very different approaches to reconciliation in several African countries—and, above all, illustrating the different roles that religion has played in each case.

Chapter 23 introduces two ambitious contemporary efforts to bridge what are termed gulfs among civilizations: a high-level United Nations report on building an "alliance of civilizations" to combat extremism and violence, and the World Economic Forum's unusual and bold initiative to create a Council of 100 leaders, whose mandate is to help understand and bridge the divide separating the Islamic world and the West.

Three short boxes present extraordinary stories that offer important lessons. In Nigeria, two courageous and creative people, one a pastor and one an imam, have come together to model and promote peaceful engagement. In India, the inspiration and teaching of Mahatma Gandhi are reignited by his grandson, Rajmohan Gandhi, who highlights the importance of his grandfather's example and passion for understanding, dialogue, and peaceful engagement among plural societies. And finally, in Brazil, Viva Rio, a nongovernmental organization working in the favelas of Rio de Janeiro, has launched a passionate and energetic interfaith movement to curb violence among youth by employing methods ranging from theater to art to Internet advocacy.

NOTES

1. *Catholic New Times*, December 15, 2002, "Hans Kung Speaks after 9/11: 'Attacking Iraq Is Likely to Worsen the Terrorist Threat.'"
2. Douglas Johnston and Cynthia Sampson, eds., 1995, *Religion: The Missing Dimension of Statecraft* (Oxford: Oxford University Press).
3. David Little, ed., 2007, *Peacemakers in Action: Profiles of Religion in Conflict Resolution* (New York: Tanenbaum Center for Interreligious Understanding).

CHAPTER **21**

Hope for Peace and Faith-Based Reconciliation in Northern Uganda

Since mid-2006, hopes for peace have been rising in northern Uganda. There is much promise there in new alliances that support reconciliation and rebuilding. Northern Uganda is a region with well-established religious institutions, and faith leaders have long been courageous advocates for peace, recognized in very different international arenas. Thus the role that religion and religious institutions can play in resolving the conflict, rebuilding the society, and ensuring reconciliation deserves special focus.

THE CONFLICT

Northern Uganda has been mired in a tragic and seemingly endless conflict for some 20 years, with the paramilitary Lord's Resistance Army (LRA) operating there and in surrounding countries. Untold lives have been lost in the fighting, and probably far more from starvation and disease. The conflict has destroyed much of the region's infrastructure,

---

This chapter is based largely on Katherine Marshall's visit to Uganda in August 2006, and on continuing discussions of the situation in northern Uganda. It benefits from discussions with many people, especially Grace Yabrudy, the World Bank country manager for Uganda, and Suleiman Namara, World Bank, Kampala.

and the economy and society are in shambles. Even when active fighting ebbs, fear of conflict is ever-present. The brutality of the conflict—which has involved the abduction of thousands of children, widespread rapes as a weapon of war, and horrendous and routine violence—has scarred virtually everyone in the region.

The conflict has also put any prospect for development, whether human, social, political, or economic, on hold. As many as 2 million people—more than 80 percent of the population—have been forced to move from villages into densely compact "camps," because they fear attack by LRA rebels, or being mistaken by Ugandan army soldiers as LRA sympathizers. Formed as temporary centers, the camps are crowded, squalid, and dangerous, with especially devastating impact on women and children.

The plight of the "night commuters" is well known: children who walk long distances to protected spaces, often sleeping on the ground, so that they will be safe from abduction. The physical misery and attendant high mortality rates are compounded by psychological stress, with almost universal trauma intertwining victims and perpetrators. In short, the camp situation is a nightmare, with obviously suffering children all around, disease and hunger, visible graves, tales of fires (the houses abut one another, so the thatch catches fire easily), alcoholism, madness, and suicide, and a tangible aura of waiting and uncertainty.

The prolonged crisis has produced a confusing plethora of institutions endeavoring to respond. Religious institutions are among the most widely present, with deep historic roots and vigorous engagement. Also jostling to cope are elected and appointed local and national officials, omnipresent security forces, UN agencies (especially the World Food Program and UNICEF) providing emergency relief, and the Northern Uganda Social Action Fund, a community development program supported by the World Bank. A bewildering array of NGOs are also offering help, such as reintegration programs for people "coming out" of the bush, including former child soldiers and abducted girls who return as mothers of several children. This remarkable work is barely alleviating the worst suffering, and an all-too-classic pattern of individual approaches, overlap, and competition is much in evidence.

THE FAITH CONTRIBUTION

The interfaith dimensions of the conflict and prospects for peace have received considerable global attention. The conflict is recognized as having deep social and religious roots, but also as inspiring courageous leadership by faith leaders. For example, global interfaith gatherings have often both lamented the conflict and celebrated the role of the Acholi Religious Leaders Peace Initiative (ARLPI), which was founded in 1998 and engages a broad interfaith group from the region. The group offered moving testimony at the global assembly of the United Religions Initiative in Rio de Janeiro in August 2002, and has participated in annual Sant'Egidio Prayer for Peace meetings.[1] ARLPI won an interfaith award at the World Parliament of Religions in Barcelona in July 2004, and the prestigious Niwano Peace Prize in May 2004.[2] The group is renowned for its persistent courage, witness, and practical support, as when bishops slept night after night in the open with the night commuters.

Archbishop of Canterbury Rowan Williams has expressed special interest in northern Uganda, highlighting the horrendous plight of child soldiers in several major statements. Cardinal Renato Raffaele Martino, of the Vatican's Pontifical Council of Justice and Peace, has often spoken movingly of his visit to northern Uganda. Ugandan religious leaders, including Catholic Archbishop Odama and Anglican Archbishop Ochola, have also spoken out vigorously in international forums. World Vision, a Christian relief and development organization, has published powerful testimonies about the plight of northern Uganda's children, as have other faith-inspired organizations.[3]

The very name of the rebel group at the center of the conflict suggests looking hard at its religious dimensions. While the Lord's Liberation Army clearly falls into the category of a cult, in terms of its theology, roots, and activities, its leaders tie their objectives to religious ideas at many levels, including a claim that a central goal is to restore religious values, based on the Ten Commandments. Understanding the conflict requires knowledge of the history and sociology of religion in its broadest dimensions, not only in northern Uganda but in the wider central African region.

Indeed, northern Uganda can aptly be described as religious in at least two senses. Most people appear to look to religion as an important source of values and identity; and the physical presence of religious institutions is pervasive. Religious institutions in all their forms have been profoundly marked by the long conflict, with battered shells of churches across the countryside at least one symbol of trauma.

Northern Uganda has complex spiritual traditions, active missionary work (past and present), a strong Catholic presence (with several different strands), successive revivalist and millenarist movements, and active interest by a range of evangelical groups today. Beliefs and practices, people and personnel (including clergy), infrastructure and networks—all have roles to play in building peace. A clear portrait of religion in northern Uganda is difficult to discern, because evidence is both fragmented and interwoven, and there appears to be much that is not clearly known or at least documented. However, the lack of concrete information should not detract from awareness of the significance of religion in the conflict, or from pursuit of faith-inspired avenues for peace and reconciliation.

The continuing suffering and stalemate have drawn mounting concern among faith leaders and laypeople. For example, speakers at the WCC assembly in Porto Alegre, Brazil, in February 2006 offered blistering critiques of the failure of those involved to resolve the conflict, and of the abysmal situation of the people.[4] When Cardinal Martino, of the Vatican's Pontifical Council on Justice and Peace, visited northern Uganda in June 2004, he told a crowd gathered in Gulu, "The flames of a bush cannot be extinguished with fire"—stressing that violence cannot be overcome with arms, and that more action to bring peace by religious leaders is needed.[5]

Some religious leaders have questioned whether faith leaders in Uganda and also globally have been sufficiently courageous and forthright in addressing the situation (that is, in their "prophetic vision"). These critics argue that many churches have been too silent, accepting the situation in a fatalist way, or asking too few questions about the national government's approach. Such questioning was apparent at a meeting of the Catholic Peace building Network in Bujumbura, Burundi, in July 2006. These critiques are part of larger debates about the responsibility of faith leaders and institutions to "speak truth to power."

Despite these myriad faith-based strands, the role of religion has rarely figured in formal policy dialogues within and among development institutions working in northern Uganda. This applies, for example, to the World Bank, whose documentation of Ugandan challenges and programs includes virtually no mention of religion. Even operational materials about the Northern Uganda Social Action Fund—admired in some circles for its inclusion of the ARLPI in its preparation—barely acknowledges the group's role or underlying religious issues. And during project implementation of the action fund, links to faith groups were tangential at best.

The Bank's broader strategic and operational framework for Uganda does acknowledge the role of religious leaders and institutions—notably in the health sector, and especially in work on HIV/AIDS. The gaps and silences on northern Uganda would appear to reflect complex sensitivities and sociopolitical relationships, accentuated by the Bank's tendency to steer away from religion as a matter of intellectual and operational reflex.

RELIGIOUS LEADERS IN PEACE PROCESSES

Despite these critiques and gaps, religious leaders are important players in the peace process unfolding in northern Uganda, with two international faith groups among the mediators. Pax Christi (Netherlands) and the Community of Sant'Egidio (a Catholic lay organization—see Chapters 4 and 22) have long maintained contacts with the LRA, and have worked for many years to bring parties to the table and move toward settlement. Theirs is a classic "track-two diplomacy" role (working in parallel with public diplomacy).

Religious leaders from northern Uganda also are active.[6] ARLPI, which took shape in 1997 and 1998, brought together Catholic, Church of Uganda, Orthodox, and Muslim leaders—a significant step in the region's rather divided religious topography. The aim was to work for peace through advocacy, training, and community-level reconciliation. Toward that end, the group—affiliated with the United Religions Initiative and other interfaith efforts—secured funding for a secretariat, primarily through the good offices of the UNDP, with branches in various parts of the north.

Apart from its willingness to speak out despite risks, the group has shown personal courage in sleeping in the streets of Gulu with children fleeing the threat of abduction. ARLPI played an instrumental role in the passage of an amnesty bill. ARLPI and other religious leaders have maintained frequent contact by satellite phone, text, and e-mail, during the protracted peace talks, including participating in several talks with LRA representatives. Reports about the negotiations circulate widely, and there is even maudlin humor, as when one leader regretted the absence from a discussion of "Brother JK" (Joseph Kony, leader of the LRA).

TURNING TO REBUILDING

With hope alive for a settlement—soon if not imminently—attention began to turn to plans for peace and development programs. The task of reconstruction is huge and will need to engage many actors: schools, hospitals, and clinics are visibly in shreds, and the agriculture-based economy is profoundly disrupted.

The Uganda government has launched technical work and consultations in preparation for a major reconstruction program. It is obvious that the voices of people from northern Uganda will be essential in formulating these plans, and both elected leaders and the full gamut of civil society groups are mobilizing to develop options and present proposals. Ending hunger and restoring physical security come highest on the agenda—for everyone, but especially for women, who have suffered so much during the conflict, including widespread rapes.

The length and depth of the conflict also present broader challenges, including the future settlement pattern: whether it should concentrate in larger agglomerations or revert to traditional scattered hamlets. The choices are political as well as practical, with the probable outcome rather messy, though hopefully driven by local preferences and realities. Layer upon layer of land-related problems complicate the picture, including perceptions that much land has been purchased or appropriated by government and wealthy people, and the likelihood of conflicting claims when families return to their original lands after long absence. Many fear that the interests of the vulnerable, especially women and children, will be neglected during frenetic resettlement, and that people will be forced to sell their land, with no alternative source of livelihood. Still, one long-term vision sees restoration of northern Uganda as the historic breadbasket of Uganda and central Africa.

RECONCILIATION AND TRUTH COMMISSIONS

Reconciliation is a central preoccupation in northern Uganda. The reasons are clear and twofold. First, the challenge of attaining that end after long years of conflict is massive. Second, the indictment of the LRA leadership by the International Criminal Court (designed to hold the leaders to account) presented an important issue during peace negotiations. (Joseph Kony reportedly was particularly concerned about his personal future, asking often if he could be safe anywhere with the indictment hanging over his head.) The basic message from northern Ugandan leaders, religious and secular alike, is that local traditions to reconcile parties to conflicts do exist, can work, and are far better suited to addressing these complex challenges and people's needs than national or international forms of justice. Limitations of the International Criminal Court are also duly noted: that it lacks a provision for locating those who have been indicted.

To respond to this crisis, ARLPI has joined with traditional leaders also interested in reconciliation. The renewed spotlight on the role of traditional leaders reflects hope for reviving and rebuilding Acholi cultural life and traditional practices. Recent discussions underscore support for traditional Acholi rites and customs for both purification and reconciliation: Acholi leaders seek inspiration there for the gigantic task ahead.

Two traditional processes are highlighted as important to reconciliation. The first—already practiced with some success—is the "cleansing" of abductees who want to reintegrate into their communities. The second, *mat oput,* is a far more complex set of rites that involve protracted negotiations between the clans of victim and perpetrator, compensation in cases of killing, purification with various roots and clean water, killing and eating of lambs, and a final feast. (Oput is the bitter root of a tree, and the rites also involve an egg, signifying purity and wholeness.)

Most religious and traditional leaders (with the possible exception of some Pentecostal pastors) contend that these traditional practices are entirely compatible with Christian theology, and that the two should go hand in hand. While some religious leaders are fascinated by ritual, even to the point of romanticizing or oversimplifying it, the underlying motivation is hard-headed good sense and is directed to finding creative paths to reconciliation. Traditional reconciliation practices vary within the region, and indeed have been in disuse for decades—hardly surprising given the massive disruption of communities. Some traditional elements need to be jettisoned (including the ritual sacrifice of a young girl), and some adapted, as they assuredly do not sufficiently include women and youth. However, the widespread agreement on the sensible merits of traditional practices is encouraging.

A broader issue is whether a national truth and reconciliation process is needed or desirable. Northern leaders see such a process as largely occurring in parallel with community-based Acholi practices. Overall, creative efforts to foster reconciliation and address demands for information (truth) and compensation will need to take several forms, to help move everyone forward after a long and tortured period.

THE FUTURE ROLE OF RELIGIOUS GROUPS IN NORTHERN UGANDA

There is wide agreement that reconstruction programs must be grounded in the culture, history, and wishes of the people of northern Uganda, and that religious groups should be involved in planning these programs at an early stage. This calls for thoughtful mapping of faith-based institutions and activities: many churches and programs are at work, often with little coordination. For example, numerous groups affiliated with the Catholic Church (65 percent of the population counts itself as Catholic) and the Church of Uganda offer social and physical services. The Uganda Joint Christian Council, a 40-year-old ecumenical body that has worked for peace, also has substantial knowledge of the situation and actors.

The Orthodox Church and Muslims have small communities, and large numbers of evangelical churches (referred to locally as "born agains," "saveds," or "dollar churches") are increasingly active. Their role deserves to be looked at carefully, as they can offer remarkable resources and inspiration, but there are also some tensions around them because they are new and compete with traditional institutions on various fronts. Religious orders are also involved across the region, especially in running schools and hospitals but also in providing wells, grinding mills, and other infrastructure. Faith-based NGOs operating in the region include World Vision, Catholic Relief Services, and Quaker organizations.

Given their deeply rooted and pervasive presence, religious leaders and institutions should be well positioned to play key roles during the peace process, making particularly significant contributions in healing, health, and education. However, capacity is a central issue, given recognized weaknesses in newly revived traditional religious and cultural institutions. (The need for capacity is sometimes referred to in Northern Uganda as the need for "facilitation.") Not far below the surface are concerns about financial support, and about relative status and recognition among various organizations.

Clearly the region and the country face a host of complex issues as they embark on the difficult road to reconciliation. Religious networks offer much potential, but come with their own limitations—including the fact that traditional healers and religious leaders are almost all men. The special contributions as well as the special vulnerabilities of women and young people should be a central focus during the reconciliation period.

NOTES

1. See http://www.uri.org/; or http://www.interfaithnews.net/.
2. The Acholi group received the Paul Carus Award for outstanding contributions to the interfaith movement. See http://www.cpwr.org/2004Parliament/parliament/carus.htm. The Niwano Peace Prize was also awarded in 2004. See http://www.prnewswire.co.uk/cgi/news/release?id=122531.
3. See World Vision, 2005, *Pawns of Politics*, at http://www.worldvision.org/.
4. See http://www.wcc-assembly.info/en/news-media/news/english-news/article/469/plight-of-children-in-nor.html.
5. For an interview with Cardinal Martino, see http://www.30giorni.it/us/articolo.asp?id=4283.
6. See, for example, Carlos Rodriguez, 2002, "The Role of the Religious Leaders," Conciliation Resources, at http://www.c-r.org/our-work/accord/northern-uganda/religious-leaders.php.

CHAPTER

22

Religion, Reconciliation, and Rebuilding

Fragile and conflict-torn states are a central problem for strategic agendas for development. Alongside heartening success in fighting poverty in very different societies across the world are horrible, long-lasting conflicts that stand in the way of progress and poverty relief. Some conflicts, like those in northern Uganda, Somalia, and the Democratic Republic of the Congo, plainly bring development to a halt and result in misery for millions of people. Others have a more simmering quality, ever threatening to derail progress and dampening even encouraging movement toward economic and social goals. The development community is justly expending much effort to understand better how its support can help in these fragile situations. An important dimension of the development challenge, therefore, is to appreciate what works best in healing and rebuilding societies in the wake of conflict, and also how conflict can be prevented and stopped.

Religion is often, though not always, an important factor in conflict and social tension, and thus it often needs to be part of the solution during

This chapter draws on the authors' participation in the Fès Forum, and on thought-provoking discussions with Helena Cobban. We owe much to lessons from her 2007 book *Amnesty after Atrocity: Healing Nations after Genocide and War Crimes* (Boulder, CO: Paradigm Publishers); and her December 2005 article "Religion and Violence," *Journal of the American Academy of Religion*. The latter is available at http://justworldnews.org/archives/AAR-presentation-revised.htm. Interactions with Hillel Levine and Coralie Bryant contributed to the thinking underlying the chapter.

periods of rebuilding. Participants in the process of reconciling conflicting parties often look to religion in a special way, both because religious elements may be seen as contributing to conflict and because religions can bring to bear deep traditions of forgiveness and peacemaking. In addition, in traumatized, post-conflict societies in which most institutions of normal life have been deeply fractured, religious worldviews and the institutions that embody them can provide solace as well as a cognitive and ontological framework that helps people ascribe meaning to a shattered world, and thus regain their own sense of agency within it. This is not to say that all religions always achieve these tasks—far from it. But most religions can offer teachings and practices that can propel or inspire processes of reconciliation.

A first step in considering practical ways to engage faith leaders in these reconciliation processes is to better understand the resources they can offer, including by looking to case studies that reveal best practices. A second step is engagement: finding practical tools and partnership frameworks that work. This chapter describes two recent efforts—one by participants at the Fès Forum in Morocco, the other by journalist Helena Cobban—to draw on religious teachings and leaders to consider how best to foster reconciliation, thereby providing a foundation for peace and development.

FORGIVENESS AT FÈS

In June 2006 the Fès Forum (see Chapter 18) devoted a full day to the topic of forgiveness, considering classical social and political perspectives as well as wisdom and practice about forgiveness within the three Abrahamic faiths (Judaism, Christianity, and Islam).

Forgiveness is not an easy topic, and religious teachings on the subject are intricate and overlapping. The idea is often pondered based on teachings about God's love and mercy, but never far removed are teachings about justice and punishment. Brad Hirschfield, a wise rabbi from New York, mapped important tensions within his own faith's teachings and traditions in the visual form of a diamond, with the four points representing vengeance and forgiveness, justice and mercy. With all their seeming contradictions, all four elements are deeply embedded in religious teachings, and they need to be recognized and reconciled. Similar tensions are also intrinsic in more secular formulations of rights and corresponding responsibilities.

Each great religion offers wisdom for ordering societies so people can live together while they contend with the constant reality of conflict, whether a banal gesture of retribution or quid pro quo after a minor incident, or murder and war, which leave far deeper scars. The diversity of these religious traditions should be seen far more as a resource than as an obstacle. Exemplifying the positive spirit of the Fès discussion, Father Kesrouani from Lebanon compared world faith traditions to the flowers of the world—each so very different, each with their beauty and their thorns.

The pain that conflict leaves behind was epitomized at Fès in the personal testimony of two women, Nurit Peled and Aisheh Hashem Nimer Aqtam, leaders in the Forum of Bereaved Families, based in Israel and Palestine. The forum's members, most of them women, are united above all by the loss of children or relatives to violence. Each has come to terms with suffering and deep personal loss, and they work for peace through summer camps, Web-linked conversations among children, and other means. These women use the sad legitimacy they have earned through loss of someone they loved to call for mutual respect and amplify their voices.

The witness of the two women was quite different in both tone and message, though their joint work and mutual esteem illustrated and affirmed the powerful potential of new, often unconventional alliances. For Nurit Peled, the very term forgiveness is strange and jarring; she cited Jewish tradition wherein a person is obliged to ask for forgiveness, but no one is obliged to forgive. She noted that Israeli and Palestinian members of the forum try to work as equals, but in reality equality is a far cry when so many Palestinians have never left refugee camps, seen the sea, or are truly free to control their lives.

Aisheh Hashem's message took the form of an appeal to our common humanity. She also hesitated even to speak of forgiveness, and her primary message spoke to the common bond between people who have experienced loss, and how it translates into a will to act and to bring peace. "In the Forum, we work hand in hand, in order to put an end to the bloodshed; our most important activity is constant joint work to push forward the peace process and achieve equality." Together, and with passion, both women called on the world to end the bloodshed.

The Fès discussion reflected a hunger to work for peace, and participants' conclusions ran in that vein:

Promote larger government roles and responsibilities. Governments and politicians need to participate more fully in discussions of and work for reconciliation. Forgiveness may in essence be personal, but social reconciliation needs active framing, inspiration, and work by state institutions and structures. Rights and justice cannot become realities without this national and international public support. The scaffold of public norms, laws, and above all leadership is even more essential in resolving situations of conflict. These responsibilities are more widely shared than is often assumed: voters and media share the stage with government leaders.

Do not deny or shy away from the tendency to blame. Blame and responsibility go together, and speaking truth to those in power about who has contributed to tension and conflict is vital. Yet it can be too easy to point the finger of blame at governments and officials, as well as "the other." Wise voices called for appreciation of the notion that each person, each society, each religion has made plenty of mistakes, and deserves its own share of blame. "Let us look first inward, into the mirror, and then outward, with caring and compassion."

Appreciate, understand, and enhance the role of civil society. Civil society also has a deeply important role in resolving conflict, and in rebuilding and strengthening communities that are still raw from conflict. Civil society's special role in helping to bring the state to account is nowhere more important than when it is linked to the pain and anger of communities in conflict.

Work with the many leaders emerging in the field of conflict resolution. John Marks, founder of Search for Common Ground, highlighted the inspiring and important world of people and institutions dedicated to conflict resolution.[1] Lessons from the post-conflict experiences of France,

Germany, and South Africa have special relevance to such efforts, especially in situations where prospects seem bleak. In its time, forgiveness is a vital part of resolving conflict and bringing reconciliation: "If we are ever going to get to peace, if the two sides are going to have to live together, there is going to have to be forgiveness." Doors and windows were common metaphors: doors seem to close yet windows to open. There are times when reconciliation and resolution of conflict occur, and others when unfolding events make those processes more difficult. Thus it is vitally important to be always ready to seize the moment to act, and to convey a constant sense of urgency.

Learn from the experiences of truth and reconciliation commissions. The remarkable contemporary experience with public instruments for public reconciliation has yet to be fully absorbed. Driss al Yazami highlighted important lessons from the world's 30 major recent or ongoing reconciliation processes, including Morocco's experience.[2] These processes must be built on with the aim of building trust and confidence. They respect and preserve memory; they also acknowledge personal choice in how individuals contribute to conflict, and they recognize clearly that forgiveness is not forgetting. Truth and reconciliation commissions rely on fact, on telling the story, on seeing clearly what happened; and this history is written, preserved. The very acknowledgment of what happened, if pursued without pressing too hard or too soon for forgiveness, can help. Recognizing that sharing experiences is important, most such commissions conduct their work in public, to shed light on what really happened and what crimes took place, and thus give victims the chance to gain recognition and respect. The work of these commissions can provide a beacon of inspiration.

Acknowledge women's central roles in working for peace. The multiple roles of women in shaping the attitudes of children, teaching, setting standards, and working together in a powerful sisterhood are all vital in resolving conflict. As panelist Aisheh Hashem said: "Women have the greatest power to influence, as mothers, sisters, and wives. Our main goal is for mothers to instill in the minds of their children that they should never become soldiers of bloodshed: they should become actors for peace."

Allow time to heal, even while recognizing the urgent need for action. While conflict rages, it is often too soon to talk of forgiveness. People need time to heal. Thus timing matters, but even during raw moments of tension it is none too soon to start to build bridges across walls, national boundaries, and ancient and modern enmities, based on knowledge of what must occur for peace to succeed.

Focus on the strengths and deep teachings of religious traditions during broader reconciliation efforts. Major faith teachings call for truth and witness in examining conflicts between communities. Many wise religious leaders emphasize that religious diversity need not entail tension or conflict, and that each faith has both the will and the tools to encourage reconciliation. Indeed, peace will not come without taking religious and spiritual factors into account. Rabbi Hirschfield urged that in thinking about the role of faith, we "try to imagine falling deeply in love with a tradition, not because the tradition is best but because it is the best way to be human. If you use the tradition to get beyond yourself; all will be well; if not, we are in for terrible times."

Draw on the many roles of education. Education serves as a potentially powerful force for changing people's exclusionary attitudes, cooling ancient mistrust and hatred, and transforming societies. The capacity to reconcile, to live together, and to build just societies is vastly enhanced through knowledge and understanding; learning about other traditions, in depth, is a critical path, as is better education for all children. Human interaction through one-on-one and group meetings is crucial.

RELIGION AND RECONCILIATION: DIFFERENT APPROACHES

All over the world, people facing the uneasy aftermath of conflict look for examples of successful reconciliation. None is better known than South Africa's Truth and Reconciliation Commission, which played an important part in that nation's extraordinary experience in putting behind it the fearful history and pain of conflict. Less well known is the remarkable experience of post-conflict rebuilding in Mozambique. And epic efforts to foster justice and reconciliation in Rwanda following the 1994 genocide challenge all preconceptions and ideas.

As a journalist, Helena Cobban was inspired by the South African experience but also drawn to Mozambique and Rwanda. She noted the many parallels in timing as all three societies emerged from ferocious conflicts during roughly the same period. She was also deeply struck by the very different approaches that their leaders and societies took.

South Africa focused on the healing power of public truth telling, in a context of public forgiveness of most who had been involved in the violence of apartheid. Mozambique did not establish a process of either truth telling or ensuring justice for people's actions during the long civil war. Instead, that country has chosen to leave the past behind and look to building a future in which citizens have the promise of real equality and are accountable to each other, and where the government is also accountable to the citizens. In Rwanda, more than a decade after the genocide, two complex processes of justice—one through the International Criminal Tribunal for Rwanda, and the other through the neotraditional *gachacha* court system designed to bring justice at the village level—grind slowly on.

Of particular interest is Helena Cobban's focus on the potentially vital role of religion in healing and rebuilding. Like the Fès participants, she wrestled with the contradictory trends within many religious teachings:

> It seems to me ... that "religions" come in two main different flavors (though sometimes these flavors come mixed together in the same institutional package.) The first of these flavors, or trends, in religions is the trend toward judging and punishing others, a focus that many, many religions seem to have. The other trend is quite different: it is the trend in those religions that seek to heal other people and ourselves. In the situations of often atrocious inter-communal conflict that I have witnessed or studied intensively—whether in Lebanon, in Israel/Palestine, in Rwanda, South Africa, Mozambique, or elsewhere—I have seen both trends at work. And I think I know, both intellectually and from my own experience, which of these kinds of religion seems to be more spirit-led and to be best for me and, I venture to suggest, for the rest of the world.[3]

In short, she comes down firmly on the side of mercy and amnesty, raising powerful concerns about the practicality and benefits of elaborate systems designed to mete out justice in the wake of widespread violence and genocide.

In South Africa, religious thought and institutions have long played significant roles in sustaining the spirit of people ground down under terrible forms of oppression. It was in that country that Mahatma Gandhi did his first spiritually motivated, nonviolent mass organizing. Many churches, mosques, and temples were central to efforts to build and sustain the anti-apartheid movement, often supported by their denominations. For example, the South African Council of Churches became a bastion of support for the anti-apartheid movement.

As Cobban notes, Christianity had a lot to make up for in South Africa, since both earlier colonial ventures—whether Dutch or English—and the later form of rule known as apartheid claimed to have received inspiration in good part from the teachings of the Christian Bible. It was particularly important that Christians of conscience could contest the authors and upholders of apartheid by relying on the very biblical discourse that the latter claimed as their own. During the apartheid era, many churches in South Africa also took real risks to help the poor and oppressed.

As recounted by Cobban, the country's Truth and Reconciliation Commission (TRC) provided a forum where individual victims could finally be heard. However, the process was not without its pain, and costs were high. Religion's role in the TRC was personified by the ideas, words, and rituals of its chair, Anglican Archbishop Desmond Tutu. He opened TRC sessions with prayer and lit candles. In both these rituals and his frequent articulation of the values underlying the work of the commission, the strong role of Tutu's religion was evident. He enriched and broadened the theological underpinnings of the TRC's efforts with frequent reference to *ubuntu*—an indigenous concept found in many different forms throughout Africa. Tutu defines it as the idea that "a person is human inasmuch as he or she recognizes the humanity of others."

Cobban was moved by the somewhat different perspective of a participant who put more emphasis on the need to look to the future rather than dwelling on past wrongs. Rejoyce Mabudhafasi, a long-time activist with the African National Congress, spoke to Cobban about her perspective.[4] During many of the toughest years of the anti-apartheid struggle, she was a semiclandestine organizer for the pro-ANC United Democratic Front. She lived through terrible times, including acts of retribution by apartheid authorities and many deaths around her. Dogs were set upon her, and she spent long periods in jail. Her response to the fact that many who did these things to her and her family were still walking free after the TRC had finished its work was: "that's okay—God will see to them." She also highlighted that her priority was rebuilding: she was "just too plain busy" to spend time settling old scores. She also did not wish to be the kind of person who would visit upon others the same kind of treatment heaped upon her. She was ready to leave "punishing" to the Almighty.

In Mozambique, too, many religions and religious institutions have played vital peacemaking roles. These include the well-known participation of the Community of Sant'Egidio in the peace negotiation process, but also the deep contributions of African traditional religions to Mozambican society. The latter, for Cobban, played the most critical part in enabling Mozambique to put the past behind it without formal processes of any kind.

Sant'Egidio's work with Mozambicans in this process remains an inspiration and exemplifies the best of Christian and Catholic teaching and action. In their engagement, Sant'Egidio's activists lived their values of caring and friendship, and their capacity to serve as peacemakers drew on their deep experience with working with the poor over long periods. The Sant'Egidio community also connected with a rich matrix of such attitudes in Mozambican society.

Mozambique's indigenous cultural and especially religious resources played a critical role in building peace, as did externally born faiths that grew in Mozambique through the twentieth century. The largely Mozambican character of the culture—owing to the shallow penetration of Portuguese colonial rulers and settlers—is reflected in its religious faith. Despite the country's great complexity, encompassing 16 or 17 language groups, each with its own approaches to questions of ontology and cosmology, many citizens subscribe to some version of *ubuntu*. In this tradition, the "self" is intimately bound up in the web of relationships with the extended family, the homestead, the ancestors who are buried there, and the spirit world to which these ancestors belong.

Thus even after the brutal post-independence civil war that raged from 1975 on, Mozambicans could draw on robust indigenous cultural resources to help withstand the rigors and privations of that war. Through the difficult times, traditional leaders and healers (*curandeiros* and *curandeiras)* continued to practice their religion-based art of individual and social healing. These included rituals through which former child soldiers—some forced to commit atrocities against their own villages to ensure they would not have any safe refuge to flee to—were speedily reinstated into their communities. These rituals aimed at spiritual cleansing and reestablishing young people's reconnection with ancestors and the rest of their rightful world. Healers used similar rituals to purify young women who had been abducted as sex slaves, to enable them to resume their rightful place in their communities.

In Mozambique, all religions—traditional and external, Christian and Muslim—helped enact at the local level the kind of "forgive and forget" policy embodied in amnesty at the national level. When Cobban traveled throughout the country, she was often told: "Now we are in a time of peace. So our main aim is to make sure there is no resumption of the war. Investigations? Tribunals? Why would we ever have wanted to do that? What for?" Anglican bishop Dinis Sengulane's book *Vitória sem Vencidos* (*Victory without Losers*)[5] exemplifies the spirit of the Mozambiquan reconciliation process. The apparent depth of that process is remarkable, and religion was important in achieving it at many different levels.

In Rwanda, initial thoughts about the role of religion during and after the genocide are dominated by the shameful involvement of many religious leaders in the genocide itself. Criminal prosecutions highlighted the fact that many Christian priests and nuns actively aided the *génocidaires*. These included an Anglican bishop and a high-ranking Seventh-Day Adventist priest who were both indicted by the International Criminal Tribunal for Rwanda. But the religious institution that was morally compromised most deeply by its involvement in the genocide was the Catholic Church, which until then had been closely associated with the country's power centers. In the tortured, multiply traumatized aftermath of Rwanda's genocide, many Rwandese felt that they had no stable institutions to help them to recover, either physically or spiritually. They desperately needed a framework within which they could restore meaning to lives shattered by the experience of 1994.

This framework needed to acknowledge that many survivors were not themselves pure innocents: indeed, people who have survived the torment of others often become enactors of torment in their turn. Strict boxes or categories that are black and white simply do not work. Once the genocide had ended, the entire population of Rwanda was left in a web of multilayered trauma. Nearly all the institutions that had given meaning to people's lives had either been taken from them by the genocide or had palpably failed them in their time of need: families, communities, economic networks, the state apparatus, the Catholic Church. Western aid organizations flooded into the country, some offering services that were vital, appropriate, and much appreciated, and some offering services that lacked those qualities.

While visiting Rwanda, Cobban stayed in a Protestant mission in a shantytown area of Kigali, the capital. The mission was run by Michel Kayetaba, an evangelical Anglican with great gifts as a spiritual leader and social organizer. His organization, Moucecore, provides faith-based training in sorely needed social leadership skills to local grassroots leaders from around the country. For example, 40 trainees of all ages and varied backgrounds, including evangelicals, were enrolled in a two-week course on faith-based community development during the period Cobban was at the mission. Hutu and Tutsi trainees worshiped and worked together.

At the human level, the ability of many, many Rwandan Tutsis and Hutus to transcend the terrible cleavage of the past is a remarkable achievement, as is the role of religion in this continuing work of reconciliation. Muslim institutions, which are well rooted in parts of the country, have played a role in this drama of reconciliation, and evangelical churches have experienced massive growth in Rwanda since the genocide. The new wave of evangelicals did not merely arrive with the evangelical aid groups that flocked to the country after 1994. That tradition was already present in the lives, experiences, examples, and organizing skill of indigenous evangelical leaders who played an exemplary role during the genocide. These leaders were mainly Protestant, though some Catholic priests also played such a role.

Helena Cobban concludes: "Many of us here would probably argue, along with the anthropologists, that one of the main things that gives "meaning" to the lives of people who are living through traumatic times is not "war," but religion. In my own experience, I have certainly seen how in times filled with fear, uncertainty, traumatization, and suffering, various different forms of religion can help to restore meaning and dignity to human lives from which those attributes have previously been stripped, or from which they were absent."

NOTES

1. Search for Common Ground is a nongovernmental organization founded in 1982 that works to change the way the world addresses conflict and conflicted situations, using an array of tools, including media and artistic modes like reality television. For more information, see http://www.sfcg.org/.

2. Driss al Yazami is director of Generic, a research center on the history of immigration based in Paris.

3. Helena Cobban, December 2005, "Religion and Violence," *Journal of the American Academy of Religion*.

4. Rejoyce Mabudhafasi is Deputy Minister of Environmental Affairs and Tourism and a member of parliament from Limpopo.

5. Dinis Sengulane, 1994, *Vitória Sem Vencidos: A História do Processo de Paz para Moçambique do Ponto de Vista do Conselho Cristão de Moçambique*, Bispo das Libombos, Maputo.

23

Bridging Civilizations and Cultures

"Dialogue among civilizations" is not normally part of the routine work of international development institutions. However, interfaith and intercultural relations, at both community and global levels, are far from irrelevant to development. In fact, the agenda of efforts to address what many term the "clash of civilizations" often overlaps with work on combating poverty and spurring development. Social justice, education, stability, and security are relevant in both arenas, as are underlying community relations in plural societies, which so deeply affect the cohesion and effective functioning of those societies.

Two notable efforts to enhance global intercultural relations illustrate this common ground. The first, a UN initiative to foster an "alliance of civilizations," has focused on interfaith dialogue and conflict resolution, as well as education, migration, and youth. The second, the World Economic Forum's West-Islamic World Dialogue, also targets education, as well as youth, issues of mounting concern to the development community. These two ambitious initiatives offer insights that are important for development work, just as the effort to advance economic and social development is a precondition for social justice and global peace.

Three quite different stories that fall within the spirit of bridging civilizations and seeking alliances across deep divides are told in short boxes: a Christian and Muslim interfaith initiative in Nigeria, with a very

This material draws on discussions with leaders of the High-Level Group for the Alliance of Civilizations, and on the experiences of Katherine Marshall, who has served as a member of the C-100 since 2003.

personal face; the continuing inspiration of Gandhi's message, through his grandson who speaks of a "wall of peace" built of civil society initiatives; and the bold symbol of Viva Rio's caravan for peace that fights gun violence in Brazil.

ALLIANCE OF CIVILIZATIONS

At the urging of the heads of state of Spain and Turkey, UN Secretary General Kofi Annan established a 20-member High-Level Group for the Alliance of Civilizations in May 2005. Its mandate was broad, and infused with a deeply positive spirit (hence the title of "alliance," to contrast with "clash" of civilizations). However, an underlying goal was to address the global problems of extremism and what was seen as the polarization between Muslim and Western societies. The effort was to work within the spirit of the earlier "dialogue of civilizations" initiatives at the United Nations. Among the high-level group members were Karen Armstrong (scholar and writer), Ismail Serageldin (who heads the Library of Alexandria), Enrique Iglesias (Ibero-American Cooperation Secretariat), John Esposito (Director, Prince Alwaleed Bin-Talal Center for Muslim Christian Understanding at Georgetown University), Andre Azoulay (counselor to the King of Morocco), Archbishop Tutu (formerly Anglican Archbishop of Capetown), and Nafiz Sadik (former head of the United Nations Population Fund).

The group formally presented its report to the UN secretary general in Istanbul in November 2006. The report focuses heavily on the Middle East conflict as a lightening rod for tensions between the Islamic world and the West. Proposals for defusing those tensions include hosting a high-level conference on the Israel-Palestine situation, and preparing a "white paper" that would include a thorough "historical narrative" aimed at establishing clear facts as a basis for dialogue and negotiations.

The report treats religion more extensively and explicitly than most UN reports—though a core conclusion (and press release sound byte) is that politics is more important than religion as a source of conflict, and that most critiques of religion as a negative influence are based on poor understanding. For example, the report holds "that although religion is often cynically exploited to stir passions, fuel suspicions and support alarmist claims that the world is facing a new 'war of religion,' the root of the matter is political."[1] In one interesting observation, the report notes that "indeed, a symbiotic relationship may be emerging between religion and politics in our time, each influencing the other."

Strikingly, the report makes no attempt to define the "Muslim world" or "the West." It focuses heavily on the Arab world and its perceptions, and makes no explicit mention of Islam in Africa or Southeast Asia. What's more, while it devotes considerable attention to the corrosive impact of Islamophobia, it gives little attention to anti-Semitism and the consequences of violence for all people on all sides. The report is therefore unlikely to be viewed over time as taking a particularly balanced approach to these complex and highly sensitive issues.

The report's limited treatment of poverty, employment, and inequity as sources of tension is also noteworthy: it mentions these subjects almost in passing. However, as a "guiding principle," the group notes that "poverty leads to despair, a sense of injustice, and alienation that, when combined with political grievances, can foster extremism. Eradication of poverty would diminish those factors linked to economic marginalization and alienation and must therefore be aggressively pursued, as called for in the Millennium Development Goals."

The report does offer a lengthy set of recommendations on topics beyond the Middle East. These include education as a key arena for addressing tensions among peoples, as well as media, migration, and youth. Of particular interest is the group's focus on the role of the Internet for good and ill: that is, in aggravating tensions, and as a vehicle for reaching across cultural divides.

Specific proposals include the development of films and television programs—co-produced across religious and cultural boundaries—showing diversity as a normal feature of society; and cross-cultural and human rights education, to ensure that students everywhere develop an understanding of other cultures and religions. The report also stresses the importance of democratic reforms and broad participation in development efforts, and proposes the creation of a new office attached to the secretary general's office to implement and monitor these proposals.

THE COUNCIL OF 100

The World Economic Forum (WEF)—whose motto is "improving the state of the world"—is an independent organization based in Geneva that, from a base of business membership, links leaders across many sectors of activity. The WEF's annual meeting in Davos, Switzerland is an elite event that brings together leaders from business, politics, media, and NGOs.

In addition to the annual global meeting, the WEF organizes annual regional meetings along similar lines. The WEF has in recent years invited young global leaders—selected through a demanding and competitive process—and social entrepreneurs[2] to participate in its meetings and leaven the leadership group.

The WEF aspires to encourage participants to take action following meetings, facilitated by initiatives that it helps launch and monitor. "Partnership" is a watchword and central feature of these initiatives. For example, the WEF's Global Education Initiative has engaged leading technology companies in developing public education systems in Egypt, India, and Jordan.

An important and unusual initiative is the WEF's West-Islamic World Dialogue (or the C-100). The dialogue's creation was prompted by a first-ever gathering within a WEF meeting of religious leaders, held, in the wake of September 11, 2001, in New York City in January, 2002. Shortly thereafter the WEF invited two co-chairs—Lord Carey of Clifton, former archbishop of Canterbury; and Prince Turki al Saud, then ambassador of Saudi Arabia to the United Kingdom—to help assemble a group of 100 leaders for the dialogue. (Princess Lolwah al Faisal, vice-chair of the Board of Trustees and general supervisor, Effat College, Saudi Arabia, replaced Prince Turki as co-chair in late 2006.)

The intent was to draw leaders from both the Islamic world and the West, and from five major sectors: business, politics/government, religious leaders, the media, and civil society/academia. The WEF describes the mandate of the C-100 as convening "senior political, religious, business, media and opinion leaders in an effort to better understand their differences and act on their commonalities. This community relies in particular on the pragmatic dynamism of the business community as a powerful enabler of positive change."

The C-100 has held sessions each year since 2003 during the WEF's annual meeting in Davos, and a larger segment of the group meets more formally at the WEF's annual Middle East meeting, the latter gatherings at the Dead Sea, Jordan, in 2005 and 2007, and in Sharm el-Sheikh, Egypt, in 2006. These meetings focus on two parallel activities: a dialogue to address major challenges in West-Islamic relations, such as religion and politics, and the role of women; and opportunities for concrete action, which the C-100 identifies and encourages.[3] For example, the C-100 has established an education working group, as education has emerged as a central priority (see Chapter 6). An executive committee oversees these efforts.

A major focus of the C-100 is an annual report on global West-Islamic dialogue. The report aims to provide a careful analysis of trends in public attitudes—supported by polling by the Gallup Organization and media analysis—and to review the large and growing numbers of initiatives which aim to further interfaith communication, particularly those involving Muslim leaders and communities. The group will present its first annual report (whose lead author is John DeGioia, president of Georgetown University) during the WEF annual meeting at Davos in January 2008.

Building respect and resolving misunderstandings is challenging for a community, even a family, but is far more so at national or global levels. In a globalized world, what are the best mechanisms for coming to some common agreement, and helping to ensure a more peaceful and just society? This can be a difficult prospect as states all have their own priorities and interests at stake. It is here where nonstate networks like the Alliance of Civilizations and the C-100 can play a role; they bring together a diverse cadre of seasoned leaders both to model the dialogue and partnership and to press forward with the difficult task of translating rhetoric on respect, shared global society, and tolerance into practice. Each effort aims to bridge the need to articulate a vibrant vision of what is possible—peace, understanding, cooperation—with the equally important need to show practical results in action that people can understand and see.

The very diversity of efforts along these lines—there may be dozens if not hundreds of dialogue and alliance building efforts, spanning every continent—are grounds both for concern and for hope: concern because the lack of a coherent thread and direction threatens to dilute the effectiveness of well-meaning efforts and concern also because transnational groups of actors do not have democratic accountability or a shared mandate from citizens. Furthermore, tensions can develop, bred by overlap and competition for public space amongst the various groups interested in dialogue and peace—the reality of individuals and groups coveting attention and recognition for their efforts is certainly an issue. At the same time, these initiatives bring hope because the plethora of efforts to bridge divides is evidence of true widespread appreciation of the need for rigorous and creative efforts to build far better understanding among different cultures.

Boxes 23.1 and 23.2 reflects the hopeful side of this equation. The courage and determination of Nigeria's Muhammad Nurayn Ashafa and Rev. James Movel Wuye (the imam and the pastor whose story is told in box 23.1) are an inspiration. The hope and work of Mahatma Gandhi (box 23.2), carried on today by his family members and friends and the many inspired by his legacy, speak to the vital importance of these difficult dialogue processes and their relevance not only for global politics but for the day to day lives of individuals. The hopeful "wall of peace" that one of his grandsons, Rajmohan Gandhi, envisions is made up of the full array of civil society institutions, which, by his definition, include faith organizations. This "wall of peace" combats "walls of division" and, both by working to further true understanding and also by their work to better the lives of people, offers the hope for the future that is the aspiration of each and every effort to bridge the gulf of civilizations. Box 23.3 focuses on a community organization also working for peace, this time communal and focused on youth, within the city of Rio de Janeiro. The premise of Viva Rio is that peace is necessary for justice, and that religious groups can facilitate both when they work together.

BOX 23.1
THE IMAM AND THE PASTOR

Two men, at great personal cost, have worked for peace across deep divides separating Christians and Muslims in Nigeria, a country on the front line of Muslim-Christian relationships. Over the last quarter of the twentieth century, thousands were killed and dozens of mosques and churches destroyed there in interreligious strife. Nigeria's profound development challenges are tightly linked to prospects for stability, so the effort to address interreligious strife is vital to the nation's welfare.

Muhammad Nurayn Ashafa is an imam in Kaduna, an important city in northern Nigeria, and Rev. James Movel Wuye is a Christian pastor. They now jointly direct the Inter-Faith Mediation Centre in Kaduna. In the last five years, the Centre's work has expanded throughout Nigeria, with teams of pastors and imams journeying together to trouble spots to build dialogue, understanding, and common ground, and to try to rout out conflict.

The Centre grew out of a turbulent history. In the early 1990s Muhammad Nurayn Ashafa and Rev. James Movel Wuye were on opposite sides; in fact, they tried to have each other killed during religious riots. Christian extremists killed Ashafa's uncle, and Muslim extremists cut off Pastor James' arm when he was defending his church.

Ashafa and Wuye met in the early 1990s at a conference on drug abuse. Warily, they began to talk, and from this initial encounter they thought that together they might have a part in bringing healing. As their dialogue continued, they began to see more clearly the cost to both Christians and Muslims of the violence—lives cut short and families destroyed, and for what? They found passages in the Bible and the Koran that showed common approaches to peace. The imam says that as they focused on what they could take on together, rather than on their differences, they saw hope for "a united front against evil." They also saw their own survival as a sign from God, Allah, and they eventually set up an organization to encourage dialogue.

(Box continues on next page.)

(box continued)

Real friendship between the two men, however, came more slowly. "We were programmed to hate one another, to evangelize or Islamicize at all costs," says the pastor. "I used to want to have nothing to do with Muslims until I met Ashafa...When we traveled together, we would share a room, and he was a heavy sleeper. Every time that happened, I felt a deep desire to kill him."[a] He found that breaking the pattern of ingrained belief was very difficult.

Imam Ashafa similarly had to overcome assumptions and ideas about Christians. A turning point came when he heard another imam preach on forgiveness and the example of the Prophet. "At that point the concepts of forgiveness and mercy were far away from my conviction," he says.

Pastor James took three years to overcome his hatred. The seeds were sown when the imam and other community leaders visited his sick mother in hospital. "Ashafa was radiating love, but I'd been blinded by hate and pain," he says.

Two men work jointly through their Inter-Faith Mediation Centre, with a particular emphasis on bringing young Christians and Muslims together. Whenever violence has broken out, they go together to the streets to calm tempers and find solutions. In 2002 they helped produce the Kaduna Declaration, a powerful document declaring a commitment to ending violence and bloodshed in the region. Twenty-two influential Muslims and Christians signed it in the presence of 2,000 local religious leaders.

In the midst of interfaith dialogue and collaboration, Pastor James and Imam Ashafa stay faithful to their religions. "I always say I will die as a Christian," says Pastor James, "and I am not compromising one inch on my principles. But we are creating space for one another." The imam says, "He is no more an enemy but a friend."

In 2006, Initiatives of Change, a diverse global network committed to building trust across the world's divides, produced the documentary *The Imam and the Pastor*, with support from many other organizations. The film and presentations on Pastor James and Imam

Ashafa—a story of reconciliation and commitment to humanity—have brought the lessons of their work and courage beyond Nigeria, prompting discussions at the World Bank and the United Nations, among other venues.

Note: This box is drawn from Michael Henderson, 2003, *Forgiveness: Breaking the Chain of Hate* (Portland, OR: Arnica Publishing). Other contributions were provided by Dick Ruffin. For more information, see the Initiatives of Change Website at http://www.iofc.org/en/.

a. This quote is from John L. Allen Jr., March 9, 2007, "In Nigeria, Christians and Muslims in Uneasy Calm," *All Things Catholic* 6 (27). See http://ncrcafe.org/node/966.

BOX 23.2
A WALL OF PEACE: REFLECTIONS OF MAHATMA GANDHI'S GRANDSON

Mahatma Gandhi's legacy speaks to the possibility of collaboration and dialogue even across widely different cultures. Never has that challenge been of greater significance than it is today. In reflections at the Fès Globalization Forum in 2005, and in Washington in March 2007, Rajmohan Gandhi highlighted how deeply relations among different religions and groups, and their consequences for social justice and welfare, preoccupied his grandfather, the Mahatma, and how central they were to Gandhi's vision for the future.[a]

In reflecting on Mahatma Gandhi's life, it is fascinating to trace how he came to his sharp focus on relations among social and religious groups. Charlie Andrews, the English cleric who worked closely with him before Indian independence, told of conversations with Ghandi that highlighted the unlikely start to this remarkable path.

Gandhi recounted that, when he was 12 years old, he started to become aware of relations with Untouchables in his community, and that awareness tied in to his growing consciousness of the role of

(Box continues on next page.)

(box continued)

Muslims in his society. Gandhi recalled a conversation with his mother in which she warned him that if he were to touch the very young Untouchable boy who came to clean the toilets in their house, he must immediately wash himself to get rid of the pollution. Gandhi was troubled but also puzzled. But, he asked, what should I do if I touch an Untouchable at school or in the street, and cannot wash? The solution, his mother indicated, was to touch any Muslim, thus "canceling" the pollution by passing it to another who was in some fashion eligible to receive it because of his or her different status.

This story is a portrait of how groups interacted then (and still do even today in many Indian communities), and of Gandhi's thinking and awareness. It also underscores how Gandhi overcame the prejudices that were so much a part of his upbringing. For those prejudices were deep and assumed: in effect, they dictated no association—physical, spiritual, or intellectual—between different communities.

Gandhi was open to and deeply concerned about people of all faiths. He spoke directly with people of other faiths, including Muslims, even at times of great tension between Hindus and Muslims. Muhammed Ali Jinnah, the Pakistani leader, was a contemporary of Gandhi, and they knew each other. During the days before Partition, Gandhi made extraordinary efforts to find solutions to the Hindu-Muslim rift, and went time and time again to visit, talk to, and argue with Jinnah.

Indeed, at one stage Gandhi proposed that Jinnah serve as prime minister of a United India (the idea was torpedoed not only by Gandhi's own collaborators but also by Lord Mountbatten, governor of India). In May 1947, Gandhi met Jinnah in Delhi for the last time; when his followers questioned him on reaching out, his answer was that he would go to Jinnah "70 times 7" times if necessary—that it was vital because they had to live in the same space. Gandhi was deeply convinced that differences between Hindus and Muslims must and could be overcome, and that all were addressing the same figure in their separate prayers to God. Gandhi's view was that Partition and the associated violence could and should have been averted. It is striking that Jinnah, in his speech of August 11, 1947, assured Hindus that they would have equal rights, and was also absolutely sure that there would be peace between the communities.

Rajmohan Gandhi shares Gandhi's conviction that, except when they are stirred up, the vast majority of humans are on the side of moderation and toleration. What is needed are leaders who can convey this historic vision, and who can mobilize people in the direction of reason and peace. When people work together against poverty, he feels, they can overcome tensions (though affluence is not a guarantee against narrow-mindedness, and the very rich finance some of the most extremist efforts). Dialogue is vital, but it must be given time. When people get to know each other, good things can happen. And today's trend toward growing civil society mobilization itself constitutes a "wall of peace" that represents hope for the future.

a. See also Rajmohan Gandhi, 2007, *Mohandas: A True Story of a Man, His People, and an Empire* (London: Penguin).

BOX 23.3
CARAVAN SAFE COMMUNITY: YOUTH, FAITH GROUPS, AND ARMED VIOLENCE

Homicide rates in Latin America are among the highest in the world, with violence a principal cause of death in Brazil, Colombia, Venezuela, and Mexico. A Brazilian NGO called Viva Rio—through its Religion and Peace project—has worked over a period of several years at the local, state, and national level, in cooperation with churches, Christian networks, and other faith institutions, to achieve small arms control and police reform and build peace.[a] The program aims to deepen understanding among religious groups and networks, NGOs, social and youth movements, the press, and the public sector

(Box continues on next page.)

(box continued)

of the problems facing low-income youth involved in armed violence in urban *favelas* (slums), and to organize solutions.

"Viva Rio sees its work as a 'laboratory' for social innovation," said its founder and director Rubem Cesar Fernandes at the World Bank in 2004. And, indeed, the group is testing numerous innovative solutions to some of the greatest urban challenges.[b]

Viva Rio was founded in 1993 to respond to the murder of eight street children in front of the Candelaria church, and the killing of another 21 people in the Vigario Geral favela in Rio de Janeiro. Viva Rio now manages more than 500 projects in some 350 favelas and poor communities in the Rio area.

These projects include peace and disarmament campaigns, educational programs, access to jobs for school dropouts, conflict mediation, free legal aid, and community development, for example through microcredit. Other projects include "child hope centers," where youngsters can practice sports, Radio Viva Rio and a network of more than 170 community radios across Brazil, Viva Favela, an online magazine, computer centers in low-income neighborhoods (launched with financing from the World Bank's InfoDev[c]), police training in human rights and conflict mediation, and community policing.

In 2005 Viva Rio helped organize and link religious groups and networks with NGOs, social movements, and police institutions around small arms control. Under the supervision of Viva Rio, this group created "posts" for collecting small arms at 240 churches, spread over 216 cities and 23 states. The program destroyed some 5,000 weapons. According to Viva Rio, "These activities created a neutral space of concrete action for peace and democracy where institutions that had never interacted before could 'do good' and cooperate with confidence." The organizing began with historic evangelical churches and Catholic churches, and expanded to include Pentecostal churches and other religious groups throughout the country. The premise is that peace is necessary for justice, and that religious groups can facilitate both when they work together.

In 2006 Religion and Peace focused on police reform through the Caravana Comunidade Segura (Caravan Safe Community). Between July and September, the *caravana* visited Londrina, Rio de Janeiro, Salvador, Recife, Caruaru, Natal, Brasília, Belo Horizonte, Curitiba, Porto Alegre, São Paulo, and Campinas, holding workshops on police reform and Brazil's disarmament statute. They met secretaries of public security and chiefs of the military police, and visited faith-based projects and NGOs. Safe Community Caravan 2007 is targeting youth—often more acceptable than arms control and police reform.

Viva Rio hopes to continue to contribute leadership and technical assistance to facilitate social reform and deepen democracy. Its partner institutions include the Conferência Nacional de Bispos do Brasil (National Conference of Bishops), Conselho Nacional de Igrejas Cristãs do Brasil (National Council of Christian Churches), Visão Mundial (World Vision), Comissão Brasileira de Justiça e Paz (Brazilian Justice and Peace Commission), and Conselho Latino Americano de Igrejas.

a. Viva Rio Website: http://www.vivario.org.br/english/

b. World Bank, June 28, 2004, "Viva Rio: Innovative Approaches Against Urban Crime, press release, at http://wbln1018.worldbank.org/LAC/LAC.nsf/ECADocByUnid/323C27F1517975A185256EBE0075AF6F?Opendocument.

c. InfoDev is a partnership program housed at the World Bank that helps developing countries and their international partners use information and communication to reduce poverty and sustain economic growth.

NOTES

1. For more on the High-Level Group for the Alliance of Civilizations, see http://www.unaoc.org/.

2. Ashoka, which has in many respects pioneered recognition of the leadership category termed social entrepreneurs, defines them as follows: "Social entrepreneurs are individuals with innovative solutions to society's most pressing social problems. They are ambitious and persistent, tackling major social issues and offering new ideas for wide-scale change." See http://www.ashoka.org/fellows/social_entrepreneur.cfm.

3. Notes on the work of the C100 including reports on its major formal meetings can be found on the WEF Website at http://www.weforum.org/en/initiatives/c100/index.htm.

CHAPTER 24

Concluding Thoughts

"When the mind joins the heart, everything is possible."
—Grandmother Margarita, Mayan elder, Mexico[1]

"I will give you a talisman. When you are in doubt, or when the self becomes too much with you, apply the following test. Recall the face of the poorest and weakest man whom you may have seen and ask yourself if the step you contemplate is going to be of any use to him. Will he gain anything? In other words, will it lead to swaraj for the hungry and spiritually starving millions? You will find your doubts melting away."
—Mahatma Gandhi[2]

"Religion without social engagement is reduced to a self-centered practice, leading to a dead end. Social engagement without religion, on the other hand, becomes a pursuit of power and self-aggrandizement"
—Satish Kumar[3]

"The greatest undeveloped resource of our nation and of our world is the poor."
—Fr. Horace McKenna, S.J.

These statements convey both the essence of the lessons that emerge from the stories told in this book and some of the dilemmas that lie ahead. These quotations also speak to the untapped potential of powerful and innovative engagements and alliances. This book started out to inform—about the remarkable but often little-known work occurring through a mosaic of partnerships—and to persuade: that they matter.

These objectives relate to knowledge and information. But the underlying motivation for the work of the people and programs included here goes deeper. The hypothesis, grown to a contention, is that by understanding and engaging with faith institutions in the fight against poverty and for social justice, secular development professionals and ordinary citizens can improve and expand the overall effort. This is a simplifying statement, but it reflects admiration for extraordinary work, appropriate cautions about enduring tensions, and concern that the challenges at stake deserve more serious attention than they have commonly received.

We are left with a combination of informational and analytical challenges, a long agenda of dilemmas that call for dialogue, and arenas that seem ready for action.

The informational issues are glaring, and illustrated in chapter after chapter. Faith-inspired work is partially known and poorly understood, data are sparse and often unreliable, and evaluation is extraordinarily limited. The knowledge gaps are significant for each and every Millennium Development Goal, from hunger to housing, from women's empowerment to the environment, and the need for more analysis in critical fields like health and education is clear and pressing. While the story and case-study approach yields important insights, it is no substitute for rigorous analysis.

A second challenge is broader and applies to both faith and development communities: the need for a basic level of mutual literacy and understanding. Surely many in secular development communities would sharply contest Satish Kumar's statement that social engagement without religion is fundamentally flawed, as would many in the world of religion doubt his suggestion that religion by itself amounts to a self-centered dead end. Worse still, many on both sides have yet to pose the relevant questions.

The authors of this book share the view that secular development practitioners today cannot do their jobs well without a basic understanding of the perspectives and work of faith organizations—perhaps not all such work, but at least in the specific region and arena at hand. This understanding will enhance the quality of programs and help practitioners gain the support and engagement essential for success, and also enable them to avoid pitfalls now too often obscured by lack of knowledge and active misunderstanding.

Likewise, faith institutions often do not understand development institutions. This is due in part to language—the technocratic and somewhat formulaic style of much development literature is at best dense and incomprehensible to outsiders, at worst off-putting. Communicating in a more accessible way, with clarity and sincerity (the heart as well as the mind) is vital. Thus training—joint and separate—and exchange between development and faith leaders and staff deserves high priority, as do efforts to support numerous networks and information systems, whether Web-based or interpersonal.

Dialogue on tough issues is a third critical need. Obvious areas of frequent tension between faith and development practitioners are women's rights and reproductive health. Other issues that are less obvious include management of water systems, corruption, and housing policies. Forums that encourage constructive dialogue between faith and development leaders and practitioners, especially on topics of contention, are essential.

Finally, there is much potential for individuals and communities the world over who are not already engaged in development and social issues to move beyond words to active engagement. This entails two challenges. The first is to mobilize people—to persuade them that poverty matters for them, and that something must and can be done about it. Faith institutions are crucial partners in this effort, given their ethical calling and mandate, and their extraordinary practical reach.

The second challenge is that once people are mobilized, the question arises: "But what can I do?" This requires answers. Box 24.1 summarizes an important effort to map how citizens can become involved in fighting global poverty. This work highlights opportunities ranging from encouraging community solidarity and mobilization to committing knowledge, skills, and resources to concrete projects. Box 24.2 also endeavors to trace an agenda for action: it distills the author's presentation at the WCRP Kyoto Assembly in August, 2006 on sustainable development and shared security.

The world of faith institutions—especially those that work in effective partnerships with secular development organizations—offers an important answer to the "what can I do?" question. In connecting secular practitioners and institutions with grassroots, local, national, and global faith networks, participants can translate development theory into action, and inform policy with on-the-ground experience and the wisdom of communities that stand to benefit from development assistance.

BOX 24.1
WHAT CAN ONE PERSON DO?

A vision without a task is boring. A task without a vision is awfully frustrating. A vision with a task can change the world."

—Brizio Biondi-Morra[a]

"There is nothing greater a human being can do than help change another person's life for the better."

—Archbishop Njongkonkulu Ndungane, Cape Town[b]

A group of faith leaders produced a book in response to the question people often pose in the face of the vast challenge of global poverty. The book, entitled *What Can One Person Do? Faith to Heal a Broken World,* is designed to link the vision of the Millennium Development Goals with practical ideas on how individuals, communities, and faith groups can respond with real effect.

The titles of the chapters reflect the inspirational quality of the text: "The Mission of God," "When Did We See You? Justice and Judgment," and "On Giants' Shoulders: Stories to Inspire." The book appeals for action in wide-ranging way, relying on both prophetic stories drawn from scriptures and practical stories about action. The underlying call is for a response that fits the capacity and calling of each individual, and exhortations to combat the tendency to indifference.

The book focuses on seven recommended areas of action:

- *Pray*: Care for and hold people and situations in prayer.
- *Study*: Build real knowledge and deepen understanding by leading study or discussion groups on poverty.
- *Give*: Donate 0.7 percent of income toward fulfilling the MDGs, and encourage others to do the same.
- *Connect*: Spend time volunteering or visiting to connect with the impoverished.
- *Raise awareness*: Organize a concert or other public event to raise awareness and funds.

- *Take action*: Participate in direct action, such as by wearing the white band of the ONE campaign, which is an effort by Americans to rally Americans—one by one—to fight the emergency of global AIDS and extreme poverty. "ONE is students and ministers, punk rockers and NASCAR moms, Americans of all beliefs and every walk of life, united to help make poverty history"[c]
- *Advocate*: Write or meet with government officials to urge them to address global poverty.

The book closes with this telling question and response: "How will our grandchildren see us? Our hope, our prayer, our plea is that together we will show to our grandchildren, the impoverished, and the international community, what faith can do to mend a broken world."

Note: This box draws on Sabina Alkire and Edmund Newell, 2005, *What Can One Person Do? Faith to Heal a Broken World*.

a. Statement at meeting of faith and development leaders in Canterbury, United Kingdom, October 2002, cited in Katherine Marshall and Richard Marsh, 2003, *Millennium Challenges for Faith and Development Leaders* (Washington, DC: World Bank), p. 63; and in Sabina Alkire and Edmund Newell, 2005, *What Can One Person Do? Faith to Heal a Broken World* (New York: Church Publishing), p. 17.

b. Foreword from *What Can One Person Do?*

c. See http://www.one.org/about/.

BOX 24.2
CHALLENGES FOR MINDS, HEARTS, SOUL, AND HANDS

The rich experience of faith development partnerships suggests five guiding themes in fighting poverty, five dilemmas which need greater light, wisdom and dialogue, and five action ideas.

Five Themes

(1) Global poverty is a tragedy and an outrage. It does and should evoke sorrow, anger, compassion, bewilderment, and humility. Poverty and violence are intertwined like a dense jungle—poverty breeds violence and violence accentuates and perpetuates poverty. It should follow that we give as much and more attention to fighting poverty as to any other issue. But, judging by newspapers, televisions, and meeting agendas, we rarely do. The often silent and hidden suffering of poor people is part of the problem; prophetic voices speaking out against poverty are an inspiration.

(2) Poverty has many faces. Its root causes are as complex as any conflict. Sadly, there are no easy solutions. Unless we appreciate the difficulties and complexities we cannot think clearly about solutions.

(3) Poverty CAN be overcome. This is not an obvious assertion because for most of human history most people were very poor and the reigning assumption was that poverty would always be with us. This fatalism lingers on. But a gift of our era is that hundreds of millions of people live longer, better lives with opportunities our ancestors could barely imagine. Europe a century ago suffered widespread malnutrition and ignorance. Thirty years ago many saw Korea, Singapore, Ireland, and other societies that are successful today as hopelessly mired in poverty. This sense that we CAN end poverty, that we have the resources to do so, leads to a very different vision and mindset than ancient wisdom often suggested.

(4) The Millennium Development Goals represent an extraordinary historic event, a first in human history. They are a commitment to a resolute, disciplined, pragmatic, visionary, creative, universal alliance to end poverty in our lifetime. We can work together to communicate this vision, to be part of the global effort to achieve them, and to help galvanize and sustain the will to succeed.

(5) And this fight against poverty must engage us all, not only in our traditional institutions and alliances but in a new array of alliances, networks, and partnerships. In this galaxy of partnerships, religious and faith institutions are vital, major actors. They have been too rarely in the past but there is a fast-growing appreciation across the world, though still with some caveats and blind spots, that faith institutions are part and parcel of this galaxy. We need to weave stronger tapestries that bring us together.

The Dilemmas

(1) The approaches and experience of interfaith dialogue and partnerships are sorely needed to bridge too large gulfs that separate institutions working for development and those inspired by faith. There are suspicions, misunderstandings, and even demonization on both sides. WFDD has made a start in building bridges, as have many others, but the path ahead is demanding and largely unmapped territory. As in interfaith dialogue, we all need to listen, to respect our large common ground of caring and commitment, to work on our differences, and to be open to learn and change.

(2) We need to bring our minds, our hearts, our souls, and our hands to the fight against poverty. No group has a monopoly of any of these gifts, even as no group alone stands on the moral high ground.

(3) Intelligence, technology, research, experience, and learning are all needed. Data and experience are the bread and butter of the World

(Box continues on next page.)

(box continued)

Bank and they can be powerful and useful. Some in the development institutions question whether faith institutions look for and accept evidence. More seriously, gaps in information about what faith communities are doing on HIV/AIDS, health, education, and caring for children are serious obstacles. Limited evaluations of their work are an even more serious hole.

(4) As communities across the world are mobilized to fight against poverty and for social justice, the question often comes back: what should I do? What can I do? When people's hearts and souls are engaged, as they were by the tsunami, by earthquakes, by Lebanon, by Darfur, by New Orleans, they want to help but often the options for action are less than totally convincing. What can young people and grandparents across the world contribute? We need better answers.

(5) There are obvious gaps between fine words and fragmented, halting, and insufficient action. Three powerful tools work well and can help bridge the gaps: open information that reaches people so that they can act themselves, real participation and respect for communities, and disciplined and creative monitoring and reporting. The media and the arts can be far stronger allies. Faith leaders belong at the very center of this effort to goad, shame, encourage, celebrate, appeal to people's better angels, and keep the light on our tasks and our goals.

Looking Ahead

(1) There is a need to build bridges where development institutions are increasingly open to partnerships: where the spirit may be willing but the flesh rather weak. Priorities are education, health, HIV/AIDS, and that critical first period of development after conflicts. Other areas include housing, finance and microcredit, water, and the environment.

(2) The "interfaith dialogue" between development and faith institutions needs to address issues that divide them. This can take several forms, including working groups to define issues, explore differences, and hopefully build more common ground. The thorniest issues include the role of economic growth in socioeconomic progress, issues around public private roles in development (for example privatization), rights of women, and reproductive health.

(3) Corruption is a nasty, widespread, and corrosive phenomenon and a major obstacle to development. But faith leaders have yet to be full partners in emerging global, regional, and national alliances to work for better governance. A disciplined effort to seek wisdom from theology and experience of "living religion" might foster action to fight this special cancer.

(4) In setting agendas (always an important task that can shape outcomes) for meetings, assemblies, and work programs, and in decision processes, women and young people should be more involved. Priorities and the way agendas are framed will be far stronger and more real if these key voices are at the table from beginning to end. We all need to address the difficult task of keeping poverty always on the global agenda as a living constant.

(5) We *know* that action on some issues can enhance welfare and five priority issues invite immediate joint action: pressing for each and every girl to go to school, to stay there, and to have help to succeed; to oppose the marriage of young children, especially girls; to speak with outrage against violence in the home and in institutions; to fight passionately against stigma, especially for people living with HIV/AIDS; and to look for every path to stop trafficking in small arms.

Note: This box is drawn from a presentation by Katherine Marshall, Kyoto WCRP Assembly, August 2006.

NOTES

1. Wendy Tyndale, ed., 2006, *Visions of Development: Faith-based Initiatives* (Aldershot, Hampshire, UK: Ashgate), p. 50.

2. K. Swaminathan and C.N. Patel, eds., 1988, *A Gandhi Reader* (New Delhi: Orient Longman), p. 134.

3. Satish Kumar, 2005, "Development and Religion: Cultivating a Sense of the Sacred," in Makarand Paranjape, ed., *Dharma and Development: The Future of Survival* (Samvad India Foundation), p. 42.

Selected Bibliography

Books and Articles

Ahmed, Akbar. 2007. *Journey into Islam: the Crisis of Globalization.* Washington DC: Brookings Institution Press.

Alkire, Sabina Alkire. 2006. "Religion and Development." In *Elgar Companion to Development Economics,* ed. David Clark. Cheltenham: Edward Elgar.

Belshaw, Deryke, Robert Calderisi, and Chris Sugden, eds. 2001. *Faith in Development: Partnership between the World Bank and the Churches of Africa.* Oxford: Regnum Books/World Bank.

Banchoff, Thomas. 2007. *Democracy and the new Religious Pluralism.* Oxford: Oxford University Press.

Berger, Peter L., ed. 1999. *The Desecularization of the World: Resurgent Religion and World Politics.* Washington, DC: Ethics and Public Policy Center.

Candland, Christopher. 2000. "Faith as Social Capital: Religion and Community Development in Southern Asia." *Policy Sciences* 33: 355–374.

Casanova, Jose. 1994. *Public Religions in the Modern World.* Chicago: University of Chicago Press.

Dean, Judith, Julie Schaeferner, and Stephen Smith, eds. 2005. *Attacking Poverty in the Developing World: Christian Practitioners and Academics in Collaboration.* Authentic and World Vision.

Farmer, Paul. 2005. *Pathologies of Power: Health, Human Rights and the New War on the Poor.* Berkley: University of California Press.

Finn, Daniel. 2006. *The Moral Economy of Markets: Assessing Claims about Markets and Justice.* New York and Cambridge: Cambridge University Press.

Goulet, Denis. 2006. *Development Ethics at Work: Explorations—1960–2002.* London: Routledge.

Haddad, Yvonne Yazbeck and John Esposito, eds. 1998. *Islam, Gender and Social Change.* New York: Oxford University Press.

Harper, Sharon M.P., ed. 2000. *The Lab, the Temple and the Market: Reflections at the Intersection of Science, Religion and Development.* Bloomfield, CT: Kumarian Press/IDRC/CRDI.

Harrison, Lawrence E., and Samuel P. Huntington, eds. 2000. *Culture Matters: How Values Shape Human Progress.* New York: Basic Books.

Harrison, Lawrence, and Peter Berger, eds. 2006. *Developing Cultures: Case Studies.* New York: Routledge.

Haynes, Jeffrey, ed. 1999. *Religion, Globalization and Political Culture in the Third World.* New York: St. Martin's Press, Inc.

Hertzke, Alan. 2006. *Freeing God's Children, The Unlikely Alliance for Global Human Rights.* Lanham, MD. Rowman & Littlefield.

Jenkins, Phillip. 2003. *The Next Christendom: The Coming of Global Christianity.* Oxford: Oxford University Press.

Kliksberg, Bernardo. 2003. *Social Justice: A Jewish Perspective.* Jerusalem: GeFen Publishing House.

Marshall, Katherine. 2001. "Religion and Development: A Different Lens on Development Debates." *Peabody Journal of Education* 76 (3,4): 339–375.

Marshall, Katherine, and Lucy Keough. 2004. *Mind, Heart and Soul in the Fight against Poverty.* Washington DC: World Bank.

———. 2005. *Finding Global Balance* Washington, DC: World Bank.

Mshana, Rogate, ed. 2003. *The Debt Problem for Poor Countries: Where Are We? A Report on Illegitimate Debt and Arbitration.* Geneva: World Council of Churches.

———. 2003. *Wealth Creation and Justice: The World Council of Churches' Encounters with the World Bank and the International Monetary Fund.* Geneva: World Council of Churches.

———. 2004. *In Search of a Just Economy: Common Goals, Separate Journeys.* Geneva: WCC.

———. 2004. *Passion for Another World: WCC Internal Encounter of Churches, Agencies and other Partners on the World Bank and the International Monetary Fund.* Geneva: World Council of Churches.

Northcott, Michael. 1999. *Life after Debt: Christianity and Global Justice.* London: Society for Promoting Christian Knowledge.

O'Brien, Joanne, and Martin Palmer. 2007. *The Atlas of Religion.* Berkeley: The University of California Press.

Palmer, Martin, and Victoria Finlay. 2003. *Faith in Conservation: New Approaches to Religions and the Environment.* Directions in Development. Washington, DC: World Bank.

Paranjape, Makarand, ed. 2005. *Dharma and Development: The Future of Survival.* New Delhi: Samvad India Foundation.

Sanneh, Lamin, and Joel Carpenter. 2005. *The Changing Face of Christianity: Africa, the West, and the World.* Oxford: Oxford University Press.

Smock, David. 2006. "Religious Contributions to Peacemaking: When Religion Brings Peace, Not War." Peaceworks No. 55. Washington, DC: U.S. Institute for Peace. January.

Taylor, Michael. 2003. *Christianity, Poverty and Wealth: The Findings of Project 21.* Geneva: WCC Publications.

————. 2005. *Eat, Drink and be Merry for Tomorrow We Live: Studies in Christianity and Development.* Edinburgh: T. and T. Clark International.

Ter Haare, Gerrie, and Stephen Ellis. 2006. "The Role of Religion in Development: Towards a New Relationship between the European Union and Africa." *European Journal of Development Research* 18(3): 351–367.

Thomas, Scott Thomas. 2004. "Faith and Foreign Aid: How the World Bank got Religion and Why it Matters." *The Brandywine Review of Faith and international Affairs* (Fall): 21–29.

Tyndale, Wendy, ed. 2006. *Visions of Development: Faith-based Initiatives.* Aldershot, Hampshire, UK: Ashgate.

Websites

Berkley Center for Religion. Peace, and World Affairs: http://berkleycenter.georgetown.edu.

The Pluralism Project at Harvard University: http://www.pluralism.org/.

University of Birmingham Religions and Development Research Program: http://www.rad.bham.ac.uk/index.php?section=1.

World Bank Development Dialogue on Values and Ethics: http://www.worldbank.org/developmentdialogue.

World Faiths Development Dialogue: http://www.wfdd.org.uk.

Index

ABC model, 54
Abuom, Agnes, 12, 152, 202, 206, 207
accountability, 19, 21, 28, 239
Acholi Religious Leaders Peace Initiative (ARLPI), 269, 271–272, 273, 275n.2
Addis Ababa Muslim women's Council, 248
Adventist Development and Relief Agency (ADRA), 73
advocacy
    HIV/AIDS, 54–56
    housing, 95, 96
    role, 55
waste management, 90
Africa Monitor, 29, 238
African Americans, 148
African Network of Religious Leaders Living With or Personally Affected by HIV and AIDS, 54
African Religious Health Assets Program (ARHAP), 37–39, 44
agenda setting, 311
Agnivesh, Swami, 57
AIDS Community Training (ACT), 1433
Akong, Patotin, 98
Alagiah, Sabapathy, 72
Al Akhawayn University, 226, 227
All Africa Conference of Churches, 151–153

Alliance of Civilizations, 264, 289, 290–291
    report, 290–291
Alliance of Religions and Conservation (ARC), 209–210, 215
al Yazami, Driss, 281, 288n.2
American Joint Jewish Distribution Committee, 259
Andrews, Charlie, 297
Anglican Diocese of Angola, 218
Anglican Diocese of Niassa, 218
Angola, forestry, 217, 218
Annan, Kofi, 290
antiretroviral therapy (ART), 142–143
aouni, 101, 102
Ariyaratne, A.T., 107, 119, 121, 122, 124
Ariyaratne, Vinya, 122, 124, 126
Armstrong, Karen, 290
Armstrong, Lance, 150
Ashafa, Muhammad Nurayn, 294, 295–297
Ashoka, 35, 302n.2
asset management, 209–219
ATD Fourth World, 160–167
Athavle, Pandurang Sastri, 253
attitudes, 126
Aubourg, Diana, 152
Aurobindo, Sri, 254
AVINA, 79–80, 82
Awakatan, 245–247
Azoulay, Andre, 290

Baba, Sri Sathya Sai, 254
Bahá'í, 247, 248
Bakarr-Conteh, Abu, 152
Barnes, Victor, 152
Beckmann, David, 146, 147, 152
best practices, HIV/AIDS orphans, 191
A Better World for All, 196
Bhikkhu, Mettanando, 35–36
Bill and Melinda Gates Foundation,
    70, 210
Biondi-Morra, Brizio, 79–80, 306
Blake, Charles, 148, 152
blame, 280
Bono, 25, 149, 150, 151
book
    organization and goals, 15, 16n.11
    rationale, 10–15
Brahma Kumaris, 35, 253
Brazil, 244, 245, 264, 299–301
Bread for the World, 146–147
Bretton Woods institutions (BWIs),
    196, 197, 200
bribery, 238
Brother JK, 272
Brown, Gordon, 24
Brownback, Sam, 155
Buddhism, 29, 35–36, 121, 249, 250,
    255
Buffet, Warren, 150
building, implementation, 99–100
Byamugisha, Gideon, 55–56

Cairo Declaration of Religious Leaders
    in the Arab Region in Response
    to the HIV/AIDS Epidemic, 57
Calleja, Bobby, 97
Calmé, Nathalie, 228
Cameroon, 244, 245, 247
Candomblé, 245
capacity, 13, 61–62
    HIV/AIDS, 63–64, 193–194
Caravan Safe Community, 299–301
Carey, George, 7–8
Carey, Lord Carey of Clifton, 24, 292
Carstens, Agustín, 201, 202, 207

case studies, 241, 242, 249, 260n.4
Cash, Johnny, 150
Catholic Church, 36–37, 236
    agencies, 29–30
    Rwanda, 286
    social teaching, 3
Catholic Medical Bureau, 42
Catholic Medical Mission Board, 52
Catholic Peace-building Network, 270
Center for Global Justice and Recon-
    ciliation (CGJR), 69, 73
Centro Magis, 80, 82, 86n.4
Chicolo, Antonio, 72
Chikweti Forest, 217
child development centers, 188
child health, Madagascar, 159–170
children, 50, 175, 268, 311
    child soldiers, 268
    HIV/AIDS, 179–180
    programs, 186–188
    street children, 256–259
    see also orphans
Chile, 248, 249
Chimoio, Francisco, 72
China
    foot binding, 112–113
    health care, 35
Chinmaya Mission, 253
Chinmayanda, Swami, 253
Chowdhry, Kamla, 241, 242, 243,
    251–254
Christian Council of Mozambique
    (CCM), 72, 75n.2
Christianity, 250, 286, 295–297
    orphans, 180
Church World Service, 153
Citibank, 209
civil society, role, 280
clothing, children, 186
Cobban, Helena, 264, 283–286
Cole, Craig, 212
collaboration. See partnerships
Common Goals, Different Journeys, 201
communication, 8, 34, 45, 91, 166,
    305

community, 174
    HIV/AIDS, 179–180, 191
    involvement, 115
    leadership, 50
    organization, 294
    orphans, 191
    roles, 61
    schools, 188
    trust in FBOs, 194
community-based organizations
        (CBOs), HIV/AIDS orphans,
        184, 185, 193, 194n.6
community building, peace and,
        121–122
Community of Sant'Egidio, 58–60,
        271, 285
Comprehensive Development Frame-
        work, 9
Concessao, Vincent, 57
conditionality, 43
conflict, 279
    Rwanda, 286–287
    Uganda, 267–275
conflict resolution, 280–281
Confucius, values, 235
congregations, 182–183, 188
    children and orphans, 185, 190,
        192, 193
consensus, 12
Consultative Group to Assist the Poor
        (CGAP), 210
cooperation, 10, 174–175, 195–208
    see also partnerships
coordination, 53, 123, 125
Coptic Church, 107–108
    HIV/AIDS, 141–144
corruption, 42–43, 311
    alliances to counter, 231–240
Council of 100 (C-100), 83–85,
        292–294
counseling, children, 187
country engagement, 29–30
covenant, 62
culture, 221–230
    see also traditional beliefs and prac-
        tices

Daaras, 256
Dada, Svadhyaya afer, 253
dam building, 3
daycare centers, 187
debt, 3, 16n.5
Debt and Trade for Africa (DATA),
        28–29, 150
decision making, 123
DeGioia, John, 293
development
    holistic view, 255–259
    institutions, 4–5
Dharma and Development: The Future of
        Survival, 243, 251–254
Diagne, Malick, 115
dialogue, 9, 221, 305, 311
    Fès, 221–230
    World Bank, IMF, and WCC,
        195–208
Dialogue among Civilizations,
        289–302
dilemmas, 309–310
Diocese of Västerås, 216
discrimination, housing, 102
Douma, Joost, 215
DREAM program, 59–60

Ecumenical Advocacy Alliance, 52
education, 77–86, 255, 292, 311
    corruption and, 236–237
    madrasa system, 84, 131–138,
        138n.1
    Pakistan, 129–138
    role, 282
    Senegal, 256
Egypt, HIV/AIDS, 57
elephant, Rumi's, 223–224
Esposito, John, 290
ethics and integrity
    alliances for, 231–240
    faith communities and programs,
        237–238
    health care, 43–44
    HIV/AIDS and gender-linked vio-
        lence, 239
    public, 233–234

teachings, 233–234
Ethiopia, 247, 248
evaluation, 40, 52–53
expenditures, monitoring, 238–239

faith, 173
adherents, 183
advocacy, mobilization and, 24–28
institutions, development institutions vs, 305
leaders, 56–58
faith-based organizations (FBOs)
integrity within, 237–238
orphans, 180–192
roles, 233
Faith in Action: Examining the Role of Faith-Based Organizations in Addressing HIV/AIDS, 52
family
gathering, 127
HIV/AIDS orphans, 191
female genital cutting or mutilation (FGC; FGM), 110, 111–113
public declaration and community engagement, 113–115
Fès Forum, 174, 221–230, 264
2006, 226–229
agenda, 225
books about, 228, *230n.4*
Festival, 225
forgiveness, 278–282
origins, 222–223
spirit of, 225–226
sustaining, 229
Fe y Alegría, 77, 78–82, 82
Federation, 80–81
finance, 14, 40–41, 43, 61, 120, 123–125, 174, 175, 209–219
HIV/AIDS, 51, 192
leakage, 232
transfer, 126
Five Talents, 210–212
Flynn, Paul K., 89
food, children, 186
foot binding, 112

Ford Foundation, 242, 243
foreign policy, 1
Forest Stewardship Council, 218
forestry, faith-consistent investment, 216–218
forgiveness, 278–282
Forum of Bereaved Families, 279
Franchitti, Dario, 150
Friday Morning Group (FMG), 6–7
funding, *See* finance and

Gandhi, Mahatma, 243, 264, 284, 294, 297, 303
Gandhi, Rajmohan, 264, 294, 297–299
Gateway Ambassadors, 150
Geldof, Bob, 25
gender-linked violence, integrity, ethics, and accountability, 239
genocide, 286–287
Georgetown University, 52
Ghana, sanitation and waste management, 87–93
Global Ethic, 234
Global Fund to Fight AIDS, Tuberculosis, and Malaria, 52, 70
Global Health Council, 52
globalization, 173, 223
Global Solidarity Forest Fund (GSFF), 216–218
Global Summit on AIDS and the Church: Race Against Time, 154–157
goal-setting, 12
Goosby, Eric, 150
Gorostiaga, Xavier, 80
governance, 20
government
FBO and, 40
roles and responsibilities, 280
Grameen Bank, 210
Green, Edward, 53
Griffiths, Lord Griffiths of Goldman Sachs, 24
Guatemala, 244, 245–247

Habitat for Humanity, 96–102
Harrold, Peter, 123
Hashem Nimer Aqtam, Aisheh,
    279–280, 281
Headley, William, 152
health care, 33–47
    central questions, 34–35
    challenges, 40–43
    children, Madagascar, 159–170
    description, 36–37
    effectiveness, 40
    future activities, 45–46
    history, 35–36
    information, 36–40
    institutions, 44–45
    relationships, 168
    role, 36, 44, 47n.6
Heartland Tour, 149–150
Hinduism, 250, 252, 298–299
    health care, 35
    orphans, 181
Hirschfield, Brad, 278
HIV/AIDS, 150–151, 154, 155–157,
    311
    challenges, 60–62
    FBO-specific aspects, 62
    information, 8, 9–10, 60
    integrity, ethics, and accountability,
    239
    Kenya, 139–144
    orphans, 177–178, 191
    partnerships, 49–64
    prevention, children, 187
    Sri Lanka, 122
    strategies, 53–54
    treatment, long-term, 55
    Uganda, 41
    workshop, 8, 9–10
home-based care, children, 187
Hope for African Children Initiative,
    182–183
hospitals, history, 35
housing, 93–102
human rights, 111, 136–137, 205
humanitarian work, 45

hunger, ending, 146–147
Idowu-Fearon, Josiah, 152
Iglesias, Enrique, 290
implementation, 305, 306–307
income generation, children, 187
India, 244, 247–249, 264, 297–299
    HIV/AIDS, 57–58
indigenous peoples, displacement, 3
Indonesia, 247, 248
information, 62, 144, 166, 304, 310
    challenges, 36–40
    HIV/AIDS, 51–53, 60
    housing, 95
infrastructure
    FBO, 68–69
    interfaith, 74–75
institutional gaps, 309, 310
integrity. *See* ethics and
InterAction Council, 234
Interfaith Center on Corporate
    Responsibility (ICCR), 214–215
Inter-Faith Mediation Centre, 295, 296
Inter-Faith Waste Management Initia-
    tive (IFAWAMI), 87, 89–91
intermediary organizations, 184,
    194n.5
International Anti-Corruption Confer-
    ence (IACC), 232
International Center for Religion and
    Diplomacy (ICRD), 107,
    130–131
International Interfaith Investment
    Group (3iG), 215–218
International Labor Organization, 259
International Monetary Fund (IMF)
    dialogue, 195–208
    IMF Surveys, 200
    joint statement, 202–204
    voice and vote, 205
Inter-Religious Campaign against
    Malaria in Mozambique
    (IRCMM), 69, 70–73
investments
    faith-consistent, 215–216
    forestry, 216–218

Islam, 286, 295–299
  education and, 83–85, 129–138
  FGC, 112
  health care, 35
  orphans, 181
  Pakistan, 129–138

Jain, Sadhvi Sadhana, 58
Jakes, T.D., 148
Jesuit Order, 80
Jinnah, Muhammed Ali, 298–299
Johnson, Douglas, 263
Joseph, Ipe, 57
Judaism, 250
  health care, 35
  orphans, 180
Judd, Ashley, 150, 151
Judd, Wynonna, 150

Kabbaj, Mohammed, 227
Karim, Abdul, 72
Kayetaba, Michel, 287
Kenya, 107–108
  faith adherents, 182, 183
  HIV/AIDS, 139–144
  orphans, 189, 190
Kim, Jim Yong, 150
Knippers, Diane, 211
knowledge. See information
Kobia, Sam, 201, 202, 206, 207
Koehler, Horst, 197
Kony, Joseph, 272, 273
Kriplani, Lekhraj, 253
Kumar, Satish, 303, 304
Kung, Hans, 234, 263

labor, 126
land allocation, 126
language, shared, 12–13
Laureau, Chantal, 164
leaders and leadership, 5, 7–8, 61,
    105–106, 120, 174
  engaging, 56–58
  faith, 56–58
  HIV/AIDS, 63
  housing, 101–102
  malaria, 74

  peace process, 271–272
Lead Us Not into Temptation, 196, 207
Learning Initiatives of Reforms for
    Network Economies
    (LIRNEasia), 127
Lebanon, housing, 96, 100–102
Les Chemins de l'Espoir, 228
Lesotho, health assets, 37–30
Lolwah al Faisal, 292
London Conference, 24, 25–26
Lord's Resistance Army (LRA), 268,
    269, 273
Lula Da Silva, Luiz Inácio, 25
Lutheran Church of Sweden, 216

Mabudhafasi, Rejoyce, 284–285,
    288n.4
Machado, Joao Somane, 72, 73
Mackie, Gerry, 112
Madagascar, child health, 159–170
madrasa, 84, 138n.1
  goals, 133–136
  impact, 136–138
  Pakistan, 129–138
  reform program, 131–132, 134
Magis Americas, 80
Makda, Hassan, 72
malaria, Mozambique, 67–75
Malawi
  faith adherents, 182, 183
  orphans, 189, 190
Many Clouds and Little Rain? The Global
    Fund and Local Faith-Based
    Responses to HIV and AIDS, 52
marabouts, 256
Margarita, 303
Marshall, Katherine, 12
Martino, Renato Raffaele, 269, 270
mat oput, 273
materials, 126
Matsolo, Dinis, 72
McCarrick, Theodore, 117
McCullough, John L., 153
McKenna, Horace, 303
Mecusserima, Ali, 72
medical care, children, 187
medicine, religion and, 35–36

Melching, Molly, 110, 112, 114–115
messaging
    HIV/AIDS, 54–56
    role, 55
Micah Challenge, 24, 26–27
Micah Network, 26
microcredit, 210–212
Millennium Declaration, 19–20
Millennium Development Goals
    (MDG), 8, *16n.8*, 19, 20, 197,
    198, 204, 304, 309
    faith communities and, 23–32
    framework, 21
    goals, 23
    joint statement, 203
Millennium Summit, 19, 20
Mills-Tettey, Rosemary, 89
*Mind, Heart, and Soul in the Fight
    against Poverty*, 10–11, *16n.10*
Missionaries of Charity Brothers, 164
missionary organizations, orphans,
    185
mobilization, 305, 310
Modi, B.K., 57
Mohammed-Alfa, Musheibu, 89
monitoring, 31, 61, 310
Monterrey Consensus, 25
morality, 43–44, 233–234
    differences, 234–235
Moucecore, 287
Mozambique, 282, 283, 285–286
    faith adherents, 182, 183
    forestry, 217, 218
    HIV/AIDS, 59, 63
    malaria, 67–75
Mukherjee, Joia Stapleton, 150
Multli-country AIDS Projects (MAP
    Projects), 60
music, 221–230

Nahdlatul Ulama (NU), 248
Namibia
    faith adherents, 182, 183
    orphans, 189
Narayan, Sri Swami, 252
National Fishworkers Forum, 249

National Re-Awakening Council, 125
Ndungane, Winston Njongonkulu,
    28–29, 152, 238, 306
New Life Education Trust, 254
New Partnership for Africa's Develop-
    ment (NEPAD), 28
Nigeria, 264, 294, 295–297
night commuters, 268
nongovernmental organizations
    (NGOs), 2, *16n.2*, 184, *194n.6*
    children supported by, 185
    orphans, 189, 193
Norwegian Lutheran Church Endow-
    ment, 216
Nyamayarwo, Agnes, 150

Obama, Barack, 155
Ochola, Archbishop, 269
Odama, Archbishop, 269
Odamtten, Yao Ewoenam, 149
Office of Social Research, 161
Opportunity International, 210
organizational capacity, 10
organizational linkage approach, 120
orphanages, 188
orphans, 173–174, 183
    Africa, 177–194
    number of, 178
Our Children Are a Treasure, 166

Pakistan, 107
    madrasa educational system
    reform, 129–138
Palmer, Martin, 215
Paranjape, Makarand, 243
participation, 310
partnerships, 11–14, 205, 264, 308
    areas for, 205–206
    forming, 58–60
    health care, 44–45
    HIV/AIDS, 49–64
    housing, 95, 100
    principles for, 12–14
Passion for Another World, 200
Pastoral Social of the Diocese of San
    Marcos, 245–246

pavul hamuva, 127
Pax Christi, 271
P.E.A.C.E., 154, *157n.5*
peace, community building and,
    121–122
Peace Build program, 97, 99
*Peacemakers in Action: Profiles of Reli-
    gion in Conflict Resolution*, 263
Peled, Nurit, 279
Peterson, John L., 21
Philippines, housing, 96–100
plan mentoring, 13
plant infusions, 163
policy-making and programs, 31
poverty, 308–309
    extreme, defined, 159–160,
        168–170
    fighting, 8
    understanding, 251
    reduction, 19, 205
Poverty Reduction Strategy Paper
    (PRSP), 8, 9–10, 204
power differences, 13
Prafulta, Jaintilal, 72
President's Emergency Plan for AIDS
    Relief (PEPFAR), 54
priorities, 12, 19
progress, monitoring, 28–29
projects, long-term impact, 125–126
public declaration, 113–115
public health, 44
The Purpose-Driven Life, 153

Raiser, Konrad, 196
Ramakrishna Mission, 249, 252
Ramazzini, Alvarro, 246
Ramsey-Lucas, Curtis, 152
rationale for the book, 10–15
Rato, Rodrigo de, 201
realism, 12
reconciliation, 126
   rebuilding and, 277–288
    religion and, 282–288
    Uganda, 273–274
reconstruction, 123

recreation, children, 187
regional engagement, 29–30
Reinikke, Ritva, 40
religion
    nature of, 250
    reconciliation and, 282–288
    role, 1, *15n.1*, 263, 270
*Religion: The Missing Dimension of
    Statecraft*, 263
religious coordinating bodies (RCBs),
    183–184
    children supported by, 185
    orphans, 189, 193
religious groups
    development and, 2–5
    Uganda, role, 274–275
Religious Health Assets survey, 52
religious orders, orphans, 185
religious teaching, corruption and,
    236–237
religious traditions, 282
reporting, 61, 310
research, housing, 95
resource allocation, 123
response, boosting, 62
responsibility, 19
Responsible Wood Angola, 217
results, 13–14
Rivers, Eugene, 148
Rodriguez Maridiaga, Oscar, 232
Roll Back Malaria Partnership, 71
Roman Catholic Church. *See* Catholic
    Church
Romans, health care, 35
Rumi's elephant, 223–224
Rwanda, 282, 283, 286–287

Saddleback Church, 153, 154–157
Sadik, Nafiz, 290
Sagadan, Danganan, 98
Saheb, Maulana Sultan Ahmad Islahi,
    58
Sai Seva Centers, 254
Salifu, Lukman Y., 90
Sambutol, Nasser, 97

Samwini, Nathan Iddrisu, 89
sanitation, Ghana, 87–93
Saperstein, David, 152
Sarobidy Ny Silaky Ny Aina, 166
Sarvodaya, defined, 121
Sarvodaya Economic Enterprise Development Services (SEEDS), 120
Sarvodaya Shramadana Movement, 107, 119–128, 244, 254
Satyamji, Swami, 58
SAVE, 54–55
Scaling Up Effective Partnerships: A Guide to Working with Faith-Based Organizations in the Response to HIV and AIDS, 52
scaling-up, 30–31, 60
  HIV/AIDS orphans, 192
Schmidheiny, Stephan, 79–80
schools, 187, 188
  see also education
Search for Common Ground, 280, 288n.1
Sebastian Acevedo Movement, 249
secular organizations, faith-based organizations and, 8
Senegal, 106, 110
  street children, 256–258
Sengulane, Dinis, 71, 72, 286
Serageldin, Ismail, 290
Seventh Day Adventist Church, 73
Shankar, Sri Sri Ravi, 57
Sharma, Arvind, 249, 250
shelter programs, 95
shramadana, 120, 121
Shriver, Bobby, 150
Simbine, Horatio, 72
Simon, Arthur, 146
Simoque, Miguel, 72
Singh, Giani Bhai Ranjit, 58
Sivaraksa, Sulak, 249
Skali, Faouzi, 225
small-scale, piecemeal efforts, 30
social and economic endeavors, 105
social capital, 105
social contract, 168

social justice, 205
social transformation, 241–261
Somarruga, Cornelio, 201
South Africa, 282–284
spirituality, 244–245
spirit worship, 245
Sri Lanka, 107, 117–128, 244, 254
  post-tsunami, 122–125
street children
  Senegal, 256–258
  Turkey, 258–259
Street Children's Campaign Partnership, 257
structural adjustment policy, 3
support, 14
sustainability, 61
Svadhyaya, 253–254
Svensson, Jacob, 40
Swadhaya movement, 244
Swaminarayan movement, 252
Swaziland, faith adherents, 182, 183

Tagore, 249
Tall, Madani, 256
tambavy, 163
Tanenbaum Center for Interreligious Understanding, 263
Tanzania, HIV/AIDS, 143–144
Task Force for Rebuilding the Nation (TAFREN), 118
teacher training, 131–132, 135
Tearfund, 52
Terreiro Ile Axe Omin Funko, 245
Thailand, 248
Three Ones, framework, 53–54
time, 282
Together Against Malaria (TAM), 73, 74–75
Tokombere, 247
Tostan, 106–107, 110–115
traditional beliefs and practices, 161–163, 166, 175, 273–274, 284
  Mozambique, 285–286
  orphans, 181

traditional medicine, 161–163
transparency, 13
Transparency International, 232
Treatment Acceleration Program
     (TAP), 59
triple bottom line, 213
trust, 61
Truth and Reconciliation Commission
     (TRC), South Africa, 282, 284
truth and reconciliation commissions,
     281
     Uganda, 273–274
tsunami, 117–118
     aftermath, 122–125
Tucker, Chris, 150
Turki al Saud, 292
Tutu, Desmond, 284, 290
Tyndale, Wendy, 241, 242, 243, 250,
     260n.2
     development and, 244–251

ubuntu, 284
Ugalde, Luis, 80
Uganda, 264
     conflict, 267–268
     faith adherents, 182, 183
     health care, 40, 41–42
     HIV/AIDS, 53
     orphans, 189, 190
     reconciliation, 267–275
     reconciliation and truth commis-
          sions, 273–274
     reconstruction, 272
Union of Religious Superiors, 52
Unions of Superiors General, 37
United Nations, 2, 16n.2
     alliance of civilizations, 289,
          290–291
United States, 108
     alliances for development,
          145–157
     anti-Americanism, 137–138
     Forest Service International Pro-
          gram, 218

values, 233–234
     differences, 234–236

Values for Development Group, 6–7
Vatican's Pontifical Council on Justice
     and Peace, 236, 270
Vehidi, Farida, 58
Vélaz, José María, 78
Venezuela, 78
Victory without Losers, 286
Vikram Sarabhai Foundation, 242
village management, 120
violence, 299–301
Visions of Development: Faith-Based Ini-
     tiatives, 243, 249
visiting, children, 187
Vitória sem Vencidos, 286
Viva Rio, 264, 294, 299–301
Vivekananda, Swami, 252
Vivekananda Girijana Kalyana Kendra,
     247
vocational training, children, 187
volunteers, 185–186
     housing, 102

Wade, Abdoulaye, 257
The Warriors and the Faithful: The World
     Bank MAP and Local Faith-Based
     Initiatives in the Fight against
     HIV/AIDS, 52
Warren, Kay, 154, 156
Warren, Rick, 68, 153–154, 156
Washington consensus, 3, 16n.4
Washington National Cathedral,
     69–70
waste management, Ghana, 87–93
water, 245
Wealth Creation and Justice, 200
Webhamuva project, 127
What Can One Person Do? Faith to Heal
     a Broken World, 306–307
White House Office of Faith-Based Ini-
     tiatives, 9
Williams, Rowan, 269
Wolfensohn, James D., 5, 7–8, 24,
     124, 197, 201, 202, 206–207
     partnership areas, 205–206
women
     groups, 247, 248, 253
     housing, 100

roles, 281
World Bank
    dialogue, 195–208
    joint statement, 202–204
    partnership with faith institutions,
        5–9
    voice and vote, 205
World Conference of Religions for
        Peace (WCRP)
    Global Assembly, 27–28
    Kyoto assembly, 24
World Council of Churches (WCC), 3,
        16n.3
    dialogue, 195–208
    joint statement, 202–204
World Economic Forum (WEF), 292

West–Islamic World Dialogue, 289
World Evangelical Alliance, 26
World Faiths Development Dialog
        (WFDD), 8–9, *16nn.6,7,9*, 242
World Vision, 269
Wresinski, Joseph, 160–161
Wright, Jeremiah, 148
Wuye, James Movel, 294, 295–297

Yunus, Mohammed, 210

Zambia
    health assets, 37–39
    HIV/AIDS, 143–144
Zarkan Zoumountsi, 245
Zimbabwe, orphans, 182